PAGANINI

The Romantic Virtuoso

Da Capo Press Music Reprint Series

GENERAL EDITOR

FREDERICK FREEDMAN

VASSAR COLLEGE

PAGANINI

The Romantic Virtuoso

By

JEFFREY PULVER

With a New Bibliography Compiled by
FREDERICK FREEDMAN
Vassar College

𝄋 DA CAPO PRESS · NEW YORK · 1970

A Da Capo Press Reprint Edition

This Da Capo Press edition of Jeffrey Pulver's
Paganini, The Romantic Virtuoso
is an unabridged republication of the first
edition published in London in 1936 by
Herbert Joseph, Ltd. It is reprinted by
special arrangement with the original publisher.

Library of Congress Catalog Card Number 69-11669
SBN 306-71199-0

Copyright © 1970 by Da Capo Press
A Division of Plenum Publishing Corporation
227 West 17th Street
New York, N. Y. 10011

Printed in the United States of America

PAGANINI

PAGANINI

PAGANINI

THE ROMANTIC VIRTUOSO

By

JEFFREY PULVER

Bisogna forte sentire per far sentire.

LONDON

HERBERT JOSEPH LIMITED

FIRST PUBLISHED IN 1936

MADE AND PRINTED IN GREAT BRITAIN BY TONBRIDGE PRINTERS LTD.
PEACH HALL WORKS TONBRIDGE KENT

*To her
whose encouragement and sympathetic
interest was invaluable, whose
unwavering faith was an inspiration,
whose worth is above rubies, this
book is gratefully
dedicated.*

CONTENTS

*Portraits of Paganini at different stages of his career face the title
page and pages 113, 161 and 257.*

PREFACE

WHEN Nicolo Paganini appeared on the wider stage of Europe he burst upon a highly respectable system of providing musical entertainment, like a thunderbolt from a blue sky. With very little warning he surprised the conventional performer and his audience by presenting himself before them as a phenomenon hitherto unsuspected—the virtuoso *in excelsis:* an executant musician who had made himself so far master of the mechanical difficulties of his instrument that he won freedom to express himself in a manner unhampered by technical considerations. This in itself, however, will not explain the effects he produced. There were men especially endowed by nature for the over-coming of technical difficulties before his time. The Lollis, the Schellers, the Bouchers, also astonished the world; but they did no more than astonish. Paganini achieved far more than that; he made his audiences *feel.* This is the aspect so often over-looked when the position of Paganini in the history of music is considered. It is because the emotional, the dramatic, the poetic appeal of his performance is ignored that he is so often placed in a class with the tricksters, the mountebanks, the show-men pure and simple—a class which, by the very richness of the soil, the art had bred as a rank fungus-growth. The majority of Paganini's contemporaries did not see him in that light. It is true that a few, fearful lest the existing order be disturbed by any new factor, considered him as a natural fol-lower of the superficial men just mentioned, and would have none of him. But they were not heard in the applause of the thousands who saw, heard, and felt the spell of Paganini. The Genoese artist on the one hand, and all the other violinists that the world had ever seen—whether good or bad, sincerely artistic or charlatanic—on the other, were poles asunder. The

9

good he did might have been greater had he been succeeded by a number of pupils instructed by his methods and inspired by his example. Technical development alone, however, could never produce another Paganini. Nevertheless the fallacy was hugged to the breasts of very many that if they exercised, drilled, and tortured themselves until all the mechanical problems connected with their instrument were solved, they would emerge as legitimate heirs to Paganini's reputation. This fallacy brought many evils to the art of violin-playing, and Paganini has too frequently been blamed for the impersonality of the latter-day technicians, for their lack of soul, for their worship of the means as an end. It was not Paganini's fault if these machine-made performers possessed none of his virtues and shared none of his natural gifts. In every respect he was different from his predecessors and contemporaries, and his art stood alone because he brought to its service a personality that in the combination of its details was unique. And to prove the truth of this assertion I shall probably need the whole of the book that follows.

Before we can hope to see clearly into the mystery of this man's art we shall have to remove from our imagination all the preconceived notions that have been placed there by a couple of generations of gossips. There can be no other way of approaching Paganini's art than through the avenue that a complete knowledge of his life gives us; and we can know very little of Paganini's life except from the writings of his contemporaries. Even these are faulty enough, for we have to allow for prejudice and bias, personal taste and feeling, and bad memory. Yet all these drawbacks still leave the contemporary sources of information more useful than later legends and hypotheses. For this reason I do not feel constrained to apologize to my readers for quoting the newspapers of Paganini's own day in evidence. Surely the men and women who saw Paganini, who heard him, spoke with him, and understood his era because it was also their own, must be the best judges of his worth and the most dependable witnesses for us to call. In the same way and for the same reasons I have drawn largely upon the writings of men like Schottky, Fétis, and Schütz, in addition to many others, who enjoyed the personal acquaintance of the artist and who, on many occasions—though naturally biased in his favour—are our only sources of information. Needless to say, I have, wherever possible, verified the statements used; and for the purpose of reference I give below a list of books on Paganini that appeared during his lifetime. The first biographical works to appear after his death were Count Giancarlo Conestabile's *Vita di Nicoló Paganini da Genova* (1851) and François Joseph Fétis's *Notice Biographique* (1851; English Edition, 1852). In the whole of the abundant literature devoted to Paganini there is not a single volume quite free from chronological and factual errors. Owing to the uncertainty of his movements during a few periods in his career, I am not sure that I have corrected them all; but I hope I have reduced their number.

I have to acknowledge the kindness of Messrs. George Hart and Son for the loan of their copy of the Landseer sketch, and of Mr. Joseph Chanot for allowing me to copy a number of Paganini's programmes in his possession. The drawing by Maclise is reproduced by the courtesy of the Trustees of the Victoria and Albert Museum. I am grateful also to Miss Watson of the Brighton Reference Library for her ready assistance in tracing references to Paganini's visits to Brighton—she has, by the way, no connexion with the Miss Watson mentioned in Chapter XXIII—and to Mrs. A. Holländer of Edgware for obtaining a good deal of information on the Viennese period from the original sources in Vienna.

JEFFREY PULVER.

London, 1936.

CONTEMPORARY BIBLIOGRAPHY

Guhr, Carl: *Über Paganini's Kunst die Violine zu Spielen* 1829

Schottky, Julius Max: *Paganini's Leben and Treiben als Künstler und Mensch* 1830

Schütz, Friedrich Carl Julius: *Leben, Character und Kunst des Ritters von Paganini* 1830

Harrys, George: *Paganini in seinem Reisewagen* . . 1830

Laphaleque, G. Imbert de: *Notice sur . . . Nicolo Paganini* 1830

Anders, Gottfried Engelbert: *Nicolo Paganini* . . 1831

Anonymous (Liverpool): *Memoir of Paganini* . . 1832

[It is upon the above works and those by Conestabile and Fétis that all the later biographies have been based. Letters to and from Paganini, newspaper reports, and the memoirs of his contemporaries provide the rest of our sources of information.]

PAGANINI

CHAPTER I

THE STAGE
(1782-1840)

ACROSS a continent resounding with the hoarse cry of *Liberté,
Egalité, Fraternité,* the rattle of Marengo's musketry, the
thunder of Waterloo's cannon, the seductive strains of waltzes,
the clink of glasses from Vienna's futile Congress, the curses at
the barricades of 1830, and the careless laughter of Vauxhall,
there flitted—a fitful shadow that came and went like a wraith
—the gaunt, cadaverous figure of a living enigma; at once
glorious, pitiful, mighty, feeble, and seemingly ageless—a vision
of the incarnate will to scale Olympian heights on feet of clay.
Over all, from the marches of Tartary to the tempestuous Bay,
hung the ever-spreading cloud that was the incubus of humanity
—the menacing outrider of the Corsican's relentless ambition.
Nero fiddled while only a single city burned; Paganini exulted
and sobbed, prayed and blasphemed upon his four fragile
strings while all Europe blazed.

What was this lank and melancholy mystery—welcome to the
arms of fair and noble ladies—the strange being who could
inspire dread and raise the hair on the creeping scalp, who
knew the recipe for wringing from the eyes of cynics the tears
of dignified sorrow? Whence came his supernatural powers?
Was he the very incarnation of the long-developing spirit of
musical expression itself, or the slave of a soul traded away to
sable majesty in return for his daemonic gifts? Or was he
merely—to be quite up-to-date in historical methods—a rare
combination of great talent, indomitable will, and a personality
half evolved from suffering and privation, and half the product

15

of his own determination to rise in the world by mounting on the shoulders of the world's follies? His fixed resolve to make his contemporaries pay for his tormented youth and sardonically to laugh at them afterwards, emerges clearly enough from the story of his activities. In the first recklessness of courageous youth he felt strong enough to brave public opinion; he did not mind being considered even a murderer if the box-office profited. The knife that was supposed to have slain his beloved cut many a purse-string, and in the knowledge of his bloodguiltlessness he allowed infamous libels to live for a quarter of a century before crushing them. At the same time he was guilty of real faults that the world did not see, and he possessed virtues that his own generation refused to recognize. He was a revolutionary only because his imaginative spirit broke the bonds of conventionality. He was called charlatan for no other reason than that he created electrifying effects by means that the artists who went before him did not discover, or trembled to develop. His pilgrimage savoured of the weird only because he told his audiences no more than he wished them to know, while the sinister smile that troubled so many was bred of his amusement at the readiness of gossiping mankind to play into his hands by inventing the legends that clothed him in romance and mystery.

He appeared upon history's stage when cries of ' Liberty ' and ' Freedom ' echoed on every side. It was thoroughly in keeping with his independent spirit that he should strive to liberate his art from the trammels of tradition, that it might rise to be more than a mere exhibition of hide-bound canons and be given a tongue to speak the language of the rejoicing or sorrowing soul rather than that of the schools. He shared that wide stage with a brilliant cast, and his backgrounds were scenes from the history of a continent in travail. His magnetic genius made puppets of the greatest, and though the strong struggled for a short space against his uncanny spell, all eventually submitted. In every act of his drama he conquered thousands and drew them after him on the invisible strings of laughter and weeping.

In every scene he assumed the hero's rôle—now cynically Mephistophelian, now intensely human, palpitating and very real. And when he vanished from the glare of the footlights he left his admirers and victims breathless, exalted, bewildered, beaten—the helpless prey to a hundred conflicting emotions. Nothing need be less surprising than that this man, who could wring a passionate and involuntary ' O Dio ' from the matter-of-fact lips of an everyday listener, should be adorned with a halo of legend, though scarce a century dead. Unfortunately legend, even when picturesque, often hides the real worth of the personality it is intended to honour. What, in effect, were the charges brought against Paganini—the accusations that made of him so unearthly a figure in the fertile imagination of the nineteenth century? His portrait as tradition has bequeathed it to us is at once repellent and fascinating; luckily it is also amusing : He was incurably dissipated, he was an inveterate gambler; he was eccentric, selfish, cruel, morbid, avaricious; he led a band of brigands; he seduced any maid whose eye chanced to meet his glance; he abducted noble women and killed their husbands; he atoned for the murder of his wife by years of imprisonment—or, if he had no wife, he languished for having stabbed his mistress; he secured his mastery over mankind and his pre-eminence in his art from the devil in exchange for a soul already sufficiently blasted and damned. Eye-witnesses soberly relate having seen Satan guiding his hands in one town, while in another, equally credible witnesses saw emissaries from hell driving away from the concert-hall along a road that was not there. That so much nonsense could be written—and presumably believed—in the first quarter of the nineteenth century is not so easy to understand; in some directions at least, the ' age of reason ' had evidently not properly done its duty. That it should be necessary at this time of day to shear from Paganini's story so rank a fungus-growth is a sad commentary on the intellectual state of the era; but even the romantic need not mourn the shearing unduly, for we shall find that once more truth can be not only stranger, but also far more entertaining than fiction. Paganini the violinist is interesting only to those who study the evolution of the violinist's art; but Paganini the man—in all his strength and weakness, his foibles and poses, his pettiness and nobility— serves to illustrate the mentality and the artistic outlook of his generation, explains the age in which he moved, meteoric and mysterious, and helps us to fathom the complexities of Europe's psychology in one of the most pregnant phases of the world's history.

A century of biographers have sought to solve the enigma of Paganini's personality by an intensive examination of his features, to deduce proofs of demoniacal possession from certain of his acts, and to find an explanation for his haggard and pain-racked face in his remorse for countless secret sins. It seems never to have occurred to them to call the spirit of history to their aid. The superficial are often misled by externals, the over-profound frequently blind to the most obvious signposts. The plain fact is that Paganini was psychologically neither mysterious nor abnormal when examined in the light shed by a knowledge of his youth and adolescence, his line of development, and his environment. His main obsessions were his instrument and his ambition to wring from it all that it was capable of expressing; his secondary obsessions were a love for money and a fair feminine face. He was a Don Juan—that much must be admitted at once—and like his prototype he drifted lightly from one love to another, each the 'only real passion' of his life. But he was no collector of women. By devoting himself entirely to one, he tired of her the sooner. Dreadful as this may have appeared to Victorian England, we must consider how the age of Thackeray's 'naughty little Mahomet' reacted. If Macaulay could explain and excuse a Macchiavelli by remembering the world he adorned, it should surely not be too difficult for us to find a not too blameworthy place for a Paganini in an era of Lady Hamiltons, of Mrs. Fitzherberts, of Lady Conynghams.

'To the living', said Voltaire, 'we owe consideration; to the dead, only the truth '. Paganini's achievements merit no less than that we deal fairly with his memory. We are no more honest when we weigh the dawning nineteenth century in the mental and moral scales of the twentieth, than we are when we measure metres with a yardstick. Judged by the standards of his own age, the virtues of Paganini become crowns of glory and his vices, if not excused, are at least explained. Virtuous heads are shaken in disapproval at the mention of his lapses from strict morality; but how many worldly men of his generation—even without his temptations and opportunities—can be acquitted of the same? We have no right to condemn in Paganini the shortcomings which we condone in most of his eminent contemporaries. For a century hypocritical eyebrows have been raised because the great violinist was weak enough to gamble, while their owners were too prejudiced or indolent to discover that he only fell a victim to a prevalent craze during his earliest youth. To justify a false conception it may be convenient to forget that Paganini lived in an age of gamblers; but it is not honest to do so. We have the right to expect of an artist no more nor less than that he should be human. Are we to bestow the title of historian on him who scorns Paganini for losing the money he had himself earned, by indulging in the games of chance he loved, while he honours the memory of the noble earl who invented the sandwich so that his play be not interrupted by supper, and forgives the peers of Hanoverian England for losing their patrimony at a single sitting and the next morning incontinently blowing out their ducal brains? The intrinsic and potential worth of no man can be justly appraised if he is torn from his environment and set upon a pedestal as an anachronistic curiosity. Paganini, no less than any other outstanding figure, must be considered in the company of his fellow-men, surrounded by his friends and enemies, illuminated by the candle-light of his period, working out his destiny in his own peculiar way. If we are to fathom his secrets and understand his personality we must seek the key, not in his posturings and eccentricities, nor in the fanciful myths that have collected about him, but in his origins, in his mental development, and in the history of his own times.

His own times were agitated enough, cursed with miseries and gilded with flamboyant pageantry and hollow glories. He was born to the generation that witnessed the last flickering display of energy by the Italian nation, when his desperate countrymen turned fiercely on the Austrians and flew into the protecting arms of a France with ulterior motives. He was a small boy when the great Revolution was unchained, and he served the Corsican's sister in more ways than one while northern Italy was the cockpit of Europe—the fateful years that preceded Waterloo. He emerged from the battle-smoke of his native land to make his tour of a Europe torn and harassed by political and social unrest, as the first and greatest virtuoso the world had ever seen.

Paganini calls for no elaborate psychological analysis. The plain tale of his life will tell us all we need know of him, and in reading it, as at all other times, we should remember the words of Johann Gottfried Seume :

No man is as great as his reputation, whether for good or evil.

CHAPTER II

THE natural beauties of Genoa, rising from her azure bay on the Ligurian coast, are those of any other Italian port. The colour of sea and sky, the scent of flowers, the song of those who work, the mandoline of the lounger, all create an atmosphere inseparable from our romantic conceptions of the land. Towards the close of the eighteenth century—by some strange miracle—peace reigned; the uncertain peace that made the ignorant fear the worst and allowed the indolent to hope for nothing. With Nature's beauties the human element of the district consorted badly; in revolt fierce, in vendetta unforgiving, in peace lazy, in morals unstable. Contemporary Italian writers tell us that though Genoa possessed ten score of churches, her men lived 'without faith and her women without shame.' In such surroundings and in such an era Nicolo Paganini first saw the light of day. The reverent tourist still seeks out ' Paganini's house' near the harbour, and when he finds it in its narrow passage, he reads on the mural tablet that in a three-roomed dwelling at the top of the pale pink building the famous violinist was born on October 27, 1782, ' to adorn Genoa and delight the world'.

Exactly what calling his father Antonio followed will probably never be discovered. Some say he was a porter about the harbour, others that he owned a small shop, while there are writers who go so far as to say grandiloquently that he ' had interests in the shipping trade'. Nicolo himself told his friend Professor Schottky of Prague that his father was a ' not particularly rich business man '. Whatever he may have been is of small consequence; the important fact is that he never grew rich by his own endeavours. He was a hard, mercenary man; but being an Italian he was fond of music. He played the mandoline, though that need not mean he was a good musician. Indeed, Nicolo tells us later that his father could not even keep time. If Antonio ever encouraged a real passion, it was to become wealthy without working; and he spent hours in elaborate calculations that were to give him an 'infallible' method of discovering the winning numbers in the lottery. He never became a world-famous musician, and was thus never blamed for being an inveterate gambler. In any case his 'system' won nothing, and there is no excuse for a loser.

Nicolo's mother, Teresa (*née* Bocciardo), a good, simple soul, devout in her superstitious way, was hardly a match for her worldly husband. But she contrived to make little Nicolo's earliest years a shade more pleasant than they would otherwise have been, and she helped to soften many of the hardships he had to endure. The boy was never robust, and poverty, ignorance, and the hygienic conditions of the times were scarcely the tonics to strengthen him. At the age of four—after some infantile ailment—he fell into a cataleptic state. After a coma lasting twelve hours he was pronounced dead and preparations were made for his burial. It was sad, of course, but babies were not unduly rare on that coast; in any case there would remain an elder boy and two younger girls to occupy the harassed mother. Poor Teresa was heartbroken. Nicolo was her favourite; and, besides, there was an unredeemed promise made to her by an angel from heaven. When the boy was born a celestial vision presented itself before her delirium-bewildered eyes. A radiant angel offered to grant her any one boon on behalf of her new-born infant. Her wish—also divinely inspired—was that her son should become the greatest violinist the world had ever seen, and she was assured of its fulfilment. To the Italian Catholic who believes, heaven's promises are never broken. Teresa looked once more at the tiny figure in its white shroud; the cataleptic child moved slightly.

He was saved from premature burial and recovered; but to the day of his death he never enjoyed good health for more than a few months at a time.

When the delicate and sensitive child first began to play the violin is not known; but we may assume that at the earliest opportunity Antonio commenced to teach him. His talent was precocious and it was not long before he had outstripped his father's limited technical and theoretical knowledge. At the age of five his ear was singularly acute, but like the youthful Mozart he suffered physically on hearing certain loud noises. From the earliest awakening of his intelligence the sound of the organ in church reduced him to tears. He could play whatever his father placed before him, and would ask for more. Forty years later he told Schottky how his father punished him for slackness and carelessness. But here was a potential source of income, more certain than the lottery, and Antonio was not the man to allow a boy's natural indolence or a child's love for games in the fields or on the beach to stand between him and future wealth. 'He soon recognized my natural talents,' said Nicolo, 'and I owe to him the first fundamental principles of my art . . . One can hardly imagine a stricter father; if I did not seem to be industrious enough, he would compel me to redouble my efforts by hunger. I suffered very much physically, and my health began to give way. And yet there was really no need for such severity. I exhibited great enthusiasm for the instrument, and studied it unceasingly in order to discover new, and hitherto unsuspected effects.' It is to Nicolo's credit that whatever he may have said of the treatment he received at his father's hands, he never spoke so harshly of him as did most of his biographers. The knowledge that Mozart, at the age of six, had composed a concerto so difficult that no one could play it, spurred the boy on to further activity, and at the age of eight he produced his first composition under his father's direction. This was destroyed, 'as were so many more of my experiments of a like nature'. While his father threatened physical violence and reduced rations, his mother encouraged

23

him with the story of her heavenly vision. Between the urging of one parent and his fear of the other, the child soon became accustomed to look no farther than the four strings of his fiddle. Within the span of his two arms lay his universe, and the performance of his daily task was the price of his bed, his food, and his peace of mind. What youthful desires were suppressed, what sides of his mental equipment were left undeveloped, seems to have been beyond the ken of both his parents.

However sordid may have been the motives that actuated Antonio, he quickly realized that if the boy's unusual talent was to be employed to the best advantage he would now need a more highly specialized form of instruction. He recognized equally rapidly that the goal of Nicolo's ambition was not to become an average performer. With his limited financial resources he turned first to Giovanni Servetto, a violinist in the theatre orchestra, whose practical knowledge of the higher technics of his instrument, however, was not of a sufficiently advanced order to retain Nicolo in his tutelage for very long. The boy needed experience as well as expert guidance, and he was fortunate enough to find both when his father handed him over to Giacomo Costa, a painstaking and conscientious teacher and *maestrò di cappella* at the cathedral of S. Lorenzo. Under his care Nicolo made far more rapid progress. Musical training and aesthetical development now proceeded side by side with the practical work. Partially to pay for his tuition he played solos in the churches—frequently three times a week—and the necessity for continually having new works in readiness gave him a vastly increased knowledge of the contemporary literature for his instrument. Moreover, it afforded him opportunities for pursuing his own experiments in composition. It was Costa, too, who introduced him to Francesco Gnecco, a composer of operas who was then enjoying a more than local celebrity. Through the instrumentality of both he entered Genoese society, learned to speak nicely, and to behave like a gentleman. In addition, these experiences broadened his narrow outlook on the world and provided him with new and critical audiences.

What general education Nicolo enjoyed, and whether he ever went to school, we do not know; he himself is silent on the point. Where he learned to write and make the arithmetical calculations he afterwards needed, no one can say. The adult Paganini was able to hold his own in debate with some of the best-trained minds in Italy, and his conversation sparkled with ready wit and classical allusions. None of his friends ever saw him read a book, and the sources of his knowledge remain undiscovered.

We reach our first safe chronological anchorage in 1793—that dreadful year of hatred and bloodshed. Luigi Marchesi, one of the most celebrated male soprani of the day, accompanied by the scarcely less highly-courted Piedmontese vocalist, Teresa Bertinotti—sometimes given as Albertinotti—arrived at Genoa for the purpose of giving a concert at the theatre. Whether the two famous singers were seeking an assistant who would fill up the programme for a purely nominal fee, or whether the fame of the child-prodigy had reached them before their arrival is uncertain. All we know is that they asked Antonio to allow the boy to appear with them. Paganini, senior, was in a position to impose conditions, and when the interview ended, the vocalists had promised to sing at a second concert—this time for the benefit of Nicolo. This was the future maestro's first public appearance. Electing to be heard in a set of variations he had himself written upon the air of the *Carmagnole*—a popular Provençal folk-tune to which a revolutionary text had been adapted the previous year—he enjoyed a veritable triumph. The Genoese audience, always enthusiastic in their acclamations for the party in power, were as delighted with the subtle allusion to the Revolution as they were transported by the dexterity of the young virtuoso. Nicolo's success at these two concerts was such that there could now be no two paths open to him. His mother's wish was being realized; heaven was keeping faith.

Nicolo was now eleven years of age and he had not yet known the meaning of a moment's freedom. His love for his instrument had increased with his public success; but his knowledge of the vast world outside of Genoa was still as limited as ever. He had become a patient practising-machine—indeed, later in life he adopted Buffon's *Le genie, c'est la patience,* as his motto—and he scarcely noticed his father's goading. The paternal severity was accepted as a matter of course. Antonio had done his best to bring his son, by fair means or foul, to his present position, and he caused him to appear in public as a real wonder-child of nine. The crafty impresario realized that a prodigy of nine would attract far more attention than one of eleven. Even Nicolo himself believed that he was but nine years old at this period, and from this innocent deception was no doubt derived the erroneous date so often assigned to his birth (1784).

The die was cast: Nicolo was to become an international celebrity. His Genoese friends—knowing Antonio's limitations—interested themselves actively in his future; advice was showered upon the father; Nicolo must have further tuition from the best masters procurable. The concerts with Marchesi and Bertinotti had attracted the attention of the Marchese di Negro to the boy's gifts, and in this nobleman young Paganini found his first useful patron. Any search after a celebrated master of violin-playing in the Italy of that era was quickly narrowed down, and the choice restricted to the one man whose reputation was great enough to merit such a pupil as Paganini. This was Alessandro Rolla of Parma.

The two years that followed the concerts at Genoa were spent in strenuous work, still under the watchful, and now somewhat troubled eye of Costa. It was most probably between 1793 and 1795 that Nicolo commenced making his discoveries on the fingerboard. His acquired technic must at this period already have been considerable; and this, serving his natural aptitude undoubtedly permitted innovations and produced effects that were looked upon as revolutionary by so conservative a teacher as Costa. This worthy man fondly imagined that the fame of a Rolla would be sufficient to chasten the extravagant tendencies of his brilliant pupil and bring him safely back to the classic fold. In consultation with Gnecco, di Negro, and Antonio, he broached the important subject. Nicolo must leave Genoa and be deprived of the freedom that is bred of the indulgence of familiars; he must go to a stricter school, to a master who would sanction none of the boy's fantastic notions. Costa was almost aghast; whoever heard of anything so fantastic as the attempt to make the violin say more than the plain, unvarnished, though truthful words of a written text? Whoever could find an artistic use for the harmonic combinations, the scintillating bow-magic, charmed from his wooden vessel by this thirteen-year-old fiddling magician? Frankly, Nicolo was more than Costa could manage; he was too inexplicable to be given a place in Giacomo's circumscribed musical scheme. Rolla alone could make him conform to traditional usage; could lead his stupendous genius along time-honoured paths; and with his inherent talents—who knows?—Nicolo Paganini might one day be as great as Corelli, or even Viotti.

CHAPTER III

(July, 1795—Nov., 1797)

NICOLO was almost thirteen when his father, in consultation with his friends, evolved a plan to make possible a period of study at Parma. On July 25, 1795, the good citizens of Genoa read a strange advertisement among the concert-announcements:

> 'Nicolo Paganini of Genoa, a boy already well-known in his own country for his skill in the manipulation of the violin, having decided to improve his talents by study under the guidance of the celebrated Signor Rolla at Parma, but not possessing the means to carry out this proposition, has seized upon this plan, and summons up all his courage to ask his fellow-countrymen to contribute towards the realization of his object by inviting them to attend this concert, arranged for his benefit'.

The entertainment was a financial success and was probably followed by others of a similar kind. No immediate move was made, and between Nicolo's public appearance and the departure for Parma, Costa was doubtlessly preparing his pupil for his interview with the great Rolla. It has never been suggested before, but it would seem to have been more than likely that Gnecco also gave Nicolo the benefit of his advice—if not actual tuition—in composition. It was either at Gnecco's house or in the palazzo of the Marchese di Negro that Rodolphe Kreutzer, then visiting Italy (1796), heard Nicolo play; and the grace and charm of the boy's performance pleased the master as much as his technical skill and powers of sight-reading amazed him. No doubt Nicolo was learning rapidly that Genoa was not the whole world, and that outside of its walls there was much to be learned. Association with the di Negro family—especially with Giancarlo who was a fertile poet and polished linguist—was removing from his bearing the *gaucheries,* and from his tongue the patois, of the pale pink house, and Paganini later on showed his sense of obligation by dedicating a few of his works to its members.

Kreutzer's praise, added to the urging of Costa, finally forced Antonio to action; and some time during 1796 he packed his own and Nicolo's personal belongings and, accompanied by the generous di Negro, set out for Florence. This was by no means the most direct route to Parma; but the Tuscan capital provided a concert-audience which increased Nicolo's funds. Thence their road took them north to Parma.

The times were anything but settled, and travellers often played hide and seek with marching columns—now of friends, now of foes. At the middle of the year Napoleon's reforms were advertised in the Genoese territory and a somewhat belated miniature Revolution, in imitation of the Parisian model, afforded a little amusement for the populace. The statue of the noble Andrea Doria was overthrown, the ' book of gold ' was publicly burned, criminals were liberated from the gaols, and a message of congratulation was sent to the twenty-seven-year-old victor of Lodi and the Bridge of Arcole. Here ended the duty of Paganini's countrymen to the man who had cleared northern Italy of the Austrians. In the meantime Antonio and Nicolo arrived in Parma.

Alessandro Rolla, an excellent violinist of Pavia who had been appointed to the court of Parma as solo viola in the year of Paganini's birth, was perhaps the most highly esteemed teacher of his day. His compositions demanded well-developed techni-cal powers for their performance, and the violinist who could play them after a reasonable amount of study was considered a finished artist. Without going through the formality of first making an appointment, father and son presented themselves at the *casa* Rolla, only to find that the maestro was indisposed and in bed. Their letters of introduction from Costa, Gnecco, and di Negro secured their admission, and Signora Rolla acquainted her husband with the names of the visitors. The almost threadbare story of what followed is this time perhaps best told in Paganini's own words : ' . . . his wife showed us into a side-apartment where I discovered, on the table, a violin and the maestro's most recent concerto. It needed but a gesture from my father to cause me to take up the violin and play the composition off at sight. The ailing musician was alert immediately and asked who it was that had elected to be heard in this manner, refusing to believe that it could be but a boy. When he had convinced himself that it was so, he cried, " I can teach him nothing new; in God's name let him go to Paër; here he will only waste his time fruitlessly " '. Was this to be the result of all Costa's planning? Could nothing be done to curb this extraordinary boy's unheard-of extravagancies? Not even by a Rolla? It appeared so.

Ferdinando Paër, then the most popular composer of operas in Italy, was busy with the writing of his *L'Intrigo Amoroso* for the Duke of Parma. He was not then in Germany as so many writers assert, but merely too occupied to accept Nicolo as a pupil at once. But he was very helpful and received the Paganinis kindly. Nicolo's account of their meeting continues to the effect that he ' recommended me to his own teacher, the old but widely-experienced Neapolitan conductor, Ghiretti, who took me formally in hand, giving me three lessons a week for half a year in counterpoint. Under his direction I composed twenty-four fugues as studies, without the assistance of any instrument—having only ink, pen, and paper before me. I made considerable progress because my own desires lay in the same direction. Soon Paër interested himself so deeply in my studies that he insisted upon my going to him twice a day so that we might work together. After four months he set me the task of composing a duetto which he read, smiling merrily, saying that he could discover no violation of pure form'. Paër then returned to his post at Venice, though Nicolo says that later on he ' often turned with great pleasure to this great

30

master, whose grateful pupil I am glad to consider myself'. These studies occupied about a year, during which time Ghiretti's influence secured for Nicolo frequent opportunities for appearing before the court of Parma. What he had learned from Ghiretti and Paër—especially in instrumentation—was later to stand him in good stead when his public appearances and his own peculiar style necessitated the composition of works for his own use. However much his own genius was responsible for many of the dazzling effects he produced, there can be no doubt but that he owed his technical facility in orchestration to the sound teaching of these two conscientious men.

It is curious that Paganini should strenuously deny ever having had lessons from Rolla himself. Carlo Gervasoni, an eminent writer on musical matters and a contemporary of Paganini's at Parma, was certain that Rolla did teach him— for some time giving him three lessons a week. There seems to be no reason for doubting Gervasoni's evidence, and the only explanation that appears to meet the case is that the undisciplined and recklessly experimenting young fiddler and the severely classical Rolla did not agree. Nicolo's mastery of the fingerboard must by now have been great enough to permit him a freedom in performance that Rolla could sanction no more than Costa had done two years earlier. Paganini's highly ornamental trimming and sparkling bowings were irreconcilably alien to the Parmesan professor's dignified musical scheme.

But the quick eye of that mercenary showman, Antonio, espied in Nicolo's amazing brilliance a means of extracting the *lire* from the pockets of the masses, even if it did not meet with the full approval of the traditionalists; and he decided then and there that his son's period of apprenticeship was ended—that he was ripe for concert-work as a professional virtuoso. But Nicolo had profited in more ways than one while studying in Parma. He had seen new sights, had met interesting people, had tasted court-life, had seen other boys of his own age enjoying life far more fully than he had ever done. He began to imagine an existence that was not all crotchets and quavers,

fugal exercises, and applause. He found himself turning for a
second glance when a pretty girl passed by. Something in him
was awakening, he knew not what. Longingly he would gaze
over the open landscape and furtively look at his father to see
if he had been observed. ' The excessive severity of my father ',
says Nicolo, ' now seemed to weigh more crushingly than ever
upon me—more and more so as my talent developed and my
knowledge increased. Fain would I have torn myself free that
I might travel alone; but my strict Mentor moved not from
my side '. Together father and son toured northern Italy, and
concerts were given with great success in Parma, Milan,
Bologna, Florence, Pisa, Leghorn, and other towns.

It was now early in 1797 and Nicolo was in his fifteenth year.
Eighteen months of absence from home had probably exhausted
Antonio's resources, but with the proceeds of the tour in his
pocket he returned with his son to the little dwelling in Genoa.
The Nicolo who found his mother thanking the saints for the
fulfilment of at least a part of the divine promise was a very
different one from the docile child who had set out for
Parma. He was elated by his success; but beneath his rapture
for his fiddle and the pride of achievement that lifted his head
high above those of the barefooted boys about the harbour of
Genoa there stirred a something that would not be stilled. The
early maturity of the Mediterranean littoral, instead of lending
him dignity, gave him torment. In his soul cried a voice, ever
increasing in its urgency—' liberty, liberty '—and he felt the
chafing of his yoke as a physical pain and the bearing-rein,
tightened by his father's firm hand, as a degrading sufferance.

Only one avenue of escape seemed open to him—the one
that lay in the perfection of his art. In his violin he saw the
key that alone could unlock his prison-gate. Furiously he
covered sheet after sheet of paper with music; feverishly he
practised a single passage a hundred times until he secured the
effect he sought. From morning to nightfall his amazing
fingers discovered and conquered one difficulty after the other,
until worn out he would sink on to his bed, and sleep as only

those who are on the verge of complete nervous collapse can sleep. His health suffered seriously. But one thought occupied his mind, one ambition fired his soul: he must master his instrument as it had never been mastered before; he must develop tonal effects that would compel the homage of all who heard him; he must become so much greater than his rivals that even comparison should be impossible. His indomitable will supported the frailty of his body and he achieved his object. And for the rest of his life exacting Nature demanded payment in recompense for her outraged laws. If we compare Nicolo's performance with that of his contemporaries and predecessors we realize that we see here no evolutionary step. However much Paganini the musician may have owed to his teachers, Paganini the violinist was self-made and self-taught. Aided by his natural aptitude he leaped over three or four stages of normal development and reached the zenith of his powers a century before his time.

CHAPTER IV

WILD OATS
(Nov., 1797—1801)

Lucca lies pleasantly enough in the valley of the Serchio, the heat of the plain tempered by the kindly breezes from the Apennines; at sundown the Zephyr from over the Gulf of Genoa gently stirred olive and vine, while on the landward horizon the mountains stood mysterious, awe-inspiring, cloud-capped, protective. Outside the ramparts the silkworm-feeding mulberry-groves afforded grateful shade to those who were free to wander. But it was not the beauty of Lucca that occupied Nicolo's thoughts by day and disturbed his sleep by night. The old republic had inscribed the magic word *Libertas* upon its panther-banner. Liberty. Nicolo was too pitifully young and too inexperienced in the ways of the world to suspect even the existence of the dreadful slavery of freedom. His mother was too modest, his father too busy dreaming of his future wealth, to teach him of the perils that lay in ambush on every side, awaiting an adolescent just as he, possessing a temperament like his. From his race he had inherited passions which sent the blood coursing through his veins and which brooked no treatment but indulgence. With his own desires for compass and his fiddle for paymaster he was ready to see a paradise in any place. Lucca was his lodestar because Lucca might provide him with an excuse for leaving the dwelling that to him was as the salt-mine to the Russian and the galleys to the Roman. The thrice ancient town perpetuated a custom that could serve his purpose. Every year, to honour St. Martin, Lucca enjoyed a musical festival open to all performers. The audiences came from all directions—townsfolk and countrymen, workers seek-

34

ing amusement, tourists thirsty for novelty and entertainment, impressarios questing after new talent. Nicolo begged his father to allow him to exhibit his knowledge before such a motley gathering. Whether Antonio saw no promising financial results accruing from the trip, or whether an imminent drawing of the lottery kept him at home, we do not know. But the request was refused. The boy sought the help of his mother, and through her mediation grudging permission was wrung from the father. Nicolo could attend the festival of St. Martin if his elder brother Luigi went with him. Here at last was some measure of freedom. Quickly the two youths packed their belongings, embraced their mother, promised their father a future of gold, and with a hurried *addio* to the two little sisters playing in the court below, they were gone. As the north-western gate in Lucca's venerable fortifications clanged shut after them late at night, it separated Nicolo from his childhood. Lucca's story contains many an interesting page; but to Nicolo that night it said nothing more than, 'This is the portal of your world'.

The chronology of this stage in Paganini's life is very hazy, and we have to fix certain dates rather arbitrarily. Thus, November, 1797, seems to be the earliest date for his appearance in Lucca—the only one that will allow us to reconcile what went before with what is to follow. His success was very great and the concert was but the first of many. He ventured to Pisa, Leghorn, and other towns in the vicinity. His fame spread, and wherever he appeared he was received rapturously and remembered with astonishment. Success intoxicated him a little; but he learned to give his audiences that which they applauded loudest, and to reserve for his own private recreation the music he had been taught to love. For the masses who swelled the ranks of his admirers he developed the amazing style that was Paganini.

Performing the works he had written for his own use, he already stood alone, separate and distinct from all other players. His second appearance in any town was the signal for enthusiasm even greater than before, which proved to him that he was giving his public what they wanted. Out of what was intended to be a single concert at the festival of St. Martin, developed a whole series of concerts, and Luigi remembering his father's injunctions, became restive if not a little nervous. But Nicolo worked as in a frenzy; every day he evolved new wonders. He played a melody with his bow while he accompanied himself by plucking the strings with the fingers of his left hand, and men stamped with delight; he whistled an exquisite air in the clearest of bird-like harmonics, and women smiled upon him; he brought off breath-taking runs in double-stopping, and the house would rise and shower flowers upon him. Nothing could now force him to turn his face northwards. Luigi went home alone, taking to his parents the money his brother sent.

Left to himself Nicolo filled each day with twenty-four hours of work, pleasure, and error. He told Schottky that 'many towns sought to retain me, sometimes as orchestral director, sometimes as soloist. But my fiery—nay, unbridled—temperament revolted against the idea of any fixed post. Travelling appealed to me, and it was not possible for me to remain in one place for any great length of time'. He preferred the care-free life of the wandering virtuoso to a more dignified existence at the little court of some petty Serenissimus. But a new spectre rose to trouble him; he began to experience a terrible loneliness. Thus it came about that after he had played and his pockets were filled with money, he became acquainted with other artists, more worldy-wise than he. They introduced him to friends whose only philosophy was the Horatian *Carpe diem,* and to others who manipulated little oblongs of pasteboard as skilfully as Nicolo did his fiddle. The son of Antonio, inheriting the hope that fortune's wheel would turn the right way, fell an easy victim for such smiling cynics to fleece. The company was so pleasant that the pigeon hardly felt the plucking—there was always a song to the guitar, a flask of red wine, a salacious joke. And on the way home to their several lodgings there was the patter of dainty feet to follow; the faint smile of invitation under the flickering street-lamp, the assignation, the perfumed caress, the intoxicating rapture of the young man's first excursion into a land of lotus-eaters. Change of air and scene, freedom from incessant drudgery under his father's jealous eye, and liberty of action, had at first improved Nicolo's health considerably. His nerves were strengthened, cobwebs were brushed away, and he began to enjoy life. But the midnight orgies into which he plunged with his new friends quickly dissipated the benefits derived. Fits of indolence, indifference, and dalliance took possession of him from time to time; and while he listened half-awake to the song of the sirens, the magic of his violin slept. Empty pockets, the cold glances of his companions, and the contemptuous sneers of his latest inamorata, spurred him to sullen wakefulness and fresh activity. A concert was arranged. Within an hour or two his four strings and a hank of horsehair had charmed a jingling solace into his purse—and the hectic round of cards and hazard, soft lips and languishing eyes, ruined finances and exhausted body was danced again. Sometimes, in a feverish attempt to recoup himself for accumulated losses, he would take a greater risk—and lose all. Often the earnings of more than one concert vanished at a single sitting. Then it was that the only thing he really valued—his violin—would be placed in sordid hands as pledge for sums borrowed to settle debts of honour.

It was on such an occasion—his violin safe in the keeping of the Lombards, his nerves taut and mistuned, his temper frayed to the last degree of irritability—that he fled to Leghorn from the memory of his losses, of unquiet nights, and of heartless love. He told Schottky that he made the excursion 'for pleasure'. It is far more likely that the subconscious urge was to escape from himself and from the temptations that were luring him on to the easy road to Avernus. The musical clique of Leghorn had not treated him any too well when he visited the town for the first time since he gained his independence: 'On one of my artistic wanderings', he says, 'I came to the port of Livorno armed with recommendations to the British consul who received me very kindly, helped me to engage a hall, and made sure that I should have a numerous audience. But Livorno, like so many other towns, had its own limited and conservative musical society, the members of which felt slighted at my failing to appeal to them. They managed matters so well that the ordinary orchestral musicians proved unfaithful to me. The concert was to commence at eight o'clock, the hall was packed, and no professional player had appeared. At length three or four mediocre spirits turned up. I was naturally compelled to alter my programme; my pride and my ambition forced me to make a supreme effort, and for almost three hours I managed to entertain the gathering with a youthfully virile performance. My endeavours were appreciated and rewarded with noisy applause'. Although a second visit to Leghorn resulted in a highly successful concert with a full orchestra, he never forgot his first unpleasant experiences there. On this, his third visit, he had no intention of playing at all; but the numerous friends he had made in the neighbourhood pressed him so insistently that he was forced to yield. A wealthy amateur—one M. Livron, a Frenchman who had amassed a fortune by supplying the needs of the French armies in Italy round about 1799—came forward and offered to provide Paganini with an instrument worthy of his talents. Nicolo was himself again; once more his chin rested on a good fiddle; again his will conquered his dissipated body; and after a wonderful display of artistry and virtuosity Livron refused to take back the violin he had lent: 'I cannot now profane it again', he said, 'keep it, my dear Paganini, and look upon it as a souvenir'. This magnificent instrument was the Guarneri del Gèsu that became his inseparable companion, a friend in all his trials and triumphs, the last object he touched before death mercifully closed his eyes four decades later. It was the fame that came to fiddle and player together that made the name of Guarneri universally known and created a demand for his instruments experienced only by the work of the Amatis and Stradivari.

A little earlier—at Parma—a fine example of Stradivari's workmanship fell into his hands. The well-known painter and excellent amateur violinist Pasini, doubting Paganini's unusual powers in sight-reading, offered the instrument as a prize if Nicolo could read a concerto that would be placed before him. The conditions were such that he could afford to ignore them. He had been so often challenged to these tests, that the work would have had to come from Paganini's own pen to have given Paganini the slightest trouble. We remember how at the age of thirteen he polished off Rolla's difficult composition in the same town, and he had been known to play strange works with the music upside-down on the music-stand. This time he was asked for a perfect performance of a piece packed with the most difficult passages that Pasini could have written for the purpose. Nicolo glanced rapidly over the pages, observed quietly: 'You may say good-bye to the violin'—and played the concerto in a manner that transported Pasini into ecstasies of delight. This was the instrument he was forced to pawn when he went to Leghorn 'for pleasure'. It was a magnificent specimen of Stradivari's art and forms the subject of another anecdote which has its important aspects.

Our reckless young fiddler had found himself in one of his frequent financial scrapes when a certain prince offered to buy the Stradivari. 'I declared I could not sell it for 250 gold Napoleons', Paganini told Fétis; 'some time afterwards the prince . . . said he was willing to give me two thousand francs. I was, at that moment, in the greatest need of money to pay a debt of honour I had incurred at play, and I was almost tempted to accept his offer'. While in this dilemma he was invited to a party at a friend's house. 'All my capital consisted of thirty francs; I had disposed of all my jewels, watch, rings, and brooches'. The gambler in him conquered once more and he decided to risk his all at hazard. 'My thirty francs were reduced to three'. Already the desperate man saw visions of himself bereft of everything, on his way to Russia, 'without instrument or luggage, to re-establish my affairs'. At the last throw fickle fortune turned her wheel in his favour and he won 160 francs—a sum sufficient to extricate him from his present difficulties. The experience provided him at last with the lesson he needed; from that moment gambling ceased to offer any attractions to him and he realized that 'a gambler was an object despised by all properly regulated minds'. He never again merited the reproach that clung to his memory so long. His speculations—with one tragic exception—were generally shrewdly managed by his countryman and lifelong friend, the lawyer Germi, and in spite of his occasional lapses which bene-fited no one but some unworthy woman, he contrived to amass roughly a thousand pounds before 1801. He offered his father the interest on this sum to assist in the solution of his mother's housekeeping problems, but Antonio would have nothing to do with such a proposition. After long discussions that degenerated into fierce epistolary quarrels, and a few paternal threats, Nicolo regained his peace of mind by sending the whole sum to Genoa.

What was happening to the inhabitants of the pink house near the harbour of Genoa at this period we can only guess. In the Spring of 1800 Massena, Soult, and Suchet were fighting Napoleon's battles in the Ligurian country; an Austrian army under Melas and an English fleet debated every inch of coast and every stone inland. Outnumbered and out-manœuvred by the Allies, the French sought refuge in Genoa, which then experienced one of the most desperate and harrowing sieges in history. The wretched Genoese, looking to France for protection, starved in protecting the French. Gunpowder, famine, and plague played dreadful havoc among a people drawn into the maelstrom of foreign quarrels. Food for the civilian population soon failed, horseflesh, cats and dogs were luxuries, and finally bats and worms were placed on the ghastly menu. Corpses were piled high in the streets; the conditions were unspeakable. On June 4, Massena surrendered, and three weeks later the victory at Marengo restored Genoa to the French. Though still rejoicing in the name of Republic, Genoa like a vassal state sent a message of congratulation to the Emperor who was then at Milan placing upon his head the iron crown of Lombardy. It is very much to be doubted that Paganini was at home during the siege; he certainly never mentioned it in his later reminiscences. Although we know pretty well what he did at this period, we are in the dark as to when and where he did it. The only dated information we have is that on September 14, 1800, he was in Lucca, and, on the evidence of Gervasoni, early in 1801 again at Leghorn. He was probably flitting from town to town, giving concerts or chasing some fair will-o'-the-wisp that in passing had caught his roving glance.

He had become more careful in money matters, taking few risks, and living very economically. It is quite likely that his reputation for meanness arose from his reluctance to give every petitioner free tickets for his concerts. He also hated tipping servants, though he paid generously for services rendered. His health was in a very precarious state, and though his will-power succeeded in winning for him a high position in the artistic world, it failed to maintain more than a very spasmodic discipline over his body. Nearly thirty years later he confesses as much to Schottky, and his explanations or excuses are worth remembering: 'At present, as a man over whose head life has often passed stormily enough, I must admit that my youth was by no means free from the errors of young people who, after the upbringing of a slave, are suddenly freed from their bonds and seek to reward themselves for long privation by heaping pleasure upon pleasure . . . My talents found great favour everywhere—aye, for a fiery young man *too* great a favour. Travelling unrestrainedly from place to place, the great enthusiasm that almost every Italian exhibits for the art, my Genoese blood which seems to flow just a little more rapidly than that of the foreigner—all this, and many more circumstances of a like nature, often placed me in company that was not of the best. I confess honestly that I often fell into the hands of people who played with more finish and success than I—though their instruments were not the violin or the guitar . . . . But these periods were luckily only of a temporary nature; I regret having passed through them, but do not desire to appear better than I actually am, and I beg of you to give your readers no more than the simple truth. There may be some among them who will refrain from throwing the first stone . . . until they have placed in the other scale the circumstances of climate, a faulty upbringing, Italian customs, and the life of an artist generally'. We are to remember that Paganini was giving Schottky the materials for his own biography.

A weak constitution and over-indulgence might easily have brought to an early grave the man who still had so much to do. He was moving downhill very rapidly when a ' lady of title ' came to his rescue. He had, in 1801, played somewhere in Tuscany, and the lady hearing, straightway fell in love with him. He reciprocated with what was again probably ' the first real passion of his life ', and, the curtain rung down for the last time amid peals of vociferous applause, the energetic and determined lady took him by the hand and led him to her Tuscan chateau. In the abundant crop of wild oats sown by this precocious youth during the past three years, one plant of better quality grew up. A saviour seemed to have fallen from heaven to drag him from the mire; but, then, heaven often chooses strange instruments for benefitting mankind.

CHAPTER V

'DIDA'

(1801—Sept., 1805)

IF Nicolo harboured any illusions of a Venusberg-like existence in the Tuscan chateau of the unknown lady, they were speedily to be dispelled. Whether she felt any really deep affection for the violinist, or whether her interest in him was called forth by his art, we have no means of deciding. That the impressionable young man fell head over heels in love with her seems to be sufficiently proven. Whatever may have been the motives of the lady, she was certainly an influence for good in a highly critical epoch of his life. It is perhaps a pity that he had no one of her character and temperament by his side later in his career. She quickly diagnosed his case, prescribed a rigid routine of regular hours, sensible meals, open-air pursuits, and rest; and being no doubt the elder and more determined of the two, she was obeyed. The violin was laid aside for the time being, the patient was encouraged to take up agricultural and horticultural work on his noble hostess's estate, and for recreation in the evening was permitted to play the guitar. That she allowed him to admire her own attractiveness only at a distance will presently be clear enough.

Who this benefactress was has never been discovered. That she was wealthy goes without saying, and that she was of noble birth and socially above suspicion—so that she could freely indulge her present whim without losing caste—is obvious. She seems to have allowed him to address her as 'Dida', for several little pieces which he composed while with her are 'Dedicato alla Signora Dida'. One of them—a Menuet and Perigourdine in A—bears the plaintive sub-title, 'Menuet that goes calling

43

for Dida' (*Minuetto che va chiamando Dida*).   Another in
Paganini's autograph—also a menuet—bears on the back of the
manuscript the avowal : ' Sighing is of no use, jaundice leaves
me a heritage of weakness, so that Doctor Botti forbids me to
play.   Patience for a little while; shall I be happy then?
Patience.   And meanwhile the days pass by.   I am becoming
stronger and I shall prove myself to be your most obedient
servant . . . '; while in a third he calls himself her 'most
obedient servant and *implacable* friend'.   Although, as both
Bonaventura and Kinsky (Catalogue of the Heyer Collection)
point out, other works of the same period are dedicated to the
' Signora Marina ' and to the generous ' Emilia di Negro ' (of
Genoa), the name of Dida occurs most frequently.

From the autumn of 1801 until late in 1804 Dida managed
to keep Nicolo near her and docile.   It was probably the longest
that any woman had held his affection and esteem.•   If he ever
learned who she was he never divulged her secret.   These three
years formed a gap in his earlier biographies that gave rise to
many unpleasant rumours concerning him.   Paganini must be
admired for his steadfastness and loyalty in preserving her
anonymity.   Even when challenged in the public press to say
where he spent this period of his life, he maintained an obstinate
silence.   His calumniators therefore decided that this must be
the time he spent in prison for the murder of his wife, his
mistress, or a possible rival.   Even these direct accusations failed
to make him speak.   He told Fétis as much of his association
with Dida as we know ; but he did not trust even this friend with
her name or status, nor did he give any indication as to the
whereabouts of her estate.

It was Dida's liking for the guitar that prompted him to take
up the instrument seriously.   He soon acquired an almost
unheard-of facility upon it, and taught his friend all he discovered.   He wrote a number of compositions for the instrument—including duets which he most probably played with her
—and it is quite likely that prolonged practice on the wide
fingerboard of the guitar increased the span of his left hand

in a way that was later on very useful to him when he returned to the violin. He took up the guitar again as an aid to composition, and many of the most effective of his chord effects were discovered on the plucked instrument. As he advanced in years he spoke disparagingly of the guitar, but he made it serve a definite purpose in his work. All through the years in which he was employed at Dida's side, the busy gossips were industriously spreading the fiction that he was perfecting his performance on a violin with a single string, because his heartless gaoler refused to replace the others as they broke. Of all the baseless stories connected with Paganini's life, the one that offers this explanation for his perfection as a 'one-string fiddler' is the most absurd.

What caused him to leave this rural Elysium we cannot say with certainty. Cynics suppose that he tired of Dida as he did of all his other lady friends, forgetting that she belonged to an entirely different category. But Nicolo was now twenty-two years of age, and with returned health and vigour he no doubt became impatient for action. He was too independent a spirit to consent to remain idle, eating the bread of charity. Moreover, he loved travel and he loved the violin; and all through his life the applause of great audiences afforded him a delight that was almost childish. Possibly Dida, realizing that she had done for him all she could, sent him back into the world with strict injunctions to lead a more temperate life. Paganini—except for recounting the story to Fétis—never mentioned her again; and, sad to relate, the cure she effected was by no means permanent. He gave up gambling, it is true; but his search for the 'one real passion' of his life went on intermittently until he was past fifty.

He returned to Genoa in 1804. After the terrors of the Napoleonic campaigns his homeland now enjoyed peace under the French tricolour. How he was received by his parents we are not informed; but we have his own word for it that he settled down to a course of intensive study on the violin—so long neglected to his own mental and physical advantage. His technical foundations had been well laid and he found that he had lost very little of his old power and assurance. He worked harder than ever and surpassed his previous achievements. Before the year closed he found time to teach a little girl of seven—Caterina Calcagno—who became, at the age of fifteen, a very accomplished violinist, exhibiting all the courage and fire that one would expect in a pupil of Paganini. We shall meet her once more in her master's company, after which she vanished from public life.

Dividing his time between composition and practice on his violin, Paganini prepared himself for his real conquest of the artistic world. The three years of Dida's guidance and affectionate watchfulness had brought him to a more settled frame of mind. She had converted him from a rudderless derelict, tossed whithersoever the winds of caprice or passion pleased, into a mature man with fixed intentions. He tells us that he spent a little time ' as an amateur ', deriving pleasure from the chamber-music of the classic masters, but most of his energies were directed to preparations for the future. He revived obsolete seventeenth-century practices such as the *Scordatura*, or unconventional tuning of his instrument, he extended the range of useful harmonics, he perfected himself in pizzicato for the left hand, he developed a series of bow-strokes that had never been seen before. He exhausted the resources of the violin so completely that even to-day we can see no possibility of anything new being discovered or invented. His inspiration was fertile and feared nothing; his outlook was romantic; his experiences of life and his technical powers allowed him to present the whole gamut of human emotions on the four strings of his instrument. If he over-sentimentalized his performance occasionally, it was only a concession to the popular taste of his time. If he descended to the production of sounds and effects not admissible to the domain of serious artistic endeavour, it was again but to please the occupants of the cheaper seats. We must not forget that an appreciation of the more elevated forms of art was by no means as common at the opening of the nineteenth century as it is to-day, and we should therefore not be too hard on a public performer who is, after all, but a public servant, if he makes an attempt to win the approbation of all classes. With a musical and technical equipment at his disposal more varied and comprehensive than that ever possessed by any other one artist, Nicolo left Genoa in 1805 to enter upon a stage in his career that was to contain his ascent to the zenith of his powers.

.   .   .   .

Leaving his home towards the end of the summer, it was Paganini's intention to visit all the larger towns of northern Italy before the winter season came to a close. How much of this plan was carried out we do not know; for though he set out firmly resolved to live the life of a free agent, owing obedience to no one, the middle of September was barely reached before he had bound himself by contract to fill a fixed post. Lucca, where he began his independent life and scored his first successes, was his primary objective, and he probably got no farther. To this visit belongs the story of his appearance at a festival in one of the convent-churches. Memories of his youthful performances in the churches of Genoa came back to him as he played a concerto in the sacred building. On such occasions, laying aside his most scintillating *tours de force* at the dictation of his good taste, he knew how to charm from his instrument a song of hope and comfort, a sermon in tender wordless melodies, that went to the hearts of the most worldly and indifferent of men. Woman paid homage to this eloquent preacher with their sighs and tears. Paganini was now a man who could speak with authority on pain and joy. He possessed the advantages conferred upon him by his experiences in the home of the sympathetic Dida, and the worshippers were so carried away by the elevation of his playing that they forgot their environment and broke out in unrestrained applause. The monks, shocked though understanding, hurriedly left their

47

stalls to remind the congregation of the decorum due to the edifice.

A public concert followed at which the new Paganini, brilliant and captivating, exhibited his complete mastery over bow and finger-board. All Lucca paid tribute to his genius by speaking of no one else, and the fanfares of fame's clarions sounding his praises penetrated to the ears of the Princess Elise Bacciochi and her violin-playing husband. They may even have graced the concert with their presence. No Bonaparte—least of all Elise—needed much time for reflection in order to reach any decision; and before Paganini realized it his signature was appended to the document that made him the servant of this imperious and in many ways fantastic woman. It is to be hoped that Nicolo, resplendent in his gala uniform and fêted by the artificial flatterers of a glittering establishment, sometimes devoted a grateful thought to the noble Dida who had made of him the courtly man he now was—but it is to be feared that he did not.

CHAPTER VI

ELISE BACCIOCHI
(Sept., 1805—1808)

WHEN the first Napoleon opened his generous hand and bestowed duchies and thrones upon his kinsfolk, he kept his eldest sister Marianne Elise waiting until last, to see what would be left over. It will be guessed that Elise, the ugly duckling of the Bonapartes, was not in the best of odour in the high places of the Empire. Indeed, she annoyed the man of destiny in many ways. For one thing she did not treat him with the respect he felt he merited; for another she had been presumptuous enough to marry without his consent. Though she failed in her attempt to ensnare in her matrimonial meshes the astute soap-maker Rabassin, she succeeded in capturing the slower-witted Pasquale Bacciochi, who was too perfect a fool to realize that the ambitious policy of Elise required a husband more than her heart needed affectionate companionship. In such a court as Elise had in her subtle mind, the blind stupidity of husbands was a distinct asset; dash and brilliance, wit and intellect, could easily be obtained elsewhere. Bacciochi exhibited only two features of romance: he came of a good family and he was poor. Napoleon did not see eye to eye with the Bacciochis on political matters, and he had had other plans for his sister. In addition to all these irritating trifles, Elise was always at loggerheads with her imperial brother; she scandalized him with her eccentricities; she slighted and insulted Josephine with and without provocation. In an elementary way she was an interesting subject to study. She cultivated the friendship of some of the most brilliant men and women of her day; her salons were crowded with the most outstanding figures in the world of art,

49

science, and literature; and the lists of her guests read like pages from a Napoleonic 'Who's Who'. But she also exposed her own intellectual gifts—employed perhaps in a blue-stocking manner—to ridicule by an excess of misplaced zeal and her eccentric behaviour.

Masson gives us a perfect account of her personal appearance with a brevity that is admirable. She was very tall and very thin, with black hair and black eyes; a large mouth and fine teeth; she had nothing feminine in her air, her figure, or her face; her spirit was grave, her body flat. She was one of those androgynous beings ' whose body modelled itself upon the intelligence and which, without having acquired the qualities of the other sex, has lost the charm of its own '. Not much need be said of her education at St. Cyr; it rested upon a very insecure foundation, to say the least. At the same time she showed a real affection for literature. If she differed from the other members of her family in most features, she possessed one Napoleonic trait very highly developed: she was intensely and insatiably ambitious. But ambition, as her brother understood the term, was obstructed by Bacciochi. Still, he was Elise's husband and something had to be done for him, if only for the purpose of removing the vociferous Marianne from the Parisian court. Napoleon well knew what this sister could do when she had made up her mind to cause embarrassment. He only needed to remember how she appeared at Madame Junot's wedding. She had presided the same morning at a literary society for ladies and had decided that its members should wear a distinctive costume. Having designed what she thought a suitable dress, she had a model made and wore it herself. ' Her head-dress ', said Madame Junot, ' was made up of a muslin veil, embroidered with gold and coloured silks, twisted about her head, with a laurel-wreath in the style of Petrarch or Dante balanced on top. A skirt and half-train, with a very long tunic over it, was the dress; her sleeves were very short, or, as I remember, none at all; a tremendous shawl was thrown over all like a mantle. Her ensemble suggested the Hebraic, the Grecian, the Roman; in a word, everything but good French taste'. A woman who could make an Emperor ridiculous by riding in the Bois de Boulogne in a flaming red habit and by appearing at the court dramatic junketings in pink tights, would be capable of anything. Bacciochi had been made a colonel; that is, a colonel's uniform had been hung upon his insignificant shoulders. Elise was still nothing but a thorn in Josephine's side. Suddenly relief came to the harassed Emperor from an unexpected quarter. The principality of Piombino had placed itself under the 'protection' of Napoleon; Lucca asked for a prince of the Bonaparte family. Pasquale Bacciochi received the title of Prince of Lucca and Piombino—a pure matter of courtesy; Elise could wear the princely trousers as easily as any other unfeminine costume. She became the ruling head of the little Italian state; Bacciochi remained what he was before—nothing.

On July 14, 1805, Elise and her husband Felice—he had to change his Christian name because Pasquale, in the language of the Italian comic opera, connoted 'fool'—made a state entry into Lucca that resembled a musical comedy version of a Roman triumph. She established her household on the model of her brother's and spared no expense. She had her *Dame d'honneur,* her *Chevalier d'honneur,* her first Chamberlain, her *Intendant-general,* her ladies of the chamber, her reader, and a far greater number of subordinates. She surrounded herself by a barrier of etiquette, made up of 253 articles, that was more minute, more detailed, than that of the Tuileries. She took her position seriously and had no mind to be considered less than a sovereign. She had her praiseworthy moments too; she founded an *Academia* and reorganized the charitable establishments; she employed Tofanelli in her Academy of the Fine Arts; she had a French and an Italian Theatre; and she engaged the celebrated Nicolo Paganini to place the crown upon her musical establishment.

The great violinist's post was no sinecure. It was his duty to conduct the Opera when the ruling house visited the theatre, to play at court two or three times a week as the princess's private chamber-musician, and to arrange a fortnightly concert for the special benefit of the court circle. In what personal relationship the princess and the musician stood to one another is not clear. Rumour made them secret lovers; and though Elise was six years Nicolo's senior, it is quite possible. Neither of them was unduly perturbed by scruples as to how the boredom of dreary days and long evenings at a petty court was to be avoided. The princess was accustomed to move in an entourage of obsequious flatterers with any one of whom she may have flirted. Even if she went farther, 'that fool Bacciochi' was negligible. Paganini, for his part, had already forgotten Dida, as subsequent events will prove. To give him the right to attend all court functions, Elise conferred on him the rank and uniform of a Captain of the Royal Gendarmerie, which made him a member of her bodyguard. Felice, though enjoying his brilliant decorations and serene titles, was pushed unceremoniously into the background to practise his violin. The only sign of favour shown him by his imperious consort was the boon of lessons from Paganini, for which she paid. Nicolo's salary at this court was not very high, and what kept this money-loving man a prisoner in Lucca is another Paganinian mystery. Perhaps we shall find a solution among the ladies.

Though it may have required a little effort for Paganini to reconcile himself to settled life on one spot, he managed to pass his time pleasantly enough. Elise took a lively interest in his extraordinary gifts and afforded him every opportunity and encouragement to extend his quest after new effects. She was not always present at his court-concerts, and when she did attend, her 'nerves' frequently prevented her from remaining until the end, for she disliked harmonics. Where she went and what she did has nothing to do with us. Paganini may have wondered uneasily; but he had quite enough to occupy his mind. As, for instance, when he was asked at midday to write a concerto for violin and cor anglais that was to be performed the same evening. The musician whose duty it was to compose it had considered the time too short and declined the task. Within two hours Paganini had scribbled out the orchestral score, and improvising the solo-violin part, produced the work at the required time. He was very fond of giving such exhibitions of his technical address. One evening, when Panesi's opera *L'Avviso dei Gelosi* was being given, he wagered that he could conduct the work and play the leader's part throughout upon a violin provided with only the third and fourth strings. The stake was a supper for twenty-five persons—and he won it. We have his own word for it that most of his performances at court were improvised, and that only the accompaniments were written out.

Nor, on the other hand, was his time at Lucca fully occupied by work. He was free—on the evenings when he did not appear in his professional capacity—to indulge in his old sport of seeking romantic adventure. He related the details of one escapade of this nature to a genial gathering of Italian friends at Prague: 'Once, at Lucca, I found myself fortified with money and youth, but lacking someone to love; and since such a barren existence went very much against the grain, I went to seek what fate refused to hand to me'. After painstaking search he at length discovered at a window a face pretty enough to attract his attention. In the time-honoured manner he bribed a hairdresser to smuggle him into the lady's presence; he revelled in pleasurable excitement; he was living a Mozart opera. 'One evening, just as I was dressing to attend the princely court, there to direct a concert, this messenger of the gods sought me out. The powdering Iris swore to await me that evening at eleven o'clock to lead me to the fulfilment of my desires. Highly delighted, I hurried joyfully to my work, and even to the present day I cannot remember how I played. Semiquavers seemed semibreves, presto became largo. At the end of the performance I flew on the wings of love and hope to the pre-arranged spot where Figaro was already awaiting me at the door. A woman received me and conducted me into a room on the ground floor where I found the maiden. Silence

53

reigned, a lamp burned dimly, and the window stood open. I hurried towards my charmer who had not yet noticed my presence, for her eyes were fixed upon the full moon. The woman, who had not left my side, approached the day-dreamer and whispered a few incomprehensible words. Thereupon the young lady turned suddenly, and seeing me, screamed so loudly that I stood as if petrified. The duenna attempted to pacify her, while the barber who had taken upon himself the duties of sentry in the street outside, hurriedly called to me to come out. A thunderous voice was now joined to the pain-racked shrieking of the virgin. I lost my head and sought to leave the apartment; but at that moment I heard someone approaching. The lamp was suddenly extinguished, everything seemed in the maddest confusion, and I—fearing worse to come—leapt out of the window, which was luckily near the ground, and hurried home. The next day I expected Figaro to appear and explain the enigma, but he did not come. I therefore decided to seek him out. The circumstances of the case were roughly these: Having been disappointed in love the poor girl had become unbalanced, and the barber, thinking she might take me for the lover she imagined to be in the full moon, had promised her servant half of his reward if she introduced me. She allowed herself to be led astray and prepared the imbecile to receive her returning lover. That is why she had fastened her eyes upon the moon; she wished to see the hoped-for apparition step out of the shining disc and then embrace her. Surprise and joy were the causes of her involuntary shrieks that so frightened me'. Well, one cannot always expect to be successful in quests of this delicate nature.

He found some consolation for this disappointment in a Countess at Elise's court, 'a charming lady who felt herself drawn to me—or so I thought—while I had long admired her. Our mutual affection increased gradually, but had to be kept secret, a condition that enhanced the mystery and interest of our association'. It was difficult for a man of Paganini's temperament to hide his feelings, but the wrath of Elise was a factor to be remembered. She was a Corsican. One day he promised his latest flame to surprise her at the next concert with a musical jest that should have a bearing upon their secret amour. Little did he dream how far this promise would take him. It led to a manner of performance that he developed to the highest possible level and which became one of his most popular specialities.

When the evening of his experiment drew near he announced to the court that he would play a novelty entitled *Scene Amoureuse*. 'General curiosity', says Paganini, 'was excited, and the astonishment of the audience was excessive when I appeared with my violin provided with only two strings. I had retained the G and the E. One was to express the sentiments of the lady, while the other was to represent the voice of her lover. I worked up a sort of passionate dialogue in which the most tender accents followed transports of jealousy. The music was now insinuating, now plaintive; there were cries of rage and sounds of joy; sighs of pain and of happiness. The piece ended in reconciliation and the two lovers, more attached to one another than ever, executed a *pas de deux* which closed a brilliant coda. This musical scena was highly successful. I will not speak of the intoxicating glances which the lady of my dreams sent in my direction. The Princess Elise, after overwhelming me with praises, said most graciously: " You have just performed the impossible on two strings; would not a single string suffice your talents? " I promised on the spot to make the attempt. The idea intrigued my imagination, and some weeks later I composed a sonata entitled *Napoleon* for the fourth string only, and played it on August 25th, before a crowded and brilliant court . . . My predilection for the G-string dates from that evening '.

This, then, is the simple explanation of his uncanny facility on the G-string, the compass of which, with the aid of harmonics, he extended to more than three octaves. It was to a compliment from Elise that he owed the idea, and not to the cruelty of his gaoler. It seems a pity to have to part with the

55

romantic prison-story, especially as the string upon which he scored so many triumphs was made of his murdered wife's intestine. The manuscript of *Napoleon,* in nineteen autograph parts, is in the Heyer collection at Cologne, and dates from 1807. Although Paganini exploited the exclusive use of the G-string to an unprecedented extent, he was not the first to employ it for an entire work. Mozart's father tells us of Michael von Esser (born in 1736) who played with astonishing ease upon the fourth string, while Friedrich Wilhelm Rust wrote a sonata (dated 1796) for a single string. The latter composition remained hidden in manuscript-form until after Paganini's death, and he certainly did not derive his inspiration from that source.

Nicolo may have expanded genially in the warm glow of courtly compliments and the applause of cultured audiences, but he was becoming a trifle bored and impatient for change. He may have considered his talents too unusual to be hidden under the Luccan bushel. The *wanderlust* awoke, and he petitioned Elise for leave of absence. Possibly he needed more money than he was paid at court; and the princess, realizing the impossibility of rewarding him as his capabilities merited, allowed him to undertake a series of concerts. Elise was no fool; she had summed up the situation and she preferred to do without him for a while rather than lose this mercurial spirit altogether. It is during this period—between 1805 and 1808— that we see Paganini most like the ordinary artist of his era. Except for his flirtations he lived a normal life; his health seems to have been good; he was well-liked in society and he enjoyed general popularity; he was interesting and companionable. As to his amorous adventures, we are still not sure whether his was a lonely soul seeking comradeship, or whether he just enjoyed the pleasures of the chase. Perhaps he could say with Molière's Don Juan: 'I feel I have a heart capable of loving the whole world; and like Alexander I congratulate myself that there are other worlds in which I can extend my amorous conquests'.

CHAPTER VII

TRIALS, TRIUMPHS, AND TRANSITION
(1808—1809)

THE Paganini who entertained indulgent friends at the court of Lucca was a very different being from the artist who appeared on the public concert-platform from this stage in his career onwards. He had developed a style that was peculiarly his own. With music of a highly sentimental type he associated a studied pose that quickly became characteristic of him; with brilliance of execution he combined a facility and a grace of performance that were the despair of imitators. The consciousness of power that a complete knowledge of his own capabilities gave him, more than the flattery and applause of a court which amused rather than impressed him, developed in his mind a species of egotism for which he was not altogether to be blamed. His natural gifts, his years of patient labour, and the experiences he had gained, taught him exactly where he stood in relation to his contemporaries. His audiences outside of the court circle, typical of their romantic era, expected a certain amount of theatrical sensationalism on the platform. Paganini was too wise a business-man and too good a pupil of his father to disappoint their expectations. For this reason he began to cultivate an inscrutable expression of sphinx-like mystery, to allow his hair to grow long and curl unrestrainedly about his shoulders, to thrust his right foot well forward and rest the weight of his body on his left hip in a most unnatural— even grotesque—manner, and to appear before his public as a man of whom much more could be expected than was actually known. As his fame spread, so did the number of the rumours

57

concerning him increase and the improbability of the stories grow. As each one came to his ears his smile became more cynical and the grin on his manager's face broadened. If the people preferred to see their artists surrounded by a veil of mystery, Paganini was not the man to teach them better sense. After all, the minority who came to hear him for his music's sake, would come in any case. If the promise of a tricky little piece that contained imitations of all the sounds of the farmyard attracted hundreds to the concert-hall, the more artistic in his audience would have to put up with it or—since it was the last item on the programme—leave before it was performed. If they felt so disposed they were always at liberty to call him a charlatan—a privilege of which not a few availed themselves. Such was the man who appeared before the public of northern Italy in 1808, to continue the tour he had interrupted when he signed his agreement with Princess Elise three years earlier.

His first journey took him once more to Leghorn, and once more this city provided him with some anxious moments. He had had the misfortune to tread on a nail and injure his heel, with the result that when he limped on to the platform his entrance was anything but dignified. Italian audiences express their opinions in no half-hearted manner. They will be impelled to hiss and whistle, and even pelt an artist with whatever objects first come to their hands, quite as readily as they will applaud enthusiastically and extravagantly. They are also not innocent of that perverted sense of humour which makes us laugh when we see a portly old gentleman slide on his back after a banana-skin has brought him down. On this occasion the Livornese decided that the limp of the great Paganini was irresistibly funny, and an audible titter passed through the house. The violinist, usually very sensitive to an atmosphere of this sort, affected to ignore his rude reception and commenced his performance. The volatile listeners had scarcely settled themselves to enjoy the music when the candles fell out of a music-stand. This was more than the audience could endure, and an undisguised burst of laughter shook the theatre. Paganini, restraining his rising resentment, continued stolidly; but after a few more bars a string on his violin broke with a vicious little snap. For the third time laughter, now quite unrestrained, rocked the audience. What alternative was now left the artist but to retreat limping and more ridiculous than ever? Paganini knew of one, and he was determined to teach these people how to respect courage and presence of mind. They were already beginning to doubt the evidence of their senses; this peculiar man was still playing—and on three strings. Gradually amusement gave place to surprise, stupefaction to admiration; and by the time Paganini was finished he had completely dominated the scoffers. The applause was deafening, and Leghorn realized once and for all that here was a man who could rise above the petty contretemps that would have demoralized a less determined spirit. For the magician who could play through a whole opera on two strings, the performance on three strings of a solo he had himself written would provide very few difficulties. But when, in the future, strings broke during his performance, ungenerous critics were not wanting who asserted that he deliberately commenced his concerts with frayed strings so that the breaking of one of them might give him the opportunity of exhibiting his dexterity. This fantastic idea, given publicity by writers ignorant of the technics of the violin, found favour with many, and once again the name of charlatan fastened itself on to Paganini. Yet anything more absurd could scarcely be conceived. Quite apart from the well-known fact that he invariably examined his instrument most meticulously before each item, to satisfy himself that his strings were in good condition, no one appreciating the difficulty of producing long glissandi, single and double harmonics, and other hardly less exacting effects, on frayed and faulty strings would entertain so stupid a notion for a moment. Those of us who are on the wrong side of forty will remember how seldom a violin recital passed off without the then ubiquitous gut E-string breaking. But in those days we did not laugh at the accident; we merely

59

applauded politely as a vote of confidence in the artist, and waited patiently until a new string had been put on or a fresh instrument fetched from the green-room. And if, in the era that preceded the introduction of the steel E-string, breakages were common with the average violinist, how much more frequently were such incidents to be expected in the case of a player like Paganini, whose employment of the left-hand pizzicato subjected the strings to so much more wear?

Whether he was kept too busy professionally to attend to the matter, or whether he allowed his contributions to the family exchequer to become irregular through carelessness, we cannot say; but while he was at Leghorn he received a very sharp reprimand from his father. The letter, opening with the sarcastically formal ' Signor Figlio ', accused Paganini of forgetting the needs of the poor members of the household in Genoa, while he himself was enjoying great wealth. Antonio wondered why his son had not visited his home and would like to know if he ever gave a thought to his parents. He was sure that his missive would remind Nicolo of his duty. How far Antonio was justified in adopting this tone on the present occasion we do not know; but there is ample evidence to show that Nicolo generally treated his parents and sisters very generously.

Data that would enable us to follow Paganini step by step on this tour are wanting; he appears to have visited several towns in northern Italy, but we are not sure of his movements until we meet him in Turin, which he made his next centre. There he gave several concerts to the great delight of Felice Blangini—musical director at the court of the Princess Pauline Borghese—who gave Fétis a detailed account of the enthusiasm aroused by Paganini's playing. His great reputation, probably assisted by a letter of introduction from Elise to her sister, no doubt opened the doors of the Borghese court at Turin to him. Pauline—the favourite sister of Napoleon, the one who accompanied her brother in exile to Elba—still possessed in 1808 the beauty that inspired Canova when he created his Venus Victrix. Busy gossip soon informed the secluded corners of the court that it was not only the musical performances of Paganini that kept him so long near the beautiful and adventure-loving princess. History has already established the main traits of Pauline's character; and knowing Paganini as we do, there seems nothing left for us to do but shrug our shoulders indulgently and place the cause of the whispered rumours in the category of old courtly customs.

It was during his stay in Turin that he fell seriously ill with an intestinal complaint that left him weak and depressed. A local doctor, mistaken in his diagnosis, almost killed him with unsuitable treatment, and Paganini, losing confidence in professional practitioners, became a foolish addict to patent medicines. Although later in life he consulted some of the most celebrated medical men of the day, no one cured him, and the disease remained to haunt him with threats of indigestion, pain, and weakness to the end of his days. The frequent recurrence of such attacks, and his failure to meet with anyone able to give him permanent relief, converted him into a valetudinarian, and he was often kept a prisoner in small towns for months at a time by his mysterious enemy. At such times concerts and private engagements had to be cancelled, and fits of melancholy would take possession of him. Gradually his features lost the fulness of youth and his cheeks sunk; his body became more angular, and on some occasions he gave the impression of haggard age. His listless movements betokened great lassitude, and his dejected and taciturn attitude almost suggested utter despair. Rest and good air partially restored him, and he was gradually approaching convalescence when he received a summons from Elise to return to his post at court.

When Paganini left Lucca early in 1808 the tranquility of the placid town was being ruffled by rumours of imminent changes. The ante-rooms of the little court were in a perpetual buzz of excitement and anticipation. Elise, deprived of the company of her fascinating fiddler, had time to turn her mind to State affairs, to remember the promises of her august brother, and to make a bid for aggrandisement. Tuscany had been added to the states now under the banner of Napoleon's Empire, and Elise felt the time ripe for promotion. A flood of correspondence passed between Lucca and Paris; expresses hurried to and fro bearing heavily-sealed packages containing often little more than recriminations and satirical pleasantries. Elise dwelt upon the political importance of her position; Napoleon retorted by coldly reminding her that Europe had more important things to do than concern herself with what Elise of Piombino was doing. After the wrangle that usually characterized her exchanges of opinion with her brother, she gained her point; her frontiers were extended, she moved her court—from the *intendant-general* to the pretty pages—from Lucca to Florence, and she received from a weary Emperor the magnificent title of Grand Duchess of Tuscany. Felice Bacciochi, of course, also packed his uniforms, his decorations, and his violin, and moved with the court; but that does not really matter. In October, 1809, articles of peace were signed between Austria and France; and it was for the fêtes in celebration of this event that Elise recalled Paganini. How long before this date he arrived in Florence is not clear. He was not really fit to resume his duties when he received Elise's orders to return, and he probably travelled by easy stages during the summer, staying at pleasant places long enough for repose and recuperation.

Fétis says that this was most likely the period at which the sculptor Bartolini produced the bust of Paganini that later became so well known. It was also the epoch which witnessed the birth of many less tangible notions regarding the violinist. Whether his growing fame caused the general public to interest themselves in him more deeply than before, or whether the fanciful legends inspired by his changing personal appearance stirred the imagination of the romantic authors of the time, cannot be decided. But Paganini was beginning to appear as the hero—or demon—of popular literature. These Italian tales were soon translated and re-issued in France and Germany, and original romances, with Paganini the mysterious demon-fiddler as chief character, were created. It was here and now that the supernatural element was introduced into accounts of the famous violinist, and the spooks raised by these eerie stories, once let loose, were more difficult to lay than Paganini imagined. Signor Amati, a very popular Italian writer of Paganini's Florentine period, supplied Schottky with a little *feuilleton (The Five Meetings)* that is typical of the suggestive stories that soon began to appear in large numbers. It also shows to what innocent sources of pure romance the later belief in Paganini's demoniacal possession can be traced.

'Near the Pitti gate at Florence', writes Amati, 'there is a steep hill, on the summit of which stands the ancient Fiesole, formerly the rival of the capital of Tuscany; but divested of its former splendours. Here the purest air can be inhaled, and the beauty of the prospect produces the effect of a dream rather than a reality. One beautiful May morning, when the flowers and the verdure lay smiling, kissed by the sun, and all Nature was radiant with youth, I ascended this hill by its most rugged path, whence the most glorious view is obtained. Before me was a stranger who, from time to time, stopped to recover his breath and admire the enchanting landscape which lay unfolded in all directions. Insensibly I approached him. Believing himself alone he spoke aloud, accompanying his monologue with rapid gesticulations and laughter. Suddenly he checked himself; his sharp eye had perceived a charming object in the distance, which soon afterwards also attracted my attention. It was a young peasant-girl who was approaching us slowly, carrying a basket of flowers. She wore a straw hat. Her hair, dark and lustrous as jet, played about her forehead; and the severity of her handsome features was relieved by the mildness of her glance. With her beautifully-formed hand she constantly replaced her shining ringlets which the refreshing Zephyr had displaced. The stranger, surprised by so much beauty, fixed his ardent regard upon her. The girl, when she came near to him, seemed transfixed at the appearance of the individual who stood before her. She grew pale and trembled. Her basket

63

shook, ready to fall from her nerveless hands. She, however, hurried on and soon disappeared behind a buttress of rock. During this interval I had contemplated the stranger whose eyes were fixed in the direction the girl had taken. Never had I seen so extraordinary a face. He merely cast upon me a passing glance, accompanied by a most singular smile, and pursued his way '.

.   .   .   .

' The next day dark clouds, driven by the winds, rolled like the waves of the ocean. The sun was scarce visible, yet, despite the weather, I went out; and having traversed the bridge *Delle Grazie,* outside the gate which bears that name, I directed my steps to the right, toward the hill on the summit of which I could already perceive the ruined castle with its drawbridge. I approached the remains of this ancient building, through the dilapidated walls of which the winds were whistling. The true impress of destruction was visible here. Here, contemplating the fearful ravages of time, and listening to the mournful melodies of the gale, the moaning of a human voice struck upon my ear and made me shudder. It seemed as if the voice proceeded from a subterranean cavity near which I was standing. I hurried forward to its mouth where I found a man—pale and with haggard looks—lying upon the moss. I recognized the stranger of the previous day. His searching glance was fixed upon me, and I recoiled from it. Perceiving that the stranger was in no need of assistance, I withdrew '.

.   .   .   .

' On the following evening I was walking by the side of the Arno, on which the moonlight flickered as it rose. The nightingale's note and the warbling of other birds of every kind preparing for their rest were serenading the departing rays of day. Sounds of a totally different nature were suddenly intermingled with these harmonious melodies of nature. Attracted by this exquisite and unknown music, I followed the direction whence it seemed to proceed, and again I found myself near the

64

singular being who had occupied all my thoughts for the past three days. Carelessly lying beneath a tree, his features were now as calm as they had appeared troubled the previous day; and as he listened with an impassioned expression to the fury of the tempest at the old castle, so did he now seem to enjoy the concert of the feathered songsters whose notes he was whistling in most astounding imitation. I could not explain the strange destiny that led me constantly into his presence '.

.   .   .   .

' My astonishment was not yet to end; for, on returning the following evening from a long walk, just as the stars were beginning to twinkle, I sat down to rest under the *Loggia degli Uffizi*. A merry party passed me and sat down on a marble seat at some distance from me. Soon after, celestial sounds fell upon my ear, by turns joyous and plaintive, evidently produced by the hand of a consummate artist. Silence followed the hilarity of the merry party, all of whom seemed as much astonished at the divine music as I was myself. They all rose silently to follow the artist, who continued walking while he played. I also followed to discover what instrument it was I had heard, and who the artist might be that discoursed so enchantingly upon it. Arrived at the square of the *Palazzo Vecchio,* the party entered a restaurant. I followed them. Here they regained their former joviality, and the leader, more than his companions, displayed extraordinary animation. To my great surprise the instrument was a guitar (which seemed to have become magical), and the performer I discovered to be the stranger I had so continually met. He was no longer the suffering being he had seemed : his eyes beamed, his veins swelled with exultation, his coat and waistcoat were both unbuttoned, his cravat loosened, and his gesticulations those of a madman. I enquired his name. " None of us knows it ", replied the individual—one of the party—to whom I had addressed myself, " I was in company with my friends, who were singing and dancing to my guitar, when this singular

65

man pushed in among us, and snatching the guitar from my hands, commenced playing without saying a word. Annoyed at the intrusion we were about to lay hands upon him, but without noticing us in the least he continued playing, subjugating us with his exquisite performance. Each time we required his name, he resumed his playing without making reply. He occasionally ceased for a while, to relate to us some extraordinary anecdote. In this manner he has brought us hither without more knowledge of him than you possess " '.

. . . .

' Some days later Paganini was announced to give a concert. Eager to hear this incomparable artist whose fame was so widespread and whom I had not yet heard, I went to the theatre which was literally packed to suffocation. The utmost impatience was manifested until the concert commenced with a symphony, which, although by a composer of eminence, was listened to with indifference. At length the artist appeared, and I was amazed to recognize in him the stranger who had so mystified me for some days—whom I had met at Fiesole, and so on. I will not attempt to describe the effect that his performance produced; the transports of frenzy his incomparable talent excited. Suffice it to say that on that one evening he seemed to combine all the delightful impressions of the graceful appearance of the peasant-girl on the mountain, the hurricane in the ruins, the warbling of the nesting birds on the banks of the Arno, and the inspiring delirium of the evening at the *Loggie* '.

. . . .

The Grand Duchess of Tuscany was equally delighted with Paganini's performance at her gala concert, and presented him with a magnificent Florentine mosaic in precious stones. Whether Nicolo was as pleased with the new conditions is to be doubted. He pocketed the jewel, but all his earlier friendship with and respect for Elise seem to have vanished. She still flattered him, but she could not draw him back to the old intimacies of Lucca. Perhaps rumour connecting her name with that of a young man called Lucchesini had reached his ears. We do not know what conditions were attached to his appointment now that the status of Elise was raised; but he undoubtedly reserved to himself the right to undertake concert-tours when he wished to do so.

As an artist he was now unconventional in the extreme, and an entertaining sidelight is thrown upon his manner of performance by the memoirs of the musician Luigi Picchianti: 'A concert had been arranged to take place in the house of Signor de Fabri. Paganini had promised to play a sonata of Haydn's with a lady. The audience had assembled, everything was ready for the performance, but Paganini was still absent. After a long wait he at last appeared breathless. With a hasty apology he took his place, violin in hand, beside the pianoforte. His accompanist attempted to give him the note for tuning his instrument. 'No, no', he said, 'let us begin; I have kept the company waiting too long already'. The performance commenced. Paganini exhibited to the full the magic of his bow, not omitting, it is true, to ornament Haydn's smooth outline with an abundance of decorations. When, at the termination of the music, all had gone in to supper, Picchianti compared the A of the pianoforte with that of the violin and found that they differed by a whole tone. This information aroused universal astonishment'. To a musician of Paganini's stature so elementary a process as an unprepared transposition of this kind would provide little to upset his equilibrium.

CHAPTER VIII

FLORENCE with its new and magnificent court could not hold Paganini for more than a few months. Before the year ended —to be precise, in December, 1809—he left the beautiful city on the Arno for a tour of Lombardy and the Romagna. On January 22, 1810, he played at Rimini and aroused the wildest enthusiasm, staying before and after the concert with the talented amateur musician Signor Giangi. The venerable theatre of ancient Cesena echoed to the silvery notes of his violin, and concerts were given in Ravenna, Faenza, Forli, Imola, and many other towns farther south and west—but in what order these appearances took place we cannot determine. It is curious that the direction of his route was still more or less decided by the travelling conditions of the time. We cannot otherwise explain why so celebrated and ambitious an artist should have been kept so long from the greater centres like Milan, Naples, and Rome. There were no railways, no telegraph, no telephone; often the roads were in a terrible state. A sufferer from an internal complaint such as Paganini's, would have endured unspeakable pain during long journeys over rutty or quaggy highways. No concert could be arranged more than two or three days in advance, and the first news that the inhabitants of the smaller towns had concerning an approaching virtuoso were generally the reports brought by travellers coming from the place at which the artist had already appeared. A business-manager would precede him by a couple of days, engage a hall or negotiate with the authorities for the use of the theatre or opera-house, and a few posters would be printed.

Orchestras, accompanists, and even the assisting artists were seldom engaged until the day of the concert. These being the conditions it is not surprising that recitals had frequently to be postponed or abandoned, and that extensive and difficult works were often performed with little or no rehearsal. When he had not previously wounded their pride or overlooked their importance, the members of the local musical society would meet the artist and entertain him, while a wealthy amateur might offer him the hospitality of bed and board. The success of Paganini in these early days was doubtlessly in no small measure due to the facility with which he could accomodate himself to existing conditions, the readiness with which he could change his programme at a moment's notice, and his presence of mind in dealing with the many unforeseen incidents that were bound to crop up. But he already enjoyed a considerable reputation and he generally arrived to find all the seats for his concerts sold. Moreover, he made friends everywhere—in musical as well as social circles—and all who learned to know him praised his good nature, his entertaining conversation, his generosity in admitting and appreciating the talent of his contemporaries, and his polished and courtly manners.

Here and there, through ignorance of local customs, he made enemies. This was especially the case at Ferrara, where he was advertised to appear some time in 1810. It seems that for ages an implacable feud existed between the townsfolk of Ferrara and the inhabitants of the surrounding country. The townsmen were considered dull and slow, and they returned the compliment by holding the countrymen to be cloddish. Anyone returning from a visit inside of the walls would never say ' I have come from Ferrara ', but merely brayed ' hee-haw '. Paganini did not know this, and his ignorance might easily have cost him a damaged fiddle or a broken crown. The episode is related in the diary of Professor Gordigiani, who was one of the actors in the comedy; and since the story illustrates very truthfully one aspect at least of the travelling artist's life it is well worth repeating :

' My friend Paganini suggested that I accompany him to

Ferrara where he was to give a concert; and I, knowing that my sweetheart, the Pallerini, would also be there, accepted his invitation and went . . . . We had a pleasant journey, for Paganini has spirit, and no one can be bored in his company. On our arrival the impressario immediately presented himself and it was decided to hold the *Accademia* the next day. Paganini then hurried to see Signora Marcolini to ask her to sing at his recital. I also made my own arrangements to discover the lodgings of the dancer . . . . I found that she was staying at our hotel, in a room adjoining ours. I took Paganini's guitar and strummed a few snatches from the ballets in which she had shone . . . . After three or four pieces I heard a faint but sweet voice reply from a neighbouring room. I was standing guitar in hand with my ear applied to the door when Paganini entered. Now, Paganini is my friend; and yet I confess I was ashamed to be surprised in this attitude. To his question, " Cosi fai in quella posizione? " I stammered out I know not what '. Fortunately Paganini was acquainted with the ballerina so admired by Gordigiani and he offered to effect an introduction. ' After a short promenade we were invited to dine with her, and I passed the day between pain, joy, and hope—between bitter and sweet . . . . The next morning Paganini went to his rehearsal, while I visited our neighbour. Suddenly the door opened, Paganini appeared, his hair in disorder, a thundercloud on his brow '. After a good deal of incoherent raving Gordigiani and the Pallerini drag from him the crushing news that La Marcolini, with the fickleness of her sex and calling, had changed her mind and would not sing. ' Happily Paganini had thought of someone who could put everything right. We asked in one breath, " Who can it be? " Here the Genoese turned very sweetly to our beauty (for he could be very sweet when he wished) and said in a majestic voice, " This is the chosen one ". Antonietta protested in astonishment, " Who, I? My dear Paganini, I think you are disposed to jest. I sing? And at *your* concert in place of the experienced Marcolini? They would laugh at me—no, no ".—" Yes, yes " we both shouted . . .

Then they argued over the aria to be sung. They must practise.
Paganini dismissed the visitors present with an invitation to be
his guests after the concert . . . The rehearsal ended in laughter
and concord'. The time for the concert arrived—Antonietta
Pallerini's first experience as a vocalist. 'Fear swings his
sceptre; the Marcolini will have many friends in the audience,
and they can easily become Pallerini's enemies'—for such was
the barbaric code of opera and concert honour in those days
of artistic partisanship. 'We retire to make our toilets.
Paganini finishes his in a moment: he jumps into his black
trousers, hops into his shoes, wraps his throat in his great cravat,
slips into vest and dress-coat, and he is ready. The toilet of
his violin is still shorter: he simply wipes the dust off it. A
carriage drives up. Antonietta, Paganini, and I enter, and we
are already at the packed theatre. After the overture Paganini
steps on to the stage; he charms all with his magic. I hurry
to the wings; my poor friend trembles like an aspen; I try to
encourage her; Paganini cheers her up, seizes her hand and
leads her before the audience . . . . The Ritornello begins. I
stand in the wings and see how the poor girl's heart is beating—
but so is mine, hammering like the deuce. She begins: her
trembling voice betrays her nervousness. She gradually controls
herself; but as the aria is short she regains her courage when
it is no longer needed. Paganini steps out to conduct her back,
but he is now not her only accompanist; a loud whistling can
be heard, following her relentlessly into the wings. Pale with
anger Paganini turns, and the crestfallen Antonietta slides into
my arms. Yes; I feel her warm tears on my hand . . . Murmurs
of dissent arise from the stalls' and the hidden whistler thinks
it wiser to desist. 'I draw Antonietta into one of the small
boxes on the stage to calm her. Meanwhile the concert draws
to a close. Paganini enters the little box and says: "My dear
Pallerini, on my account you were insulted . . . for me you
suffered, and thus it is my duty to avenge the insult as quickly
and as well as I can. Have the goodness to stand in the
wings; I shall soon begin my last piece and I hope I shall be

fortunate enough to convince you that Paganini will not be
content to appear ungrateful to his friends, but rather that he
defends their honour ". We try to dissuade him, but he does
not heed us. Striding on to the platform he calls to us, " Venite
e sentirate ". Curious to see Paganini's revenge we hurry after
him and stand in the wings. Now, in accordance with the
promise made on his posters our friend begins his musical joke
in which he imitates various animal-noises on the violin. Before
commencing he asks the audience not to judge the performance
too critically, but to look upon it, half as a carnival jest and
half as an interlude to banish gloom. In a magical manner he
imitates the crowing of cocks, the chirping of crickets, the
howling of dogs, the creaking of hinges, and more of the kind.
All these puerilities are performed in the most perfect fashion
imaginable, though they contrast strangely with the artistry of
the rest of the programme; but where is his revenge? It draws
near. Paganini turns and, throwing us a side-glance warning
us to be attentive, advances to the edge of the platform. Close
to the footlights he makes a gesture that imposes silence upon
the public and prepares them for something extraordinary.
From right to left he draws his bow over the E-string, behind
the bridge, and suddenly from left to right with all his force on
the G-string, and there results an unmistakable and perfectly-
imitated " hee-haw ".—" Questo e per quello che ha fischiato—
This is for him who whistled ", he cries '. A tremendous
hubbub ensues. ' But Paganini is not to be shaken and repeats
his " hee-haw " several times ' before he feels satisfied. ' He
wishes to return to the stage and repeat the compliment to the
whistler, but Pallerini restrains him by throwing her arms about
his neck and breathing a grateful kiss on his cheek. Helen was
the cause of Troy's destruction; Antonietta nearly caused the
destruction of the Ferrara theatre '. The affair threatened to
become serious; several of the audience attempted to climb on
to the platform, swearing vengeance. The orchestra fled.
' Paganini holds his violin like a shield and his bow like a sword;
I, another Patroclus, did not move from the side of Achilles '.

Their friends came to their rescue and the appearance of a magisterial officer saved them. The fainting ladies were gradually revived and the ' magistrate had some bitter things to say to Paganini. The latter protested that he had done nothing wrong, that his programme had announced several imitations; but to no avail. He was forbidden to give a second concert . . . . and Paganini said he would not play again in Ferrara if they begged him to do so; there were other towns that knew better how to appreciate him . . . . With the greatest caution we left the theatre by a back-door, and returned to our inn accompanied by our sympathizers. Good wine soon caused our sufferings to be forgotten and fury gave place to laughter '. But it was quite a long time before Paganini could be made to understand that it was always unsafe to say ' hee-haw ' to a Ferrarese audience.

It may be asked in all seriousness how such an item could come to be included in the artistic programme of a true musician. The answer lies in the concatenation of a number of circumstances. In spite of the poetic heights reached by the great masters, the cult of purism was not yet beyond its infancy It was by no means unusual, even half a century later, to find the cheapest of descriptive and ' programme ' music in concert-programmes, cheek by jowl with classic masterpieces. The early nineteenth-century carnival-spirit in Italy caused the most serious of artists to descend temporarily to the most childish of follies. In addition, Paganini probably thought it a wise policy to throw a sop to the gallery when he had any sort of excuse for doing so. He did not make a regular habit of indulging in such musical jests, and as time went on they became ever rarer.

From the moment at which Gordigiani's anecdote leaves us in Ferrara we lose sight of Paganini until we meet him in Parma on August 16, 1811, playing variations on the G-string in so finished a manner that amateurs and professionals alike were reduced to speechlessness. Gervasoni who was present tells us that the audience almost stood on their heads in amazement. Nicolo was now recalled to Florence and he appears to have

73

remained at his post in Elise's court throughout 1812. Things were not going so brilliantly with the Napoleonic Empire. It had reached its zenith in 1810 when Napoleon wielded absolute power over western Europe. In 1812 his seizure of Oldenburg armed Alexander; in June the French army crossed the Niemen; in September Borodino was fought; in October Napoleon ordered the retreat that began too late. This was the first blow of the many that were so soon to shatter the Corsican's mighty empire. Paganini had in the meantime become the darling of the Italian audiences and Elise meant less to him daily. All that he needed was an excuse to break his contract with her and be a free man again. Although he took next to no interest in political matters, he associated too frequently with men of affairs to be blind to the coming storm. It would be a far better policy for him to pursue if he could regain his independence of action before his imperious Grand Duchess lamely surrendered her fortresses to the Allies.

While Napoleon and his grenadiers were wending their painful way back from frozen Russia his opportunity came. The incident which led to his rupture with Elise is related by Fétis from materials supplied by eye-witnesses: 'At a great court gala, where a concert preceded a ball, Paganini, who directed the former, appeared in the orchestra wearing the uniform of a Captain of the Royal Gendarmerie. The princess, as soon as she perceived this, sent her commands that the uniform was to be replaced by an evening dress. He replied that his commission was elastic enough to permit him to wear the uniform, and refused to change it. The command was repeated and again it was met with refusal; and to prove that he defied the orders of the Grand Duchess, he appeared at the ball in his uniform. Nevertheless, convinced that although reason and right were both in his favour, absolutism prevailed at court, and his defiance might endanger his liberty, he quitted Florence during the night and directed his steps towards Lombardy. The most tempting offers, and the promise of the Grand Duchess's leniency, proved unavailing to induce him to

74

return '. Fétis, remembering that he was writing for Victorian readers, adds a footnote in the smallest of type : ' The sentiments which induced the Grand Duchess to overlook his insubordination, and from certain innuendoes which had escaped the pen of Signor Conestabile, inferences may be drawn which delicacy dictates should not be mentioned unreservedly '. Elise was growing too old to attract Paganini on any sentimental grounds ; her court too unstable now to afford him a safe asylum ; he may even have suspected that her contrition was feigned. Deeming discretion to be a safer guide than valour he turned a deaf ear to Elise's pleading, forgot the charming Countess and her successors, and made for Milan, beyond the reach of the Empire's arm. When next he approached the Tuscan capital, Waterloo had been fought and the glory that was Napoleon had flickered out.

CHAPTER IX

'THE GREATEST VIOLINIST IN THE WORLD'
(Spring, 1813—Winter, 1814)

OCTOBER 19, 1813—when Napoleon's retreat after his defeat at Leipzig commenced—may be accepted as the date on which the ultimate fate of the broken Napoleonic Empire was sealed. The Confederation of the Rhine had come to an end. Before the close of 1813 the French forces in Germany and Poland had surrendered; almost all the provinces conquered by the Corsican went back to their earlier allegiance or gained their indepen‑ dence; Murat, adding treason to misfortune, held a clandestine correspondence with the Austrians. And in the general fall Elise's star also set without even a final blaze of splendour. Paganini, from his purely utilitarian point of view, did not bolt any too soon.

The year was at the spring when Nicolo reached Milan; and to efface from his memory the events of the past few days he attended a performance of Sussmayer's ballet *Il Noce di Benevento* (Virgano) at La Scala on the evening of his arrival. One scene in particular made so strong an appeal to his sense of the grotesque, that he seized upon its theme and composed the set of variations known as *Le Streghe* (The Witches). He in‑ tended it to form the climax of his first Milanese concert. It is a work of diabolical difficulty and it became the touch‑ stone of technicality for the virtuosi who came from the Bohemian School of Ottakar Sevčik nearly a century later. But another attack of his Turin malady laid him low, and it was some months before he was able to walk abroad again with any ease. His convalescence was slow and he suffered con-

76

siderably from melancholy and loneliness. For the latter he knew only one cure, and the thought of it was generally enough to make him forget his physical tortures. It is quite likely that the all-engrossing enthusiasm he developed when he threw himself into his love-adventures, diverted his mind from himself and drew him from the slough of despond in which his illness usually left him. This Milanese comedy of his is best rehearsed in the naive words he used when he related the episode to his friends in Prague some sixteen years later :

' I found myself in Milan in the most miserable of moods and by no means in the best of health; no form of amusement held any attractions for me. My heart was empty, and from this emptiness was bred my melancholy. One day I met a friend who told me that the beautiful Rosina, a countrywoman of mine, was in Milan. My blood raced through my veins when I heard the glad news; my nerves were tautened, and from a most listless being I was suddenly converted into one ready for immediate action. Where does she live?—" I do not know; but after supper I will meet you at the Café de Servi and give you her address ". We parted. The time hung heavily; the hours would not pass; I wandered from place to place, from café to café, from corso to corso. After dinner I tried to sleep, but Rosina prevented my eyes from closing. I had known her and loved her long, and now, just when I needed affection so sorely she, charming and graceful, had come to Milan with a promise of consolation for my long privation. How could I sleep with such happiness in sight? I returned to the café, but my friend was not yet there. In desperation I played billiards, drank one cup of coffee after the other, glanced at my watch and at the clock on the wall, scrutinized the faces of all present, and so the time dragged slowly on and my friend arrived. In the middle of a game I left the billiard-table and hurried to meet him. Where does she live?—" Here in the Contrada della Passerella ".—What number?—" Oh, that I do not know ".— On which floor?—" The second ".—Addio, and I was in the street. I hastened from one house to another, sought again and

again, but Rosina was not to be found . . . . At length I stood
before a house I had not yet searched . . . . In haste I climbed
to the second floor and knocked at the door; no answer. I
tried the door; it opened, and I found myself in the entrance-
hall. Several times I called out: " Si puole? " (Is it permitted?). Silence everywhere, and I stepped in. The second
room was empty, and very quietly I opened the door of the
third which was shrouded in semi-darkness. I was undecided
whether to advance, and was already preparing to retrace my
steps when I heard a somewhat feeble voice. Had it been a
masculine voice nothing would have stayed my retreat; but it
was that of a lady, and sounded young and fresh into the bargain. In a bed, half hidden by hangings, lay a beautiful woman
who asked whether I was the doctor. I replied that I was, took
courage, and stepped nearer. I put the usual questions of a
visiting physician, felt her pulse, and in general did my best
to play my hastily-assumed rôle as well as possible. Her lovely
hand rested in mine—a hand that, quite unconsciously, I was
pressing harder and harder, until the lady, examining my face
with greater attention, withdrew it and said: " I did not know
that Signor Paganini was a doctor also ". Being recognized but
unwilling to betray the real reason for my presence, I assured
her that I realized how wrong, how punishable, was my action
in coming thus disguised, but having seen her somewhere and
fallen so deeply in love with her, I was forced into my present
adventure. I was about to become still more confidential when
I heard someone enter. The charming lady at once released
my hand, and I stepped back several paces. An elderly gentleman approached, came to a standstill, stared at me, and asked
the invalid whether this was Signor Dottore. On her affirmative
reply the good man asked me to be seated. He also took a chair
and commenced to cross-examine me on the subject of the
lady's indisposition. My embarrassment can easily be imagined.
I, who knew nothing of medicine except what I had learned
from my own bitter experience, now found myself face to face
with an individual who believed in illness and death, possessed

innumerable prescriptions, introduced frequent Latin and Greek words, and spoke like a specialist. Naturally, I allowed him to speak on, now and then nodding my head in acquiescence and always agreeing with him. But the farce had to be brought to some sort of conclusion. Already a sheet of paper lay prepared for my prescription and the old man put on his spectacles to read what I was about to order for the patient. To extricate myself from this dilemma I said at length that it would be better to allow Nature to do her work, and that, should there be no improvement by the following day, it would be early enough to call in the aid of my art. When my inquisitor heard this he almost fell on my neck: "Yes; that is the best treatment; I do not like to see doctors writing prescriptions at once, before they have studied not only the complaint but also the temperament and nature of the patient". Then followed renewed compliments and requests to be seated. I was in hell, and feared I might be seen by someone who knew me, or what was worse, surprised by the arrival of the real doctor. To increase my agony the old man now commenced a long and monotonous recital of his own troubles . . . . At last it struck seven and I rose quickly . . . . Hat in hand, I said a lady who was very ill was awaiting me, and promised to return the next day. He begged me to come after dinner, at four o'clock, as he would be busy all the morning and yet wanted to enjoy my company. I was only too glad to agree to anything and would have promised him the treasures of the Grand Mogul, only to be free. Quickly, quickly, one more touch on the lady's pulse; then I wiped the perspiration from my brow and hurried away. In the hall I met a servant.—"Are you the Signor Dottore?"—Certainly.—"Then you must have received the note I left for you at the chemist's?"—Of course. The door was opened for me and I strode joyfully down the staircase. I could hardly await the moment when I would see the street and be able to throw off my doctorial dignity. It was certainly not Rosina, but she seemed quite as pretty as Rosina, and really far more witty and intelligent. I was entertaining myself with these

79

thoughts when I met the friend who had announced the arrival of my countrywoman. " Well, have you seen her? "—No; not Rosina, but another; listen, I have a remarkable story to tell you.—" Not now ", interrupted my friend, " I have no time; I have to visit a sick lady ".—In which house?—He pointed it out.—Oh, I said, another doctor has already been there.— " What, another doctor? "—Yes; *I* am the doctor; now you must hear the whole story . . . . The following day at about eight o'clock, I visited my invalid. She was up when I arrived and tried to be serious. But I said that since she had made me her physician I was not desirous of relinquishing the honour. On that account she must allow me to feel her pulse. Most opportunely a servant entered, and the lady was compelled to submit in order to prevent suspicion falling upon me and herself at the same time. I paid her several visits every day, but only at times when the old chatterbox was not there. Little by little the invalid became more communicative, agreed that she had seen me in a house at Reggio, told me that she was a widow, and that she had accompanied her father whom a lawsuit had brought to Milan. With her return to health and youthful vigour came love, and for the first and last time I owed Aesculapius a deep debt of gratitude '. Childish as this story may sound, it gives us a very clear insight into one compartment of Paganini's mind; and reprehensible as we may consider his conduct, it must never be forgotten that it belonged to his period and that in the eyes of his contemporaries he was no more vicious than the majority of men—especially those of his years and profession.

By the autumn of 1813 he had regained his health sufficiently to venture upon the first of his concerts at Milan. It took place on October 29, and became a definite landmark in his career. The chief city of Lombardy was then a centre important enough to attract the foreign correspondents of the greater European journals, and from this date onward accounts of Paganini's activities—more or less enthusiastic—were disseminated abroad. His first appearance in Milan filled every seat of the huge Scala building, and the delight of the audience bordered on absolute frenzy. The sensational ' Witches' Dance ' variations in particular called forth the wildest applause, and in this work—so typical of its creator—style, subject-matter, and performer were perfectly matched. Paganini became international ' news '; his comings and goings were reported in foreign papers, and his name was never absent for very long at a time from their columns. ' We hear that Paganini . . . ', ' It is reported that Paganini . . . ', ' An interesting story has just reached us concerning the great Paganini . . . ' were the usual openings, and the public of most European countries were so well acquainted with all he did, and much that he did not do, that it was asked on every side when he would be induced to leave his native land and exhibit his talents to the wider world.

For the time being he was in love with Milan. The Milanese took him to their hearts and felt that with their applause they had secured for him an unassailable position in the world of art. The Milan correspondent of the *Leipzig Musical Journal*, reporting on the first concert said: ' On October 29, 1813, Signor Paganini of Genoa, who in Italy is generally admitted to be the first violinist of the day, gave a recital in the Theatre *alla Scala* at which he played a concerto by Kreutzer (E-Minor) and concluded with a set of variations on the G-string. The attendance was extraordinary: everybody wished to see and hear this performer of miracles, and everyone was really astonished in the most striking manner. Signor Paganini is in a certain sense without doubt the greatest violinist in the world. His performance is veritably incomprehensible. He commands certain passages, leaps, and double-stops, which have never before been heard from *any* violinist . . . . ; he is one of the most artificial violinists that the world has ever possessed. I said ' artificial '; for in simple, expressive, and beautiful playing there are probably several artists in other countries who can equal him . . . That Paganini created a furore can well be understood. There are some unbiassed connoisseurs here who remark with perfect justice that he did not play Kreutzer's work in the spirit of its composer; indeed, that parts of it became unrecognizable in his hands . . . . On the other hand, his variations on the G-string (which he was compelled to repeat by the universal clamour) threw everyone into a state of indescribable excitement—for truly nothing of that kind had ever been heard before. Naturally this artist, unique in his kind, could not satisfy his public with one single recital, and within the space of six weeks he was forced to give eleven more concerts, some in the Scala and some in the Teatro Carcano . . . . Paganini has also played several times at the Milanese court'. This report seems to be an honest summing up of all the contemporary evidence—including that of the traditionalists who were not yet ready to give him the laurels bestowed upon him by the popular voice—and it places Paganini before us in a very fair manner. That he had his superiors in point of tone-production, he himself was always ready to admit; and that he realized his own shortcomings in the works of other composers, is proved by his later decision to play no compositions but his own, as no works but his own really suited his peculiar and highly specialized style. It was when he mounted his favourite war-horses—the sentimental works for the G-string and the *bravoura* variations—that he became the inimitable magician, the performer who left all hearers dumb with amazement. But it was not only by his astonishing technical skill that he so captivated his audiences; it was rather an amazing personality added to his mechanical resourcefulness that turned sober listeners into frenzied devotees. He spent a good deal of time in Milan on this occasion, and within the next five years gave no fewer than thirty-seven concerts there.

At the end of the year or the beginning of 1814 Paganini—after a very long absence—visited his home. The scene in the house with the pink front, if indeed his parents still lived there, is left entirely to our imagination, for we can obtain no information from any source. A present of honest gold Napoleons no doubt secured him a hearty welcome from his father. The good Teresa, to whom her Benjamin was bound in the deepest affection, was probably expressing her gratitude to faithful heaven for a further instalment of fulfilled promise. The *Gazette of Genoa* printed an account of Nicolo's successes and added : ' Applause and money rained on him from every direction. The advocate L. G. Germi, who had always been more friendly to him than a brother, has written an acrostic sonnet in his praise '. This was but one of many such poetical offerings to Paganini's genius. He and Germi doubtlessly had much to discuss, for the lawyer required instructions as to the investment of the money earned in Lombardy, arrangements had to be made for allowances to the maestro's family, and other business of that nature. Paganini placed implicit confidence in his legal friend and he never regretted it. After his short holiday in Genoa he returned to Milan early in 1814, and remained there until the autumn.

From May onwards he gave another lengthy series of concerts, this time in the Teatro Ré. Our useful correspondent of the Leipzig journal already quoted, remarks that ' it is surprising that this great artist remains so long on one spot, and does not extend his tours to foreign countries where he is certain to arouse great admiration and find much gold. Perhaps he is biding his time '. The same paper reports that Paganini's little pupil, Caterina Calcagno, now sixteen years of age, gave a concert in Milan on March 24th; and in another account dated September 21, writes that ' the celebrated violinist Paganini is still in Milan—why he does not go abroad no one knows '. It was during this period that Paganini founded or joined the Milanese musical society known as *Gli Orfei*, conducting its rehearsals and enjoying the classical music he could not use at his own concerts. Though Schottky places Paganini's association with *Gli Orfei* in 1814, Fétis gives the date 1820. Both had their information from the violinist himself and it is evident that on one of the two occasions his memory must have played him false. It is well established that he was very fond of chamber-music for his own recreation and often took part in trios and quartets at the houses of good amateurs. Of all the classic masters Beethoven was his favourite, and some of the last hours of his life were made the happier for him by his participation in that titan's quartets. It was most likely to have more frequent opportunities for hearing and playing this class of music that he was impelled to assist at the reunions of the Milanese society.

In October Paganini left Milan for Bologna where he played in the theatre; but though his success there was as great as he merited, the main interest of his visit lay in his meeting with Rossini. The two musicians were introduced to each other in the house of the Pegnalvas, where Paganini frequently played for his own and his host's pleasure. Gioacchino Rossini, ten years the violinist's junior, was already famous. *Tancredi* and *L'Italiana in Algeri* had already been performed, and Rossini was looked upon by the Italians as the greatest living composer of operas. *Aureliano in Palmira* and *Il Turco in Italia* belong to the year of his meeting with Paganini. The two men speedily found that they had many ideas in common, and a close friendship sprang up between them. They had the greatest admiration for one another—Paganini agreeing completely with popular verdict which bestowed the title of ' Sweet Swan of Pesaro ' upon his friend, while Rossini declared that ' it was fortunate Paganini did not devote himself exclusively to lyric composition, for he would then have been a dangerous rival '. The two met again on more than one occasion during their wanderings, and many were the mad pranks they played together. Paganini's performance so inspired Rossini that for several months he set himself the task of improving his own playing. He was rewarded by some measure of success; but he abandoned the attempt when he discovered how remote were his chances of attaining to the position held by the Genoese fiddler. The world could more easily do without one more violinist than lose a *Tell* or a *Barbiere di Seviglia*. In writing his numerous sets of variations Paganini borrowed more themes from the works of Rossini than from those of any other composer.

Towards the end of the year Paganini's movements again become difficult to follow. All we know for certain is that during the winter he was once more attacked by illness and kept inactive at Ancona.

CHAPTER X

THE year 1815 held for Paganini one of the most unpleasant experiences of his early career. It is some time since we found him philandering with women. He was too busy building up his reputation in Lombardy to waste his time over love-affairs. But, visiting Genoa early in 1815 he must have had more leisure than was good for him, and he flew to his usual antidote. The devil quickly discovered work to occupy his idle moments. In the time that had elapsed since his departure from Florence he seems to have grown far less fastidious. During the days of his court service princesses and countesses had not been too good for him; now it was only the sex of the companion that appeared to count. In one of the ill-famed passages where respectable citizens did not walk, he picked up the disreputable daughter of a tailor in a small way of business—one Ferdinando Cavanna; and the father, thinking to enrich himself by his daughter's backsliding and the violinist's folly, involved Paganini in a sordid lawsuit that occupied the courts of Genoa for nearly a year. It is from the official records of the case that we derive the bulk of our information on the tragi-comic subject.

According to Cavanna's complaint, Paganini had promised to marry the seventeen-year-old girl after having taken her into an empty schoolroom and there abused her 'innocence'. On the pretext that his parents had refused their consent to the marriage—for in Italy everyone, irrespective of age, was required to obtain the parental sanction first—he took her to Parma. Once there, he ceased to talk of marriage and, instead, vainly attempted to undo the wrong he had done the poor

86

Angelina by the use of drugs. He then, it was alleged, bundled her off home to her infuriated father. On May 6, Cavanna had him arrested and put in prison pending payment of damages. To secure his release Paganini offered twelve hundred *lire,* and Cavanna petitioned the court to liberate the prisoner. An agreement was signed by both parties, by which Paganini was to pay six hundred *lire* down and the balance four months later. Thereupon—after eight days of durance—the violinist was enlarged. Once more free, he stopped the payment of the promised sum and refused to part with any money at all until the court had reached a verdict. Alternately Cavanna and Paganini summoned each other to the courts, the former endeavouring to tie the violinist down to a definite promise, and the latter doing his best to squirm out of all responsibility by Machiavellian tactics. Cavanna, not satisfied with the way matters were being conducted, once more complains to the bench that although Paganini exhibited some feelings of humanity and right, and had even made arrangements with a sister to bring up the child of the ill-matched alliance, he now ' orders the case to proceed with the object of having his agreement annulled '. In the meantime Angelina had been going on with her share in the case. On June 24, she submitted to an operation for the removal of her dead love-child. This precipitated matters. Paganini had no reason for believing himself to be the father of the unfortunate infant. By working out a simple subtraction sum we can easily establish that he was not in Genoa at what the law calls the material time. In September and October of the previous year he was at Milan and Bologna. In his defence he admitted associating with Angelina and agreed that he had taken her to Parma. But he also asserted that the girl had offered herself to him voluntarily, which, when we study her past, we can readily believe. Paganini produced her birth-certificate which showed that she was not seventeen but twenty. His counsel's case was that Angelina was a naughty girl; that she was in the habit of going to men's rooms; that her father had more than once threatened

87

to turn her out of his house on account of her bad behaviour. It was further alleged that she enjoyed more freedom than a respectable girl should have, and that she had frequently been seen in the small hours of the morning in the company of foreigners and soldiers. Genoa was a seaport with a seaport's reputation, and only girls of one kind would walk abroad unchaperoned in such places during the hours of darkness. Further, the neighbours had little good to say of her, and it was found that even in her father's house she had clandestine meetings with nocturnal visitors. The *Testimoniali di Remissione* (September 28) add that she did all these things even during the time she was acquainted with the defendant. By this time the end of September had been reached, and, faced by so able a defence, Cavanna's lawyer reduced the charge. The courts never seemed to see clear daylight in the case, and eventually Paganini had to pay damages—for what had technically become a breach of promise of marriage—to the amount of three thousand francs, which was a cheap escape for him. Paganini, of course, felt that he had been the victim of a gross injustice. Writing to the faithful Germi in July he said that he owed nothing to the wretched girl who had offered herself to him in the manner usual to her kind, and that any one of her numerous ' friends ' could quite as likely have been the child's father as he himself. There was nothing left to do but pay the sum fixed by the court and forget the whole miserable affair. Forget it he did, for it was not long before he was writing to Germi about a pretty girl he had met, who was . . . .

From a letter addressed to Genoa it would appear that Paganini paid his first visit to Venice in the same year, and surprising as it may seem—after his experiences in Genoa during the summer—the main theme of his writing was—a girl. He met Antonia Bianchi, a very young vocalist, then probably still in the chorus, and immediately fell in love with her. He was not too sure about her being the ' first real passion ' of his life, because rumours concerning her frightened him a little : ' I was distinctly inclined to care for the Signora at Venice, but I received letters speaking so badly of her conduct that I cannot now think of approaching her. She has given up her music, and says that my friendship means nothing to her '. The liaison thus inauspiciously formed, developed later and was destined to exercise a very great influence on his life. Antonia was fated to bring him much misery and leave him an heir. We shall make the closer acquaintance of this singing spitfire in a few years' time. In the meanwhile Paganini gave some concerts in the city on the lagoons and again fell ill. These attacks were now becoming increasingly frequent and severe, each onslaught leaving him weaker and more depressed. Perhaps one ought to treat him with a little indulgence in his sexual peccadilloes. He harboured within himself a master whose orders he felt compelled to obey; a dictator of tyrannic ruthlessness whom his will-power never succeeded in dethroning. Recovering slowly in the early months of 1816, he returned to Genoa for convalescence. He had, with the help of his mother's nursing, only just gained sufficient strength to make travelling safe for him, when he heard that the celebrated French violinist, Lafont, was appearing in Milan. His relentless ambition drove all thoughts of weakness, disillusionment, and self-pity from his mind, and he hurried into Lombardy to judge for himself the performance of the man who had come to challenge his own dominion in his beloved Milan.

Charles Philippe Lafont, Paganini's senior by one year, was an excellent violinist and Rode's successor at St. Petersburg. In 1815 Louis XVIII recalled him to Paris as solo violinist in the royal chamber-music. He made extended tours on the Continent and eventually met his death in a post-chaise accident hardly a year before Paganini died. The international reputation he enjoyed must have been a very high one to have brought the Genoese back to Milan in such breathless haste. Personal acquaintance soon reassured Paganini that he had nothing to fear from the Frenchman's rivalry, and indeed, the two got on rather well together. Whenever it was possible Nicolo cultivated the friendship of other musicians, and bad feeling between him and the other great violinists of his day—such as existed between the popular singers and to some extent the composers of the period—never developed. It has often been said that his reputation was so great that he could afford to be patronizing where his artistic rivals were concerned; but it has seldom occurred to his more recent biographers that he was perhaps big enough in heart and mind to admire the qualities and admit the excellences of his contemporaries. His own account of the meeting with Lafont, affording us as it does a further opportunity to peep into the generally hidden recesses of his character, is worth reading. ' In Genoa ', he says, ' I heard that Lafont had arranged to give concerts in Milan and I immediately set out to hear him. His performances, in truth, provided me with much pleasure, and a week later I gave a recital myself, in the *Teatro alla Scala,* so that he should have an opportunity for hearing me '. This *accademia* took place on March 7, the programme including the concerto in E-flat and some G-string variations. ' Lafont then suggested that we appear and play together. I declined this invitation, however, saying that such partnerships were always dangerous, since the public looked upon them as duels, and especially so in this case because he was the first violinist of France while I—though much too generously —have been looked upon as Italy's best performer on the instrument. But Lafont would not admit the force of this argument, and nothing other remained for me to do than pick up his glove and leave the arrangement of the programme to him. In order to avoid an advantage in weapons I voluntarily waived my right to play on one string '—which was a very handsome gesture. Paganini, indeed, was very unwilling to enter into the plan Lafont had outlined, knowing that in the minds of the audience it would degenerate into a mere competition. Not that this need have worried him unduly, for such contests had long been common—even between the greatest masters. He asked Rossini's advice, and the Swan of Pesaro is supposed to have said, ' You must do it so that he should not think you lack the courage to match yourself with him '. The

90

test began by Paganini playing one of his concertos which was followed by Lafont's performance of a biggish work. ' These ', continues Paganini, ' were succeeded by a concerto of Kreutzer's for two violins, which Rode and Kreutzer had played together in Paris. Where the two violins were engaged at one time I remained faithful to the original text, note for note, so that he was ready to wager that we had both come from the same school; but in the solo passages I allowed my imagination free rein and played in the Italian style—the only one that came naturally to me. It is true that this procedure did not please my friendly rival. He followed with a set of variations (on a Russian theme) which were countered by similar variations of my own (*Le Streghe*), after which the recital ended.' There is no false modesty or egotistic arrogance in Paganini's own judgment : ' Lafont could perhaps lay claim to a stronger tone than I commanded; but the applause of the audience gave me to understand that I was not too far behind him. At the same time I do not hesitate to acknowledge Lafont as a great and highly distinguished artist.' The Frenchman was certainly treated with more fairness by his foreign rival than by his own countrymen. Imbert de Laphaleque thought that ' any artist who ventured to match himself with Paganini, without having previously heard him, never omitted to regret his indiscretion. We are sorry to have to report of our own excellent violinist Lafont that, in this respect, he passed through a very gruesome experience.' He undervalues his countryman quite unnecessarily without adding to the lustre of Paganini's name. The newspaper correspondent from Leipzig came to the decision that in beauty of tone and grace of performance the two players were fairly equal—with Lafont perhaps a shade better; technically the Frenchman was far behind the Italian. Fètis thought that Lafont had ' acted imprudently in the circumstances, for although it may be admitted that he possessed more purely classical qualities, and a style more in accordance with French taste than Paganini, and although his tone was fuller and more equal, yet, in original fancy, poetry of execution, and mastery of difficulties, he could not place himself in juxtaposition with his antagonist. In a concert at the Conservatoire of Paris in 1816, the palm would have been awarded to him; but with an Italian public, athirst for novelty and originality, his failure was certain.'

How long Paganini spent in Milan on this occasion we do not know. During the summer his health, only hastily patched up in the spring, broke down again. He suffered great pain and again flew to a patent medicine—this time possibly the so-called panacea ' Leroy ', though he may not have commenced taking this drug until later. All that such mixtures could do for him was to excite his nervous system and upset his digestive apparatus. Except when he thought his condition desperate, he avoided doctors, a lack of confidence that made little difference in his case, for he scarcely ever followed their advice even when he did consult them. He went to Venice again to rest, and though he gave some concerts there, he seems to have appeared rarely during the comparatively long stay he made. It was probably in the August of that year (1816), while in Venice, that he wrote the G-string work called ' Maria Luisa ' in honour of the ex-Empress of France. Napoleon was at St. Helena, and his wife had come to Italy in the April of this year as the Duchess of Parma. And at Parma Paganini came in contact with her during the last years of his life. She it was also who eventually caused the insulted bones of the great Italian to be brought home to his native land.

When Ludwig Spohr, one of the most outstanding figures in the history of the violin, left Vienna in 1816, he arrived at Venice in time to meet his great artistic antithesis there. In October Paganini and Spohr met and, widely as they differed in style, outlook, mode of life, and temperament, a great personal liking sprang up between them. Paganini often told Schottky how much pleasure the meeting with Spohr gave him, and in his generous manner he pronounced the Brunswicker to be the ' first and the finest *singer* on his instrument '. Spohr had heard so much of the strange man he had now met for the first time that his curiosity was aroused. He wrote in his diary: ' Yesterday Paganini returned from Trieste, having thus, as it would appear, abandoned his plan to visit Vienna. To-day he came to see me, and at length I personally met this extraordinary man, of whom I have been reminded daily ever since I reached Italy. No player has ever charmed the Italians as he has done, and though instrumental music is not their favourite form of art, he gave no fewer than a dozen concerts at Milan, and has appeared in no less than five here. Without going into the methods by which he hypnotises the public, one hears on all sides from unmusical people that he is a genuine master in the art of witchcraft, and that he produces sounds from the violin never before heard. The connoisseurs, on the other hand, say that his tremendous left-hand facility, his double-stops, and his excellence in all sorts of difficult passages cannot be denied; but they add that the qualities which intrigue the masses are spoiled by charlatanism which cannot make up for the absence of a good tone, a long bow-stroke, and a tasteful cantabile style. That which satisfies the Italian audiences and has won for him the title of ' the incomparable ' . . . . is found to be a series of bewildering tricks such as those with which the once famous Scheller was wont to astonish the natives of town and country—harmonics, variations on one string, a peculiar kind of pizzicato for the left hand, without the help of the right hand or the bow, as well as sounds quite alien to the instrument, such as imitations of the bassoon, the voices of old women, and other noises. . . . ' He had not yet heard Pagannini play —Nicolo excused himself when asked to play privately so that Spohr might hear him, saying that he was suffering from the consequences of an accidental fall—nor was he to have that experience until he was fourteen years older, when the two met again in Germany. It would hardly be fair to Paganini if we were to measure his reputation by Spohr's verdict. Though honest as a man and charming as a friend, the German was notoriously narrow in his views, and incurably and rigidly

93

traditional in his musical methods. To him springing, bounc-
ing, and ricochet bow-strokes, harmonics, left hand pizzicato,
and the rest of the newer sensational effects, were anathema,
and we have no right to expect from him anything but a pre·
judiced judgment upon what was to him a phenomenon of the
most unusual order. He treated the French manner of playing
with unfeigned contempt, and in his eyes the Italians were
expressive only in an artificial way. To Paganini anything that
succeeded in making his audience feel what was going on in
his mind and soul was legitimate; Spohr disallowed everything
that went beyond the teachings of the classics upon whom he
had modelled himself. The two artists were poles asunder—
as men and as musicians—and nothing on earth could ever
bring them on to common ground.

Paganini remained in Venice until July, 1817, for a news·
paper report, dated on the 23rd of the month, says: ' The
famous violinist Paganini, who has been in Venice for over a
year, has at last left, going to his birthplace Genoa '. Travelling
by way of Milan he hurried home. It is possible that he heard
of his father's failing health while in Lombardy, but whether
he reached Genoa in time to see Antonio alive, we do not know.
Anders is our only authority for the information that the old
man died in 1817. It was most likely for the purpose of seeing
his mother comfortably settled that Nicolo travelled to Genoa
as quickly as possible.

The chronology of events is again uncertain from this
moment until Paganini's appearance in Rome at the end of the
year. If the source of the anecdote printed in the *Athenaeum*
is trustworthy, the violinist was now giving concerts in Verona:
' In 1817, Paganini being at Verona, the leader of the band at
the principal theatre of the town, Valdabrini, himself a very
clever violinist, thought proper to say that Paganini was but a
quack, who no doubt excelled in some pieces he had been in
the habit of playing, but that he (Valdabrini) had a concerto
of his own composition, which Paganini could not execute.
This came to the ears of Paganini, who lost no time in causing

it to be intimated to Valdabrini that he should be glad to try his powers at reproducing the inspirations of the leader of the band of Verona. This trial, which he reserved for his last concert, offered a powerful attraction for the public. The day of rehearsal was fixed—Pagannini did not fail to attend; but he came there less to prepare himself than to conform to the established usage; the music which he executed, on the occasion, was not that which he intended to perform in public. According to his custom, while playing with the band, he introduced a multitude of extempore graces and delicious passages (the instantaneous product of his own fertile imagination) with incredible success. It was not a spiritless rehearsal, but a preceding concert, which nevertheless left the wonders of the intended performance yet unknown to the orchestra. With Paganini it is necessary to be ever prepared for surprises of this nature; the musicians whose duty it is to accompany him, are sometimes so struck that their astonishment interrupts their performance, and they remain bewildered, forgetting in their admiration the task prescribed them. The disappointment of Valdabrini in thus hearing music so different from his own, was excessive; the rehearsal being over, he accosted Paganini— " My friend, it is not my concerto that you have been playing; I have not recognized any part of my own composition in your performance."—" Be easy, my friend," replied Paganini, " when the hour of the concert arrives you shall hear your own music; then alone I shall beg of you a little indulgence." The concert took place on the following day. Paganini commenced by playing several pieces of his own choosing, reserving that of Valdabrini to finish the soirée. The whole audience expected something extraordinary; some thought that he intended to make some change in the instruments of effect in the band; others, that he would reproduce the motivi of the music of Valdabrini, while he would make the most brilliant additions in his own manner. Nobody was in the secret as to what was really to take place. Paganini at last appeared, holding a piece of reed-cane in his hand. All wondered what he was going

95

to do with it; when he suddenly took up his violin, and making use of the reed for a bow, he played from beginning to end the concerto which its author had deemed could not be executed unless after much practising; he not only executed the most difficult passages, but introduced delightful variations, without ceasing for an instant to give proof of the purity, grace, intensity, and fire, which characterize his talent '.

' I have wept only three times in my life,' Rossini is reported to have said; ' the first time when my earliest opera failed, the second time when, with a boating party, a truffled turkey fell into the water, and the third time when I first heard Paganini play '. It was therefore with great joy that the two friends met in Rome towards the end of December, 1817. Rossini was preparing the production of *La Cenerentola* while Paganini meant to give several concerts during the carnival season of 1818. They had a very good time together, though Paganini's health was bad again. He consulted a doctor, which proves that his condition was worse than usual. The diagnosis this time pointed to ailments of a more serious nature, and the physician felt compelled to attribute most of Paganini's troubles to an inflamed state of the nervous system and to a spinal column attacked by an unnamed, or unnamable, disease. Moreover, he suspected the presence of sepsis which the unsuspecting Don Juan of Genoa had probably inherited from one of his many injudicious love-affairs. Personal hygiene was not yet a highly-developed science, and effective antiseptics had not yet become common property. After writing a full account of the doctor's diagnosis for the benefit of the long-suffering Germi, Paganini did his best to forget his spinal column and his troublesome alimentary canal in a little hectic carnival fun. He was ready for any sort of escapade. There is the story that he and Rossini hunted up Meyerbeer, and that the three of them, disguising themselves, sang and acted in the traditional manner. It is quite possible that Meyerbeer had already met Paganini in Venice when both were there in 1816. While on the Adriatic shore on that occasion Meyerbeer was deeply influenced by

96

Rossini's work, and it is more than likely that Rossini's admiration for Paganini drew all three together in a common bond of friendship.

An interesting light is thrown upon Paganini's first concert in Rome by an embittered correspondence that appeared in *The Times* (1833). A teacher of languages, one Moscati, for reasons of his own addressed the editor of that highly respectable newspaper in this strain: 'When in 1817 he (Paganini) made his first appearance in Rome, he had no shoes to his feet, and no coat to his back. A young artist, called Adducci, borrowed from me some money to dress him up and to enable him to give a concert at the Argentina. He did not succeed; the few scudi of the evening he gambled away the same night, and the next morning he had not a paolo at his disposal, and I was never paid. From that time I have never spoken to Paganini' . . . . which must have been a sore deprivation for Nicolo. The editor remarked sourly that to become great after having had no shoes to his feet, redounded to Paganini's credit. The latter, thus encouraged, wrote a spirited reply, saying that he was in no way embarrassed by the want of money in 1817. He had 'Letters of credit on Torlonia the banker.' Moreover, ' the Adducci family were in very easy circumstances ' and could have lent him the money, had it been necessary, without having to borrow from Moscati. The concert *was* a success and the gambling story was a libel. All the same, Paganini's first concert in Rome does not appear to have been a very brilliant affair. He came there as a stranger, the locale chosen for the *accademia* was very unsuitable, and the audience far from numerous. But, his qualities once made known, his subsequent appearances were attended by the accustomed success. According to his letter to *The Times,* he applied to the ecclesiastical authorities for permission to give concerts on Fridays, 'nights on which the Pope does not permit theatrical representations. I was at first refused; but, as the curiosity of the public was excited, I subsequently obtained leave for a single Friday evening, which concert was eminently successful; so much so, that in consequence of its obtaining so many admirers, I received permission for concerts on the two remaining Fridays of the carnival, which were, if possible, more fully attended than the previous one; nay more, I received an order from the Government to return at Easter, and perform before his Majesty, the Emperor of Austria, who was then expected, and for which I received a sum of 3,500 collonati (or Spanish dollars) for two concerts. . . .' He often played in the palazzo of Count de Kaunitz, the Austrian ambassador. There he met Metternich, and a warm friendship developed between the violinist and the celebrated statesman. Metternich, at every encounter, urged Paganini to tour abroad and show himself at Vienna. Nicolo was himself now very desirous of extending his conquests, and would have welcomed the first opportunity for foreign travel. Curious it is that he was prevented by one circumstance or another from carrying out his plan. Sometimes it was a series of engagements in Italy, sometimes it was a love-affair; most often it was his health, which had the unfortunate habit of breaking down when he most needed all his strength. In spite of all his endeavours, ten years were to elapse before he crossed the frontiers of his own country.

CHAPTER XI

' VIE DE BOHÊME '
(1818—Feb., 1822)

WHEN Paganini left Rome in the spring of 1818 he was allowing definite plans for the future to form in his mind. Metternich, Kaunitz, Meyerbeer, Rossini, and many other experienced men of affairs and touring artists had opened his eyes to the possibilities awaiting him in foreign countries—and yet he did not seem able to tear himself away from his homeland. It may have been the state of his health that made him look towards the future with a more practical eye; it may simply have been the influence of his maturing years. The fact remains that he began to regard money in a different light. Hitherto the means of gratifying his desires and the price of pleasure, it now became the guarantee for an old age of ease and the comforts of a domestic fireside. What many mistook for avarice was merely a provident concern for the future. He began to realise that an artist's life—as it had to be lived early in the nineteenth century with its uncertainties and dangers, its difficulties and inconveniences—was of comparatively short duration; that his own artistic career, in view of all he had lately discovered about his physical state, seemed destined to be more limited than that of the majority of virtuosi; that unless he earned more and spent less there was the painful prospect of his mother suffering unnecessary privations in her old age, and of his sisters having to fight life's battles alone while their respective husbands amused themselves in other ways. Paganini's affection for the women of his family never varied; his sisters never appealed to him in vain for help, his mother usually being the intermediary who placed their difficulties before him. The tenderness which he reserved for his mother was of an almost unique order—constant, deep, nearly feminine—and only for one other being, his son, did he exhibit so self-sacrificing a devotion. He wished to exhaust the gold-bearing lodes of his motherland before crossing the frontiers and, working in a more systematic manner than before, he went north to Turin and played his way southward.

The tour then commenced at Turin, and a newspaper report tells us that 'during Lent in 1818 Paganini gave two concerts in the Teatro Carignano. The theatre had probably never before been so completely filled, and certainly never before has the violin transported the public into such ecstasies of enthusiasm. Had he given another ten concerts straight off the reel, the house would assuredly have been equally sold out. . . . Nothing more can be added to what has already been said of him'. Nevertheless, he found time to dally with a girl of about fourteen, precociously developed as were the maidens of the Italian lower classes, and he confesses that he grew lazy on her account. But although he told Germi that he asked the girl's father for her hand in marriage, the flame died down when he met a couple of ladies of more mature years some four months later. In April we meet him in Piacenza where he made the congenial acquaintance of the great Polish virtuoso Lipinski.

Carl Joseph Lipinski, eight years younger than Paganini, was a violinist of outstanding qualities; he possessed what Paganini lacked—a big, powerful, tone—and his facility in the performance of double-stopping commanded the respect even of the Genoese. In 1817 he set out to tour Italy, with the hope of meeting his celebrated Italian contemporary as an added incentive. Baulked by fate from encountering him in Venice, Verona, and Milan, he was playing in Piacenza when a concert-announcement informing him of Paganini's arrival was placed in his hands. The Pole was enchanted with the Italian's performance. There is a local story to the effect that after the playing of an Adagio, Lipinski was the only member of the audience who applauded—the natives probably reserving their energies for the more brilliant movements. This unusual action drew all eyes in his direction. He explained himself by saying he was a foreigner who had travelled far to hear Paganini, and after the concert an acquaintance effected an introduction. Nicolo, having arranged to give six concerts, made a stay of some duration and the two violinists became greatly attached to one another. They were frequent visitors at each other's lodgings and passed away many pleasant houıs by playing music for two violins; and when the supply of suitable compositions failed, they improvised duets together. At the last of the concerts at Piacenza Paganini was joined by Lipinski in a double concerto. It has often been asserted that their appearance upon one platform was in the nature of a public contest such as Lafont had staged at Milan. But there is absolutely no foundation for that statement; the two men were friends who genuinely and generously admired each other's genius, and friends they remained in spite of the ill-advised enthusiasm of a few partisans when the two artists met again at Warsaw eleven years later. Paganini himself said : ' Lipinski had heard me in six *accademie,* joined me in a concerto for two violins in the theatre, and often played with me on other occasions, for I had formed a really cordial affection for this unusually skilful and pleasant man '. There can be no denying, however, that their public association greatly increased Lipinski's reputation in musical circles.

Travelling *via* Modena, where he appeared once, we find Paganini in buoyant mood in Bologna at the end of June. The stay in Piacenza and the companionship of Lipinski seem to have done him good, for on July 1st he is discovered writing cheerfully to Germi : ' At the concert in Bologna on Friday last, the Cavaliere Crescentini, a musician, visited me in my rooms, and asked me to honour him by being his guest at his country-seat. I went, and found much entertainment in the company of Madame Colbran, and of another really charming amateur, beautiful as any Eve, who bewitched me with her rendering of " Per mare, per fonte cercando di luce " '. Isabella Angela

Colbran had a little earlier basked in the full sunshine of fame; she was accounted one of the best singers of her time, and had enjoyed some instruction from the Crescentini who now played the host to an ideally Bohemian house-party. Later on she sang dreadfully out of tune, and as Rossini possessed a sense of humour she married him.

In the winter Paganini returned north for four further concerts at the Carignano in Turin during December, 1818, and January, 1819. His movements are again difficult to follow, and we are not sure of him until he appears for a number of recitals in Florence during the spring of 1819. His style had by now become so individually characteristic of himself that all attempts at comparison with other great artists were abandoned. The Florentine correspondent of the *Leipzig Musical Journal* contents himself by reporting: ' He follows the method of no single master; his manner is peculiar to himself; his method of performance has no equal; and in short, everything that can produce delight and amazement is at his command '.

It was probably during this visit to Florence in 1819 that Meyerbeer heard Paganini play. The story goes that the German was so enraptured by the Italian's performance that he followed the magnetic Nicolo from place to place, and did not leave him to attend to the production of one of his own operas until he had heard eighteen of the concerts. What astonished Meyerbeer most—as it surprised Imbert de Laphaleque—was that ' in a country where everyone is a musician, where they have music at every moment of the day, and where consequently they care little for concerts, Paganini attracted crowds everywhere and excited universal enthusiasm.' Meyerbeer, indeed, when he was in Paris eleven years later, at a time when the French capital was awaiting the arrival of the Genoese wizard with incredulity and impatience, said to Castil-Blaze : ' Imagine the most astounding effects that can be produced from a violin; dream of the most extravagant prodigies that can be performed with the bow and with melody;

Paganini knows how to surpass all your imaginings with his realities '.

During the summer of this year Paganini paid his first visit to Naples, a city he had long wished to know, a centre where he expected to meet with more serious criticism than hitherto. Without making a lengthy detour through the musical and political history of Naples during the eighteenth and early nineteenth centuries, it will be almost impossible to realise how different was the attitude of the Neapolitans towards the arts. They preferred their own brand of opera, they possessed their own favourite artists, their own dialect, their own kind of humour; they were conservative and very jealous of their reputation as performers and critics; above all, they hated having to endorse the verdicts of others. A stranger from the north who had been ill-advised enough to court the favour of Lombardy, Piedmont, and Tuscany for so long without passing his examinations, as it were, in Naples, might be certain of a cool reception when he put in a belated appearance on the beautiful bay. Politically things were not too settled either, and every arrival was a potential spy; revolutions were brewing; in every way Naples felt that this was a moment when she should be left alone. Paganini's fame had, of course, reached the ears of the musicians and critics by various channels, but it had been welcomed by a frown of mistrust from the former and an amused smile of incredulity from the latter. If the Neapolitans were to be impressed by this stranger—even if the incomprehensible north had gone into raptures over him— he would have to be very good indeed.

The reception accorded the Genoese artist by the leading professional musicians of Naples was not of the friendliest nature. To put it frankly, they were afraid of being taken in by hear- say, and one of the tests to which Paganini was by now accustomed was prepared for him. A young composer, one Danna, regarded locally as the most promising technician of the younger generation, was given the task of putting together a quartet the first violin part of which was to contain every conceivable difficulty. Paganini was to be asked to play this part without rehearsal—the intention of the Neapolitans being no doubt to make the warmth of his public reception dependent upon the result, while their expectation was the failure of the so-called magician to perform the work satisfactorily. We need not assume that this clique was going out of its way to be gratuitously spiteful; to put it colloquially, Paganini had often enough—on posters and in conversation—' asked for it.' Indeed, from the earliest years of his career he had invited the most extravagantly difficult tests in order to prove his extraordinary powers of sight-reading. He was accordingly asked to honour the professional musicians of Naples by his presence at a musical reunion; and doubtlessly suspecting the real reason for this polite gesture, he went with his inscrutable smile of self-satisfaction playing about his expressive features. The monstrous part was handed to him; he glanced through it as casually as he had looked at Pasini's concerto in Parma, and sat down to play. In company with three well-known players he went through the composition in brilliant style, astonishing all present by the perfection of his manner and the accuracy of his reading. As if by magic the attitude of the Neapolitans changed, and they were sportsmen enough to award the palm ungrudgingly where it was merited. Led by the violinist Onorio de Vito, the cellist Ciandelli, the composer Danna, and the internationally famous court-conductor and violinist, Giuseppe Maria Festa, the musicians of the conservative town applauded vigorously. Paganini's status was established, and his performance no less than his personality brought many valuable friends to his side. In particular Festa, as conductor of the San Carlo theatre orchestra, could be very useful.

Commencing his series of concerts at the Fondo theatre, where performances were generally given during the summer months, he later transferred his activities to the larger San Carlo. Once more he was unanimously acclaimed as a miracle. Paganini's own satisfaction was hard to conceal; it was characteristic of him to become highly elated at such successes and his own version of the triumph is tuned in an enthusiastic key : ' Nothing could be more flattering to me than the applause and praise I was given at the three concerts I arranged at the royal theatre—and this by an audience notoriously difficult to satisfy and one that takes pride in its power to pass correct judgment in musical matters. I need say no more than mention that on the first evening I played at the great theatre of San Carlo, the public broke a rule by applauding me ; a rule which obliges them not to give any sign of approval or dis- approval when the court is present, until their Majesties have themselves commenced to show their feelings. However, they did not wait for this, but with incessant clapping and cries of ' eviva ', applauded me most enthusiastically, and made me come three times from behind the curtain '. He is in a most genial and expansive mood and tells his old friend Germi that ' I am living here with every regard to economy, so that you need suffer no uneasiness concerning my squandering of health, money, and peace of mind. This spot is lovely and enchanting ; a beautiful climate, magnificent views, the best of food and wines, the greatest luxury in carriages, public gardens, smiling happily like those of the Hesperides, attractive ladies. . . . But Paganini lives, half a stoic and half a careful Genoese. I am to give two more performances, and when the hot season has passed I shall go to Palermo '. Once again—as is usual when he is in this ' unbuttoned ' mood—he outlines his future plans : ' From Sicily I hope to make another musical excursion through Italy on my route to Vienna, whither Prince Metternich has invited me. Thence I shall travel to Paris and London. From these productive tours should spring honest repose which I wish to ensure for myself when the years of impotence arrive. Here, my dear chap are my plans, if Heaven gives me life '.

These sentiments had hardly been expressed before he was compelled to retire from the public gaze by another, and serious, attack of his intestinal trouble. In addition, an incessant cough —either nervous or gastric—persisted in robbing him of all repose. With the nervousness of the chronic invalid he feared every draught and cool current of air, and to be in a more sheltered position he took lodgings in the district of Petraio under St. Elmo. Here, as he told Fétis, he ran into the very conditions he most desired to avoid, and becoming worse, the rumour spread that he was suffering from consumption. Believing that Paganini was dying of this scourge, then held by the Neapolitans to be contagious, his landlord asked him to move at once. The poor man, prostrate with abdominal pains and other complications, could scarcely rise in his bed, much less leave it. Fearing for the health of his own family, and thinking that other guests might be frightened away—for death is no advertisement for an apartment-house—the landlord ' had the inhumanity to turn him into the street with all he possessed '. Luckily Ciandelli, the cellist who had taken part in the test imposed upon Paganini at his arrival, happened to pass, and ' incensed by the act of cruelty he was witness to, and which might have proved fatal to the great artist, he belaboured the barbarian with the stick he carried, and then had his friend conveyed to a comfortable lodging where every attention was paid to him '. Paganini soon recovered sufficiently to complete his professional engagements.

This recovery, however, was but of a temporary nature—another example of his indomitable will to keep his appointments with his public. The illness he had just passed through left him in a deplorably weak state, and a complete rest was imperative. That he went to Palermo for this purpose seems a logical conclusion to draw. From Sicily he wrote to Genoa that ' I wish to regain my health for the tour I have planned to undertake in Germany, Russia, France, and England; and then, perhaps, we will take a wife '. The last remark shows that he was once more optimistic. At the same time he sent Germi the respectable sum of thirty thousand francs to be invested for his mother's benefit, adding that he did this so that he might ' have a lodging ready in the event of my going to see her at some time or other, and to enjoy one of the stews that her hands can cook so divinely '. This letter was written early in 1820. According to what he told Fétis, he was back in Milan by March and stayed there until he went to Rome in December. What he did in Lombardy during these eight or nine months we do not know; but there is no lack of information on his doings in the Eternal City.

He arrived to find Rossini busy with the staging of his *Matilde de Shabran*, an opera upon which fortune did not lavish her smiles. Trouble dogged the footsteps of the unlucky composer all through the rehearsals, and the last straw was added when the conductor became suddenly indisposed—according to some authorities the victim of an apoplectic stroke. The opera seemed doomed to postponement. Paganini, however, had had a good deal of experience in this class of work when he conducted the operas for the Princess Elise at Lucca, and he came to his friend's rescue at the most opportune moment. He threw himself into his task with enthusiasm and electrified all concerned with the production into instant action. Playing the first violin part an octave higher than it was written, the better to be heard by the rest of the orchestra, he soon made the band acquainted with the music and the way in which its composer wished to have it interpreted. Indeed, Rossini's and Paganini's ideas in such matters were usually so alike that hardly any differences of opinion between the composer and his leader-conductor were to be expected. When one of the horn-players absented himself on account of illness, Paganini played his part on a viola. As a result of all this intensive drilling, coaxing, and driving, the opera was ready for performance on February 24, 1821. It was given at the Apollo Theatre, recently reconstructed out of the old *Teatro Tordinone* by Paganini's banker Torlonia. There were, of course, the usual ' first night ' scenes in which conflicting verdicts were volubly given; but the Rossini party was in strong force and the opera was launched on its career. De Laphaleque tells us that the orchestral players at Paganini's disposal were ' unskilful ' and that Paganini ' wrought an absolute metamorphosis. It astonished all the cognoscenti, and Rossini himself, who never relates the story without lively pleasure '. Paganini, both before and after this performance, had his own concerts to give, and one newspaper report says that he was greeted by tremendous applause, and that he exhibited an ' unbelievable finish and facility in the manipulation of his instrument, and on this occasion he played his Adagios with more feeling than was the case two years ago '.

In May Paganini was again in Naples, playing at the *Fondo* and the *Teatro Nuovo*. Here the celebrated musicologue Kandler heard him and wrote to the *Morgenblatt:* ' At last I have heard and admired Italy's first violinist. This Hercules among the Italian players has already given two recitals, the first on July 20, the second on September 1, while a third has been arranged for the middle of the same month. At the first *accademia* he played three movements of an old concerto of Kreutzer's, in which—apart from his *coups d'hazard* at the cadences—he satisfied even the most orthodox of experts '— thus reversing the judgment of the Milan correspondent. Or had Paganini looked upon the earlier criticism as a lesson and kept more strictly to the written text when performing the works of others? Kandler then gives the customary and highly enthusiastic account of Nicolo's technical miracles. He was now rapidly approaching that stage in his career when his experience with audiences and the more balanced artistic judgment that added years bring with them, gave him that quiet assurance, that polish and finish, that complete command of his dynamic resources, which, taken together, were in a few short years to place him on the highest pinnacle of fame. But first his inconstant heart was to be scored with a few more lacerations.

While in Naples on this occasion Paganini once more experienced the ' one real passion of his life '. He writes to Germi in haste, with all the effervescence of an eighteen-year-old boy for the first time in love, that he has decided to follow the dictates of his heart and take a wife. His description of the chosen one would suggest that he has discovered the world's ideal of maidenhood. She has beauty and education, and though ' she has no dowry, I am content to live in happiness with her '. He had made up his mind to marry her, and would Germi be a good fellow and send the necessary papers? His mother's consent was, of course, needed, and since the estimable and beloved old lady could not write, he suggests that she appear before the notary with her right thumb bandaged so that she might be excused the formality of signing the document personally. Having disposed of this obstacle in a manner satisfactory to himself, poor Paganini suddenly feels the crushing burden of all his thirty-nine years and would not like his Venus to think she was marrying an old man. Well, let Germi go and ' make arrangements with the priest of San Salvatore to enter me well below the forties '. Later on, to pass away the time of waiting, he writes again to add that ' beauty and education are the two dowries that my taste requires. . . . In everything Paganini avoids mediocrity '. In the following month he goes into ecstatic raptures over the manifold virtues of his fiancée, and can hardly await the moment when he can possess such a paragon of feminine qualities. Apparently he did not wait. The pair evidently eloped—it was a modish procedure in those days—without observing the enslaving and old-fashioned custom of marriage. After four days ' which seemed like four years ' he discovered that she was not all he imagined her to be, and left her in the care of a peasant woman who was prepared to swear that the girl had been with her the whole time. Oh, fie. Germi received this last information from Parma. It is not at all unlikely that the Neapolitan flame flickered out even before Paganini's papers arrived, and that the heroine of the Parma letter was already a new ' first real passion '. Paganini was like that.

Concerts, illness, and disillusionment in love, had frayed his nerves a little and he sailed to Sicily for repose. At Palermo, to while away the tedium of loneliness, he tried the Sicilians with a concert. The audience were scattered sparsely about the hall, their appreciation was only lukewarm, and Paganini, frowning at the whole crooked world sailed back again in no cheerful frame of mind. But at this period in his life he recovered rapidly from such little disappointments, and was quite ready to agree with the report written by the Palermo correspondent of the Leipzig paper, which said that the coolness of his reception was due to the indifference of the Sicilians to instrumental music generally. Paganini appears to have spent the winter of 1821-22 in Parma.

CHAPTER XII

The Shrovetide revels of a Roman carnival, congenial spirits, and a Paganini who was allowed for a short time to forget his internal organs. These were the bases of the masquerade played by Nicolo and Rossini when they met in Rome during February, 1822. They were joined by the celebrated Italian statesman Massimino d'Azeglio who possessed the inestimable virtue of being able to relax gracefully, and the vocalist Signora Liparini—and together this spirited quartette planned a carnival jest that attracted attention even in Rome. Paganini and Rossini were disguised as blind beggar-women, and the former, tall, thin, somewhat cadaverous in appearance, and the latter with his comfortable pot-bellied rotundity and full-faced air of prosperity, must have presented an excruciatingly funny spectacle. Rossini had composed a little ditty to a text that can only be lamely translated by this attempt:

> ' We are blind,
> And were born so;
> We can live,
> By alms alone;
> Do not refuse the poor a gift,
> On this day of Carnival.'

La Liparini and the patrician d'Azeglio sang to an accompaniment strummed by the two ill-assorted musicians on a pair of cheap guitars. They made the round of the theatre foyers and the corso, and were even invited into the fashionable houses —most of which were thrown open for the festivities—to present their well-acted 'turn'. Paganini with his sunken cheeks and his natural angles brought into sharper prominence by his feminine rags, must have been lugubrious enough to raise the laugh that the dying clown of romance calls forth when his real tears course down his painted face. But Rossini, with his well-lined paunch, chanting of starvation, was irresistible. Especially so when a wag, joining the party in the true spirit of carnival, pretending to mistake Gioacchino's natural girth for something far more interesting, though in his case less natural, offered the poor burdened 'woman' a chair with gestures of comic tenderness. Genius will out, and this four-some of born entertainers was as successful in the midst of the masking crowd as Paganini the violinist ever was behind the footlights of the Scala at Milan.

Paganini does not seem to have arranged any concerts during this short visit to Rome, for soon after Shrovetide he left for Venice. Here again his stay was brief, and he may only have looked in to see if the Bianchi was in town and still unwilling to place a value upon his friendship. His movements and his reasons for them at this juncture are alike vague. Some un-usual plans were evidently occupying his mind, for we next discover him on the road to Milan *via* Piacenza. Whenever Paganini was in doubt in northern Italy, he always made for the Lombard capital. Here he arrived in March, made arrangements for a concert, and decided upon his future plans. The Milanese were delighted to have their favourite among them again. A newspaper of March 23rd, said: 'The celebrated violinist, Paganini, after a long absence, is again in Milan and proposes to give a concert shortly. Afterwards he intends to undertake an artistic tour of Germany. I asked him jokingly whether he had made any progress on his instrument since he was last here, and he replied, "Yes; I can now do without the accompaniment of the orchestra",—and in fact, I learned from him and from others that he can play difficult variations and supply his own accompaniment'. This latter-day miracle was his polyphonic performance and his left-hand pizzicato accom-

PAGANINI

paniments. The report concerning his plans to go abroad at last—the result of his recent preoccupation—was this time not without foundation. He had long been pondering over the idea—certainly since Metternich invited him to Vienna—and he possibly went to Rome for the purpose of seeking Rossini's advice. Once more, however, there was a disappointment in store for him and his foreign admirers.

It was possibly on this visit to Milan that Paganini renewed his acquaintance with another old friend—the famous poet Ugo Foscolo; and the details of the meeting tell us much concerning the violinist's culture and general knowledge, surprising in a man who had enjoyed no systematic education in his youth. The writer Amati, rummaging among the papers of a Milanese friend, found the following memoir: ' I dined with the Countess F. . ., a wealthy and very intellectual lady, to whom the celebrated Ugo Foscolo paid court. The poet, who combined a lofty imagination with a fiery soul . . . . suspected, and perhaps not without reason, that he had a rival. His jealousy knew no bounds and, throwing all respect to the winds, treated the Countess not only as one under suspicion, but like one proved guilty of infidelity. She gave him his congé. The hours now seemed like centuries to the love-sick man, and fearing that he might quickly be replaced in the lady's affections, sent her a note which, though full of recriminations, begged for forgiveness and announced a visit for the morrow. His only condition was that they should be alone. The beautiful Countess could not resist the temptation to take her revenge, and invited a number of others to dine with her, among whom were Vincenzo Monti and Paganini. Although we were asked for four o'clock, we were all assembled by three. Foscolo, who could not or would not come earlier, was the last to arrive. Hoping to find the lady alone, he was not a little surprised to see so numerous a gathering. . . . At the door of the salon he stopped and, losing his temper, was preparing to withdraw when he heard the silvery voice of the Countess which had the effect of Orpheus's song: the tamed lion turned and came nearer.

Paganini and I were on the terrace; Ugo was unwilling to remain where Monti was playing the experienced gallant, and joined us. The rage on his countenance vanished when he saw Paganini. He shook him by the hand and said, " I went to your concert last night; you are a god, and Homer hovered before my eyes when I heard you play. The first magnificent movement of your concerto seemed to portray the landing of the Greeks before Troy; the Adagio in its nobility was a colloquy between Briseïs and Achilles; but when shall I hear the despair, the lamentations over the hearse of Patroclus? "—I thought that Paganini would fail to find a reply; but without hesitation he said, " As soon as Achilles-Paganini finds a Patroclus among the violinists." We were then called to table. Paganini stepped into the dining-room with Foscolo, who to spite his beautiful hostess, lavished all his charm and attention on the virtuoso. Monti also appeared to be pointedly attracted to the violinist. Paganini found the greatest talents of Italy paying him homage; and yet he was (as Petrarch said) *umile in tanta gloria.* His answers betrayed a man who had lived in the great world and who lacked nothing that spirit and reading could confer. It is wonderful. Between Foscolo and Paganini there is a similarity, not only in externals, but a still greater agreement in the style of the two masters. I often imagine I hear in Paganini's playing one of the last letters of Jacopo Orti, and in his music the deep passions, the melancholy calm, the rage, and the masculine decision of Foscolo come before me again . . . . Between the two there is complete harmony of character and thought '. The morals to be drawn from this reminiscence are obvious enough. Paganini, in spite of the fact that no one ever remembered having seen him reading a book, exhibited an unexpected knowledge of classic literature and mythology; that though his upbringing was in very ordinary surroundings and guided by a father with no very elevated imagination, he possessed fine feelings, ready wit, and polished manners; that in spite of the attempts of so many writers to present him to us as a surly, taciturn, uncultured, and rude man, he emerges from many contemporary accounts—at this period of his life at least—as a courtly gentleman, ready for elegant conversation and the exchange of epigrammatic sword-play; that he was not only willing to mix with intellectual society, but was a much sought-after guest in the salons of the wealthy, the wise, the noble, and the artistic. This is a very different Paganini from legend's monstrosity: the sordid, money-grubbing, self-sufficient Paganini of the prison-cell and the brothel.

We hear nothing more of him until January, 1823, when, on the way to Pavia, he was taken seriously ill. So desperate was the fight waged by his doctors that his recovery seemed very doubtful. His mother appears to have come to attend to his needs, but the cough which was now added as a regular con-comitant of his older troubles proved more difficult to combat than ever before. At about this period he began taking advan-tage of the hospitality offered him by an old friend, the Field-Marshal Pino, at whose villa on the Lake of Como he often rested after attacks of illness. It is doubtful that he went there on this occasion, for as soon as he was on his feet again he hurried to Turin where he was awarded the most tumultuous applause at several concerts. It is a cause for more than ordinary surprise that the frequent spells of ill-health which incapacitated him from time to time should not have influenced his playing detrimentally. Yet it would seem that he was greeted with greater enthusiasm after each successive attack. Only on his body was their mark visible, and he now rapidly began to resemble the portrait of a sunken-cheeked, haggard, and suffering man, with which so many descriptions have made us familiar. His engagements at Turin filled, he now for once followed medical advice, and went home to Genoa to rest and recuperate, to be nursed by Genoese friends who were proud of their countryman, and to gain strength from the stews that his mother's hands knew how ' to cook so divinely '.

Paganini's convalescence after this illness and the relapse he suffered later in 1823, kept him from the concert-platform for about a year. It must have been while resting at Genoa that he became interested in Sivori, now in his eighth year. This boy, the son of a Genoese business-man, evinced a desire to play the violin even earlier in life than did Paganini himself, for he was barely out of his swaddling-clothes before he imitated the action of performing on that instrument with the aid of two pieces of wood. It has even been said—probably by some-one wise after the event—that Paganini's influence on the child was already pre-natal and that his mother's excitement at one of Nicolo's concerts precipitated the gifted child's birth. Now, nearly eight years later, Paganini had the leisure consciously to help the boy by experimenting with the teaching-method he had evolved from his own experiences. This system—the mysterious ' secret of Paganini '—was jealously guarded, and only two or three fortunate people were permitted to benefit by it. From time to time Paganini promised to give this secret to the world, but postponed fulfilment of the intention so often that in the end death surprised him before he could carry out his plan. Whether there ever was a ' secret of Paganini ' or not, it is impossible for anyone to say; and, in spite of numerous more fantastic theories, it is quite likely that the whole of Paganini's system of practice was based upon some of his own dicta, such as the one about genius being patience, the one concerning the avoidance of mediocrity at all times, and his own method of studying each difficulty until it was mastered. But this theory does not explain the rapidity which Paganini claimed for his system. He tells us himself that ' this young man (Camillo Sivori) was only about seven when I taught him the elements of music. At the end of three days he could play several pieces perfectly, and the world cried, " Paganini has performed a miracle ". At the end of fifteen days he appeared in public. I owe it to Truth to add that the perfection of his musical sense facilitated the lessons I gave him. As for the rest, when my system will be known, artists will commence to study the nature of the violin far more thoroughly, for it is an instrument a hundred times richer than is generally supposed. My discovery is not due to sheer accident, but the result of thorough research.

One day they will come to my system of studying. The existing method, which is more likely to embarrass pupils than to further their progress, will fall before my system, which only calls for regular exercising for five or six hours a day . . . . '. At the close of his stay he wished to take the boy with him and continue his lessons; but as his intention was to go abroad as soon as his health permitted, the elder Sivori objected. But he followed Paganini's advice to place Camillo with his own old master, Costa. The little fiddler provided Nicolo with gentle exercise during his convalescence, and his needs called into being a short concerto and six sonatas for violin, viola, cello, and guitar. When these works were played—either to provide practice for Camillo or to entertain guests—Paganini took the guitar part. We may wonder whether the touch of that instrument brought any tender thought of the adorable Dida to his busy mind; perhaps he dedicated one faint smile, reminiscent and regretful, to the memory of three happy years.

In the autumn he went to General Pino's villa on Como to profit by the change of air and scene. He told Schottky that Pino's friendship was almost paternal, and he owed the old soldier a deep debt of gratitude for the many benefits he received in the villa on the beautiful lake. The two men often played duets, and Nicolo once remarked how closely the ancient warrior's manner of performance was modelled on his own. From this health-giving spot on the Swiss border he made the comparatively short journey to Milan. Whether he intended giving concerts there is not known. If such was his plan it was immediately frustrated, for he suffered an alarming relapse. Dr. Borda bled him five times, tried a mercurial treatment, and left the patient as bad as he found him. Temporary relief— this time of somewhat longer duration—came from an unexpected quarter. Writing to Germi on November 26th, 1823, Paganini said that he was still alive only by an apparent miracle performed by an American doctor : ' I had given myself up to taking opium in large doses, and although this reduced my coughing, I found myself robbed of all my faculties. I could scarcely stand on my feet, and I could hardly digest a single cup of chocolate in the twenty-four hours. In addition, I developed a little asthma, my abdomen became enlarged, and my colour was cadaverous. Luckily at this moment I met an American physician in a café. He assured me that I should be buried within a month if I did not follow his advice. He said he recognized my complaint and told me that the cough came from nothing but a weakness of the nervous system '. The treatment prescribed was a common-sense one at any rate : plain food, good wine, fresh air, and rest, to which were added some herbal remedies. ' In a few days I revived and now I feel quite well. At the end of the week I shall return to Pino's at the Villa Nuova, where I shall be well looked after and where I shall be able to indulge in the riding which the American doctor recommends'. He probably stayed on the Lake of Como until the beginning of the following year.

Early in 1824 Paganini arrived once more in Venice. As usual after a long convalescence he felt lonely when he had left the circle of congenial friends who had nursed him back to health. A long time had elapsed—for him—since he last exercised his talents for flirtation. We know his invariable cure for loneliness. Whether he had met Antonia Bianchi since he parted from her disgustedly in 1815 we do not know; she was a native of Como, and it is quite likely that he came across her when he was a guest at the Villa Nuova and she at her home. The circumstances of both had changed considerably in the past nine years, and so presumably had their feelings for one another. When they now met in Venice their old friendship—in spite of Paganini's moral scruples—ripened into something which they both believed to be love. Whatever shortcomings Antonia may have possessed, and she had many, she was at least clever enough to hold the elusive fiddler for a longer time than any other of the girls with whom he fell in love could do. But she succeeded in this only because she trusted him less than the others had done; because she was cursed with a jealous disposition so highly developed that it very soon caused a great deal of friction. In the first rapture of a new episode of this nature, Paganini never did see very clearly, and he was hardly likely to notice such seemingly negligible traits in her character. He was far too busy preparing her for the artistic life he intended her to lead at his side. A singer unknown outside of Venice, she was forced to submit to a course of intensive study under the guidance of her masterful lover. That young scamp Cupid saw to it that she also was blind to this masterfulness until he left her to seek new targets for his archery. But she improved in her music and in the management of her pleasant singing voice, and as soon as Paganini considered her sufficiently accomplished to appear with him on one platform, they set out on their travels together. This liaison evidently put off the long-projected tour abroad, and fate ordered events in such wise that it was another four years before they left Italy.

Returning with his new companion to Genoa, Paganini, probably feeling better in health than he had done for years, threw himself whole-heartedly into the professional life that was to him the ideal form of existence. His mother and sisters had received Antonia cordially, and Teresa, with the indulgence reserved for a favourite son, called her his 'amiable companion'. In the theatre where, as a child-prodigy, he appeared for the first time in public with his 'Carmagnole' variations, he opened his new series of concerts. Playing on May 14th, and 21st, and assisted by a young cellist named Signora Barette, no more than fourteen years of age, and La Bianchi, who had now risen to the dignity of a 'guest virtuosa', aged—professionally—twenty, Paganini created a veritable furore. For once the prophet found honour in his own country, and his Genoese reception must have given him the greatest satisfaction. The local paper—the *Gazzetta di Genova*—in comparing his performance now with that of earlier occasions, writes: 'We have heard it said that since his long illness he is greatly improved; we say that his touch is rather more refined in the sweetness of its expression. In this respect we believe him to be unrivalled, as is certainly the case in his happy execution of the most difficult passages, which are performed with such self-assurance and ease that neither the ear nor the eye can follow the voluble succession of notes. He stands alone with his violin in our midst—a veritable Apollo '. Even the correspondents of the foreign newspapers, exempt from all suspicion of local patriotism, are equally enthusiastic : ' On the 14th and 21st of May, Paganini delighted us with his incomparable playing in the Teatro Sant'Agostino. Each of the two concerts consisted of twelve pieces in three Acts of four each, and lasted full three hours without causing the audience to experience the slightest sense of monotony— which, in this country, where concerts are concerned, is saying quite a lot. The contrary would be nearer the truth; the performance of the concert-giver was greeted at each of his appearances with renewed enthusiasm . . . . *How* Paganini played his pieces I cannot attempt to describe. Those who have never heard him, cannot . . . . *etc.*'.

Milan, for the many kindnesses shown him in the past, deserved a visit, and Paganini next directed his steps to the well-known boards of the old Scala. The Milanese friends he had made during the past eleven years—and they were very numerous—were overjoyed at his re-appearance after the illness that had almost made their city his grave. His recital of June 12th, was no less than a triumph, and the excitement of the audience was indescribable. Thence he returned to Genoa to give two more concerts on June 30th, and July 7th, and at the end of the year was again on the shores of the Adriatic.

In January, 1825, Paganini appeared twice before the public of Trieste and twice he sent them speechless with amazement. Benesch, of local fame, after one of the performances said to Jähl, a German musician resident there, ' We had all better make our Wills '. ' No ', replied Jähl, ' I cannot—I am already dead '. Regli tells a story that gives a little more food for speculation : ' During his stay in Trieste, the artist was one day sitting at table with a numerous company. As the meal was approaching its end, he suddenly leapt to his feet, and in a desperate voice raved: " Save me, gentlemen: save me from the ghost that follows me everywhere. Look at it there, how it threatens me with the same blood-stained dagger as I used to rob him of life . . . . And she loved me so . . . . and was innocent . . . . Oh, two years in a dungeon is not sufficient atonement; my own blood should be shed to the very last drop ". With these words he seized a knife lying on the table before him. Naturally we hurried to disarm the seeming maniac. But Paganini, with a sardonic smile, returned calmly to his seat, remarking coolly that he had only wished to heap ridicule on those who had been spreading the old and well-known fairy-tales concerning himself '. He had a weakness for acting little melodramatic scenes, and he may certainly have produced this one for the purpose he indicated. On the other hand it may have been a simple attack of hysteria, a reaction such as comes not infrequently to nerve-ridden subjects. We know that when in melancholy moods he was given to the habit of speaking to himself. There remains a third possibility, and perhaps the most likely one : he did it merely to provide the reporters with another ' Paganini anecdote ' and thereby further increase the pressure of work at the box-office. Regli apparently suspected the same source for the outburst, for he continues, ' The fact remains that the theatre, in which he gave a recital on the following day, was packed to suffocating-point—thus achieving his object '.

Paganini and Antonia now crossed Italy to Naples where a concert of unusual brilliance was given at the *Fondo* theatre on April 15th. What the special occasion was, we do not know; but some of the most celebrated vocalists in Europe took part in the programme. Besides the bewildering display of virtuosity with which Paganini dazzled the audience, there were also heard the popular Tosi and Novelli, Fioravanti and Luigi Lablache. The last was later on to enjoy a European reputation, and Paganini more than once appeared on the same London stage with the famous basso. The enthusiasm of the Neapolitans at this concert knew no bounds, and Paganini was greeted with loud shouts of ' *eviva* ', honoured by complimentary poems, and crowned with the laurel-wreath that is fame's reward for patience, courage, and determination.

At the beginning of the summer, his brow encircled with triumphant bays, he packed up his and Antonia's belongings— tenderly this time—and sailed a third time to Sicily. His concerts at Palermo now met with more appreciation, and we may wonder, if we like, whether the natives had suddenly acquired a greater love for instrumental music, or whether they had learned from the Neapolitan papers that it was ' the thing ' to hear and applaud the magician from Genoa. But although Paganini may have given some concerts there for the purpose of earning his expenses, they were not the real reason for his present visit to the island. He went there because he thought the climate would have a beneficial effect on Antonia's health and that of the love-gage which he had entrusted to her. This thought transformed him. He walked about as a man in a dream; now sitting silently and meditating on the future, now absurdly optimistic and deliriously happy. One after the other castles in Spain went up—all jerry-built, but all tenanted by a contented trio. Here was an entirely new Paganini—a real, live, human, natural Paganini. As a tropical dawn it came upon his consciousness like a blow—this was what he had lacked throughout the restless years that had passed—his enigmatical soul was yearning for a dark-skinned, brown-eyed bambino that would eventually call him ' Papa '. The insouciant years of his fatiguing quest after the ideal woman fell from him like discarded rags. He forgot Rosina and Dida, Elise and the Countess, Angelina and the Milanese widow, the siren of Naples and the ' object ' of Parma; all he knew and cared about was that Antonia was going to endure exquisite pain to give him heavenly joy—the Saints preserve her—Antonia was going to present him with a child. But Nature will not be hurried even for a Paganini; and to kill time and provide funds for an increased ménage he made occasional trips to Naples and Rome, to play and be applauded, and to return to his love-nest in

Palermo with the proceeds in his pocket. Paganini was very happy.

On July 23rd, 1825, the child—a boy—was born; and the pride of its father and the hopes he entertained for its future were reflected in the heroic names he selected to be bestowed upon the innocent infant—Achille Cyrus Alessandro, affectionately known as Achillino.

CHAPTER XIII

By December, 1825, Paganini was back in Naples, his health much improved by his long stay in Sicily. But his temper was not as good as his health. Antonia was busy with her baby and had little time for Nicolo; the baby no doubt cried sometimes, and Paganini was forced to dream his dreams out of earshot. That meant out of sight too. Antonia probably felt neglected and said so in language that Paganini could not possibly misunderstand. Her old jealousy flared up in an alarming manner, and as her recriminations waxed hotter, his affection grew cooler. A rift became evident in the harmonious lute, and they wrangled incessantly. When Paganini raged, she wept; when he suffered silently, she became physically violent. By December 17, he felt that he had to share his troubles with someone, and wrote to Germi—who was probably wondering why Paganini had not written about a new 'first real passion' for so long. Nicolo says that the Bianchi is still with him and that she possesses a serious fault. 'For no reason at all she flies into a frenzy'. One evening she dashed his violin-case against the ground several times in a fit of mad anger, and reduced it to splinters; the violin itself was only rescued from destruction by being torn from her grasp by his servant. Two days earlier the pair were guests at the house of a Spanish family. Their hostess and her son were discussing with Nicolo the peculiarities of some freakish lady-violinist when the Bianchi, 'out of jealousy', asked to be escorted home. 'When I requested to be told the reason, she boxed my ears'.

Indeed, she proceeded to box the ears of all within range of her arms, screaming loudly the while. ' She nearly blew up with temper and we feared that she was losing her sanity '. It was a sad disillusionment for Nicolo. Hard as it was to believe, and humiliating as it was to his pride to be forced to admit it, Antonia Bianchi was after all not yet the ideal woman with whom he could live in peace and contentment in the castle he had built for her in the air. Only the baby kept them together. But exciting scenes such as those just mentioned seriously affected Paganini's nerves, and his distressing cough returned—being no doubt of a spasmodic asthmatical nature. La Bianchi could scream and rave, break any article which he valued or hurl it at his head, with no serious after-effects to herself. Nicolo on the other hand was physically and psychologically so constituted that his quarrels with Antonia racked his head with pain, started a paroxysm of coughing, and filled his heart with bitterness. There can be little doubt that he would have left her had she not the child as a restraining influence and taken advantage of his love for it. And to Paganini's credit it must be placed that he endured untold agonies of mind for the sake of little Achillino. By April they had patched up their differences and Paganini, always ready to make peace, wrote again to Germi to the effect that ' the Bianchi has much improved in her singing, and will make the grand tour of Europe with me, which I mean to undertake as soon as my unbearable cough leaves me '.

During this visit to Naples an interesting light is thrown upon Paganini's dealings with his family, by some accounts sent by Germi for his inspection—documents that go a long way towards refuting the commonly believed charges of hardness, selfishness, and avarice so often levelled against him. According to Germi's communication, Paganini had, within a short period, given no less than five thousand francs towards the Genoese housekeeping expenses, over and above the usual allowance. When telling Schottky of this, he complained bitterly of the ingratitude of certain recipients of his generosity, adding that the more he gave away the more venomous became the attacks of his calumniators. ' I swear by all that is holy ', he said, ' that I have always supported my family to the best of my ability '; and when his father died he remembered his ' duties as a good son ' and provided for his mother without intermission. One of his sisters who had married a glass merchant, had had five thousand francs from Paganini, which soon vanished; while the other sister—whose gambling husband deserted her from time to time—had also been the means of dissipating large sums of his hard-earned money. On behalf of this second sister his mother had often appealed to him; and he, believing that the money asked for was wanted to supply Teresa's needs, parted with considerable amounts, which the well-meaning but foolish old lady passed on to her son-in-law, who speedily lost it in play. Paganini told Schottky that these particulars were kept secret from him, and that even when his mother lived with him alone for seven months—presumably when she nursed him in his long illness—she had not mentioned a word about the domestic state of his sisters' affairs. It annoyed him intensely to learn the truth from strangers when he reached Genoa. He realized that he was being victimized for the benefit of his dissipated and gambling brothers-in-law, and determined ' to have nothing further to do with the ingrates for a time, and to recognize no duty but that due to himself '. In the outcries of these relatives is probably to be found one of the sources of the defamatory rumours concerning the artist. But his intentions sounded more severe than his performance was, and he remained ever helpful to his sisters' children and, above all, to his mother.

In the summer Paganini and the Bianchi travelled through northern Italy, but how many concerts they gave is not known. They certainly performed at Trieste and Venice, where Paganini made the enjoyable acquaintance of Count Parucchini. After this we lose sight of the couple until early in 1827 when they turn up in Rome. Five highly successful concerts were given at the *Argentina* theatre, each of which—as Fétis records—was a separate ovation.

His triumphs were so outstanding, and the interest taken in him by the public so pronounced, that the Vatican felt impelled to distinguish the already widely-celebrated Genoese by one of the temporal honours it was able to confer. Blind to the patent fact that Paganini, according to the views of the Church at any rate, was ' living in sin ', His Holiness Pope Leo XII., on April 3rd, issued the decree under the pontifical seal which created him a Knight of the Golden Spur. It is an interesting document addressed to ' Our beloved son Nicolo Paganini ', and contains a few remarks that are worth reading, and still more remembering when we reach the sombre story of the great violinist's obsequies. The decoration was bestowed upon him because he was second to none in the art of playing upon his instrument, and it carried with it all the temporal and spiritual rights and privileges of knighthood. It is dated ' Romae apud Sanctum Petrum sub Annulo Piscatoris die III Aprilis MDCCCXXVII, Pontificatus nostri Anno Quarto ', and is signed ' Pro Domino Cardinali Albano, F. Capaccini, substitutus '. The honour was a high one, especially in Catholic countries, and one that Paganini shared with Gluck and Mozart.

Carrying his new dignity proudly Paganini left Rome for Florence, where the nobility—old friends of his from Napoleonic times—welcomed him with unfeigned gladness, and looked forward to his performances with a fixed determination to find him even more marvellous than he was before. Billed as ' Il Cavaliere Paganini ', he delighted the Florentines at the *Pergola* with playing that surpassed their wildest expectation. But before he could do this he was destined to pass through an experience that very few fathers, with a higher reputation for tenderness than his, would care to face. By some mischance little Achillino broke one of his legs, and it was of course essential that the limb, once set, should be kept perfectly still. No one, not even Antonia, succeeded in preventing the fretful child from making the restless movements that could easily undo the surgeon's work and perhaps leave the boy with a deformed leg for life. Only Nicolo, with his intense love for his son and his infinite patience and self-sacrifice, could accomplish the seemingly impossible task. For over a week he held his precious baby upon his knees, singing to it, stroking it, amusing it, and guarding its fitful sleep. The limb mended, but Paganini was a wreck. A disease broke out on one of his own legs, and the strenuous days he had just passed through brought on a recurrence of all his old troubles.

Going to Bologna, he placed himself under the care of the excellent physicians, Professors Valorani and Tomassini, and it was several months before he was again fit to travel or think of serious work. But during his convalescence in Bologna he found opportunities for indulging in a good deal of chamber-music. He became intimate with the Cavaliere Milzetti who was a very fine amateur cellist, and together these two, in association with other musical friends, played trios and quartets; and in the enjoyment of Beethoven, Paganini gradually regained his strength. The local musician Pancaldi relates a story of one of his compositions which was played by the Milzetti coterie: 'The well-known Radicati had said that the numerous difficulties, unusual positions, and so on, which the work contained, were not in agreement with the nature of the violin. Paganini at once seized his instrument and performed the part so wonderfully that his colleagues as well as the audience were completely enthralled. The virtuoso handed me back the manuscript with a flattering compliment and remarked drily: " I, at least, do not find it contrary to the nature of the instrument " '. Paganini had obviously recovered his health and spirits.

A visit to Genoa followed. Paganini had probably made up his mind in earnest to undertake the foreign tour before his health—which now seemed very uncertain—prevented it altogether. A journey to his birthplace to see his mother, and a consultation with Germi were necessary; many arrangements of a financial nature would have to be made before he went abroad. While at home he had an opportunity for checking the progress of his young protégé, and found Sivori justifying the faith he had reposed in him. The boy, now twelve years old, had advanced rapidly, and Paganini recommended the father to change his teacher. The ideals which compelled the youthful Nicolo to rebel against Costa's traditional methods, made the adult Paganini suggest that Camillo be placed under his friend Dellepiane. He probably gave the boy further lessons in his own way while he was in Genoa, and he foresaw a brilliant future for the gifted youngster. Sivori eventually developed into one of the greatest technicians the world has ever seen, second only, in some respects, to Paganini himself. He remained the only pupil of Paganini's to achieve a universal reputation, and the friendship that was inaugurated in Genoa lasted until the death of the master. We shall meet Sivori again in the last phase of Paganini's life.

At the end of the year or the beginning of 1828, Paganini went to Milan, intending to make of the city he loved so well the starting-point of what was to be by far the most ambitious tour he had ever undertaken. He played at several semi-private music-gatherings and gave two important concerts at the Scala, at one of which he performed for the first time the concerto in B-Minor (Op. 7), containing the Rondo—*à la Clochette*—that was to become so celebrated. The Adagio of this work, with its imposing and affecting melody, owed its inspiration to a visit to the theatre. Paganini had seen the popular Italian actor, Demarini, in a tragedy; and his acting in a prison-scene—according to de Laphaleque—' in which, after recounting his misfortunes, he implored Providence to put an end to his sufferings by relieving him of the burden of life, had been sublime. Paganini had retired to bed, unable to overcome the emotions the great actor had roused; he could not sleep, and despairing of rest he rose and found on his violin expressions which relieved the intensity of his feeling'. The concerto, with this expressive slow-movement, and the brilliant rondo with its original bell-accompaniment, became one of Paganini's favourite war-horses; and with it he aroused unbounded enthusiasm all over Europe. This performance was in the nature of a dress-rehearsal, for the work was the first composition he played outside of Italy, the one with which he commenced his conquest of a continent.

The preparations for his great adventure were now complete. He sent Germi a final letter acquainting him with the domestic situation; less perhaps to gain his sympathy than because a financial matter was mentioned of which his lawyer should be aware. Although Antonia and he appeared in public as a happy and collaborating couple, their private life was by no means blissful or even peaceful. If they quarrelled in Palermo and Naples because Antonia was jealous enough to resent every innocent conversation which Nicolo had with women, how much more opportunity was there in Milan, where every noble lady petted and fêted the fashionable lion with the interesting head, the large heart, and the flowing locks. Antonia did not feel too sure of him, and the thought of what might happen abroad probably made her nervous. Although he had flirted with no one since they had left Venice together, there was no telling when a nature like his might grow tired of her outbursts of ill-temper and her Xantippian tongue. There was no marriage-licence legally to keep them together; no obligation on Paganini's part to provide for anyone but the child. Antonia did not like her position. When love dies, a woman abhors the thought of being dependent upon a man who needs little more than the mistrust of his mistress to drive him to infidelity. It is quite possible that had the Bianchi been a woman of the stature that Paganini had sought, she might with the help of Achillino have kept her lover at her side until the end of his days. But she was fond of ostentation and superficiality, jewellery and amusement. Paganini, never regularly generous, disliked spending money on a woman who demanded it as her right, just as much as he enjoyed the pleasure of lavishing his gifts on one who claimed them through her love. Though he gave her elegant clothes and magnificent diamonds, she accused him of being mean. He retaliated by suggesting that she only cared for his money. As usual after their quarrels, they remembered their professional engagements, their public, and the little fellow with the string of heroic names, and they patched up their differences. To allay her fears and to prove his honourable intentions, Paganini settled an annuity on Antonia, and once more peace reigned—a Crusaders' truce. Writing to Germi, Paganini permits himself the luxury of speaking without compliments : ' La Bianchi has made peace at last. I have given her a document which guarantees her one hundred Milanese *scudi* a year for life '.

When Paganini left Milan on March 2nd, 1828, he stood at the very zenith of his powers. Italy had showered upon him all the praises of her picturesque and musical language, had placed him in the honoured company of her most illustrious sons, had enriched him with gold for his labours and with gifts and a title for his personality and his genius, and now she proudly sent him across her frontiers to carry the fame of Italian art beyond the confines of her own dominion. Correspondents representing the foreign press had taken the fanfares of the Italian clarions and had translated them for the benefit of music-lovers in Austria, Germany, France, and England. All musical Europe was agog with excitement. Paganini was coming.

But was it a happy Paganini? After years of toil and a ceaseless war with illness he had realized his ambition as far as the violin was concerned; he had become the greatest virtuoso the world had even seen. Heaven's promise to Teresa Paganini had been redeemed to the very last syllable. Yet in his heart Nicolo was unsatisfied. All his life he had sought for a woman who would be his companion; one who would cheer him in his melancholy moments and nurse him tenderly when his health failed; one who would be proud of him and take him home from the glittering theatre with its applauding crowds to a happy, peaceful, fireside; one who would watch over the cot of his son with the tender love that should be natural to a woman. All his experience was of women who either threw themselves at him to his disgust, or yielded to the first opportunity of a passionate moment. Dida was possibly an exception—but Nicolo had been too young and she most likely inaccessible for reasons of her own. In Antonia Bianchi he had raised an artiste from nowhere; he had taught her; he introduced her into the society in which he was an honoured ornament. She preferred to shine in the splendour of the diamonds he had given her, and the fame she did not merit. Both were masterful and passionate. The Paganini household could endure two suns no more than Asia could hold two Alexanders. In the excitement attendant upon preparations for travel, Paganini had no time to dwell upon his disillusionments and the bitterness in his heart that gradually became more and more clearly visible in the lines of his face. He had to think of his programmes for a greater world and perhaps severer critics—and, besides, he had Achillino.

When he arrived in Vienna on March 16th, 1828, he found a city after his own heart. The Viennese were gay and cultured, good-natured and generous, hospitable to foreign artists and genuinely musical. The Emperor admired Paganini's art, and many noble houses were ready to open the doors of their salons and welcome the man who had beaten an entirely new track for his instrument's advancement. His idol Beethoven had been dead only a bare year to his infinite sorrow. Schubert lived long enough to be an enthusiastic member of his audience. Paganini from this moment ceases to be an Italian artist and a local celebrity; he becomes a cosmopolitan and belongs to the whole world.

CHAPTER XIV

VIENNA À LA PAGANINI
(March—Nov., 1828)

WHEN Paganini arrived in Vienna on March 16, 1828, the atmosphere of the city was not a particularly easy one to define. In a way, the period was one of transition and the most contradictory tendencies vied with each other for supremacy. While some of the traditions of the Napoleonic era were dead or dying, others fought with newer ideas a desperate struggle for continued existence. The incubus of Europe, the fear of Napoleon, was gone, and the bereaved Marie Louise was home again in Vienna. In all the arts new growths were visible—the product of freedom. Writers were casting about for new ideas or new ways of expressing the old. Everywhere the demand was for novelty. But as a leavening agent the *Biedermeier* with his staunch, simple, honest, sentimental nature flourished; and side by side with him were the admirers of Hoffmann and his unearthly *Capellmeister* Kreisler. In literature as in music, the mysterious and the bizarre were born. The public of Vienna were thus not only many-headed, but also many-hearted and many-minded. Great men who were born to be universal possessions are not influenced by such phases; they have to express themselves as their inherent nature demands. Schubert was in this year writing some of his most beautiful songs, and gave his only concert which provided him with the funds that enabled him to buy a ticket for Paganini's concert. It is not surprising that to such a variety of tastes, a personality like Paganini's should be welcome. His reputation, for good or evil, had gone before him. The air was full of rumour, speculation, scandal. He performed such miracles upon his instrument that an ordinary, natural, source for his talents could not be considered for a moment; he was possessed of a devil who aided him—for a price. He had eloped innumerable times—the stories never lost in the recounting—he had murdered wives, mistresses, rivals, husbands, according to the fancy or taste of the individual. He had been in prison for years—in fact, for a far shorter term than he deserved. He looked a devil. He *was* a devil. Hundreds of anecdotes, probable and fantastically improbable, had gone the rounds of the journals and the cafés. Except the wiser heads who kept their mouths closed and smiled a cynical smile, everyone awaited the appearance of this eighth wonder of the world with open-mouthed expectation.

Small marvel, then, that on the 29th of March the imperial and royal *Redoutensaal* was almost filled with an audience tense with excitement. A restless buzz of conversation agitated the hall. At the back of the platform rose the two staircases that met halfway up and there joined to form one that led to a door on the level of the gallery. On this door all eyes were riveted. On the stage a brilliant company of celebrities—all who were great in art, literature, and science—were seated. There was Mayseder, the most distinguished representative of the Viennese school of violin-playing, a man whose talents were much admired by Paganini; there was Joseph Böhm, the master of Joachim, one of the greatest teachers of his instrument that ever lived, and who shared with Paganini the distinction of having been the first to play the whole of a concert programme from memory; there were Jansa and Slavik and Strebinger and Saint-Lubin—the last of whom continued his studies after he had heard Paganini play. There would be no lack of authorita- tive technical criticism for the violinist from Genoa, and if he were caught attempting his charlatanic tricks on this audience of connoisseurs, his artistic doom in the Austrian capital was sealed. Suddenly all sounds were hushed. Slowly the door on the gallery-level opened, and there stood a figure in black dress-clothes—tall and thin, pale-faced and long-haired, looking inexpressibly weary. For a moment he stood motionless, sur-

134

veying the scene below. Then he descended the staircase. As if released from a spell the silent mass of spectators burst into spontaneous applause that continued until their tense feelings had been relieved and the artist had reached his place before the orchestra. Paganini's success was assured. These people had not yet heard a single note from the instrument he carried in his hand, but one glance at that queer figure, that immobile and expressionless face, those dull and seemingly dead eyes, and every soul present felt that here was a man from whom marvels could be legitimately expected. And when he commenced to play he became transfigured. The expressionless face became alive; the dead eyes gleamed now joyously now with sorrow; he was not playing his music—he was living it. Here perhaps was the secret of Paganini's mesmeric power over his audiences. Like the exceptional actor who lived his part, Paganini was, for the time being, the incarnation of the music itself. This, then, is the explanation of his own dictum : ' To play with compelling power, one must feel deeply '. To the virtuosi listening to him he was no violinist whose art could be acquired by study and practice ; they realized that to him the violin and the bow were not extraneous instruments, but members incorporate with his own body; that to play like Paganini it was necessary to be Paganini. What words can describe the scene of delirious enthusiasm that followed his playing of the concerto with the expressive Adagio and the scintillating bell-rondo? We of this generation can form no conception of how he played—for we cannot hear him with the ears of his own generation. Whoever is hardy enough to make the attempt to describe the scenes that, time after time, followed his performances, must exhaust his vocabulary and leave his reader doubting his veracity. There is no need to strain the imagination. The words of contemporary critics are far better able to present Paganini's talents to us than are all the fanciful extravagances of a modern hero-worshipper.

For many reasons it will repay us to consider the report of the Vienna *Allgemeine Theater-Zeitung* for April 5th :

PAGANINI

First Concert of Herr Nicolaus Paganini.

On Saturday, 29th March, Herr Nicolaus Paganini gave his first concert in the great *Redoutensaal* at midday. The programme consisted of the following items :

1. Overture to the Opera 'Fidelio' by L. v. Beethoven.
2. Concerto (in B-Minor) for the violin . . . composed and performed by the concert-giver.
3. Aria by Paër, sung by Signora Bianchi.
4. Sonata Militaire (*Napoléon*) for the violin (on the G-string only), composed and performed by the concert-giver.
5. Rondo, 'Non lusingare a barbaro', by Romani, sung by Signora Bianchi.
6. Larghetto and Variations for the violin on a Rondo from the opera *Cenerentola* by Rossini, composed and performed by the concert-giver.

The price of admission was two gulden, silver, for the hall and four for the gallery. The latter was fairly well occupied; the hall was full, but not overcrowded.

In every province of human activity great spirits appear from time to time, endowed with marvellous powers, whose participation in the general work belonging to their peculiar sphere exerts an influence that is felt long afterwards. If this impetus is to serve the whole sphere by increasing its effective power through the channels of permanent and beneficial cultivation, it must emanate from a being in whom all the radii are concentrated as at a nodal point. Such spirits are geniuses; they occur infrequently; and long periods of time must separate one from another, so that the advance of the whole may be even and regular—for the too frequent repetition of such impulses would tend to produce, not clarity, but clouded confusion. Geniuses of this kind are the frontier guards of epochs, the wardens of the marches in the history of art; they are the law-givers whose appearance often causes ferments which, however, ennoble the old mixture with new ingredients. Such a genius in the highest degree is Paganini. . . .

This artist handles his instrument according to rules that are his own, and for this reason his achievements remain inexplicable to violinists of even the first rank. . . .

Gifted by nature with the liveliest charm and placed by destiny in environments where he could devote himself to the study of the instrument of his choice without interruption; supplied

136

with an artistic sense which can make use of conditions that impede and confuse ordinary mortals, Paganini experimented with exercises that led him more and more certainly to new constructions and their effective combination. Only in this way could he tread paths that none before him knew, because they were not there. He literally detached himself from himself by his continuous pacing to and fro in a fixed direction. In this manner he developed a mechanism that raised him to heights from which he could survey the whole realm of his art as none of his predecessors could do. . . .

Such is Paganini. Those who have not heard him cannot form even the slightest idea of him. To analyse his performance is a sheer impossibility—and numerous rehearings can help but little. When a new planet appears, travelling along an orbit of which neither the curve nor the radius can be determined, repeated observations still lead only to hypotheses. When we say that he performs incredible difficulties as clearly and as surely as another—if he is an artist—can play an easy theme; that he produces double-stops, harmonics, pizzicato interspersed with bowed notes, double harmonics, unbelievable staccati, and combines them all with the most artistic of passages in the most rapid as in the slowest of tempi; when we say that the violin in his hands sound more beautiful and moving than any human voice; when we say that his fiery soul pours a quickening glow into every heart; when we say that every singer could learn from him—we shall not have said enough to give an impression of a single feature of his performance.

The writer of this will not deny that he was vexed at the announcement on the programme of the bell-accompaniment and the G-string alone; these things smelled too strongly of charlatanism. Still, when one hears how the violin speaks to the bell and how the bell responds to the violin; when one hears the fantasia on the G-string alone—everyone will beg most abjectly for pardon, as the present writer does.

Paganini's compositions are of no artificial texture; they are just pure music. The intellect is never called in to arbitrate; the heart alone holds undisputed sway. In his compositions as in his playing, the vibrations of deep feeling are discernible, in which an immortal spirit soars up into the Infinite, winged with irresistible yearning. Even his more joyous tone-paintings are scenes in which the moon is mirrored in downland pools and the heart cries for eternal day. His jests are the smiles of a sweetly-dreaming child-angel. His Adagio is the song of the

137

spheres. He must be heard—heard. Then perhaps he will be believed.

The fact that Madame Bianchi could win applause by the side of a Paganini, proves that she has not listened to him and his performance in vain. As to the nature of the applause awarded him we need not speak, for he played before the public of Vienna.'

Comment upon this verdict would be as impertinent as it is unnecessary. The present day, judging Paganini only from his printed music—bare notes without his manner—is apt to accept him only as a technician. That he was more than this is shown by the frequency with which writers recommend singers to learn from him, and it is a point that should always be remembered when reasons for his universal appeal are sought. The *Musikalische Zeitung* said that Paganini's reputation ' attracted an innumerable multitude of curious artists, in spite of the high price of the concerts, *viz.,* ten and five florins of Vienna currency. But in his case rumour has said too little rather than too much. Only one opinion is expressed by connoisseurs and laymen : that Paganini stands in his own domain solitary and alone, unequalled by any of his contemporaries. . . . What we heard was beyond belief and cannot be described in words ', . . . yet the writer exhausted his vocabulary over an account of Paganini's achievements. His verdict upon the performance of the slow movement is of more value to us : ' In his playing of the Adagio the artist appeared as if changed by a magician's wand; there was no trace of the earlier *tours de force.* A soulful singer with a noble style and tender simplicity, drawing forth heavenly sounds which came from the heart and went to the heart, his performance was the very essence of truth and a triumph of nature '. This writer mentions the Bianchi too ; but only as a matter of courtesy : ' After the indescribable enthusiasm that greeted Paganini's artistic achievement, Signora Bianchi, the virtuoso's travelling companion, came on the scene. She sang an aria by Paër quite well, fluently, and with much taste. But, in view of what had gone before and the expectation of what was to follow, she could not succeed in securing more than the ordinary signs of politeness that the laws of hospitality demand. The second concert, to take place after Easter, is awaited with the greatest impatience'. A fashion journal gave its readers the highly important information that Paganini's first concert placed about twelve thousand florins, Viennese currency, into his pockets.

Great as Paganini's satisfaction must have been when these and similar reports were translated for his benefit, there was one innuendo in the *Allgemeine Theater Zeitung* that caused him great uneasiness. Added to the many rumours of his imprisonment, such suggestive words as ' placed by destiny in environments, *etc.*' and ' continuous pacing to and fro in a fixed direction ' could quite easily convince people, who had hitherto laughed at scandal, that there was some truth in the allegations. He had now reached a point in his career when his dignity could not afford to be lowered by the breath of calumny. What was before an advertisement might now ruin him. He had cleansed his programmes of everything tending to cheapen them ; his fame and fair name would now have to be protected from slander. Paganini found the task much harder than he had anticipated. The young serpent could easily have been crushed ; the older one, whose coils extended beyond the range of his weapons, was quite a different foe. On April 10th, he wrote a paragraph denying the truth of the many rumours that were being circulated, and asked the editor to print it. Some days later it appeared in German and Italian :

' Paganini, while thanking the writer of the article in the *Theater Zeitung* of the 5th instant—on his first concert before the highly honourable and intelligent Viennese public—feels that he is bound to explain to that public the meaning of one of the remarks made ; an expression which might otherwise be taken to allude to certain rumours spread in a careless and false manner —the ultimate sources of which are unknown. He is therefore constrained, in the interests of his own honour and the truth, to assure the reader that at no time and under no government whatsoever, has he ever been compelled for any reason to lead a mode of life other than that which becomes a free, respected, citizen who has always faithfully observed the law. This can be verified wherever necessary by all the authorities under whose protection he has with honour lived for his family and the art in which he is now fortunate enough to appear before the public of Vienna—as understanding in matters of art as it is considerate—the first before whom he has had the honour to play since leaving Italy.'

NICOLO PAGANINI.'

'Vienna, 10 April, 1828.

This announcement occasioned a good deal of comment and discussion—which probably did the box-office no harm—but no authority, either local or national, came forward with the necessary documents to prove the rumours true. At the same time, few people believed them false, and they clung about Paganini to the day of his death, and to his memory after it.

Nevertheless, this silly gossip did nothing to diminish his popularity in Vienna, and when his second concert took place on April 13, the *Redoutensaal*—according to an eye-witness— was filled three hours before the time of the concert. 'Ladies and their cavaliers stood closely packed together. . . . Everyone who made any pretensions to *bon ton* or cultivated music, felt it their duty to be present at such a banquet of the arts. Even members of the Imperial family honoured this rare talent with their presence. Paganini constituted an epoch in himself and aroused unprecedented enthusiasm. But he offered on this occasion so much that was surprising, marvellous, and enchanting, that only those who heard him can understand and explain this magic effect. To everyone else the dead letters, the cold words recounting the event, must remain mystic hieroglyphics.' Even the austere *Oesterreichische Beobachter,* infected by the virus, allowed itself a little more warmth of expression than was usual : ' Far removed from our minds as it is to attempt a comparison between Paganini and the great virtuosi living in Vienna and enjoying their fame with every justification, we would rather assert that Paganini can be compared only with himself ;

he stands alone and has nothing in common with the other players but the violin and the bow. According to the unanimous verdict of all our experts, he has been raised to a height that should cause giddiness. With a power that conquers all, he calls forth from his instrument passages, music, and sounds that had hitherto not even been dreamed of; with relentless severity and iron hand he dominates the violin, which at times seems to be ready to break down under the burden of the difficulties laid upon it. Carried away by the currents of his own imagination . . . . he seems now to be breathing out his soul in heartrending sighs, now to be a supermundane being inspiring fear and amazement in the audience that scarce dares to breathe '. It is from these contemporary accounts that we obtain our most just portrait of Paganini. Many virtuosi, from Kubelik and Kocian onwards, have performed the music of Paganini, sometimes with technical perfection; but they lacked the magic that was Paganini, and an appreciation of the master's style, based upon his music only, must be incomplete if it is not actually false. We do better to read Ludwig Halirsch : ' In times like ours, in which the art has wandered into side-tracks of every nature, he is a doubly elevating apparition . . . . and in this respect Paganini's artistic greatness must influence his contemporaries with especial force. He stands out as a material witness to the spiritual domination of his art. In him, as in none other of his co-workers, is preserved the purely romantic spirit of music in its mysteriously-working influence on our subconscious minds. . . . In so far as imagination encompasses the realm of feeling with her magic bow, so far does this rare being command it; and where is the stony heart from which he, with the Moses' staff of his harmony, cannot lure the silvery spring of pleasure and the sweet drops of sympathetic tears? In Paganini's whole being, as composer and virtuoso, breathes the most elevated spirit of poetry in the noblest significance of these words. It is not the magic of a momentary charm; it becomes more firmly rooted the more his greatness is appreciated by more frequent hearing. The present writer has known him for seventeen years, has often heard him in Italy, and has missed none of his concerts here . . . . and with each new achievement on the part of the artist the conviction has grown deeper: that Paganini is the greatest instrumentalist known in the history of music '.

Further concerts followed on April 16th and 18th, and with each one the enthusiasm of his audiences increased. All Vienna became intoxicated; nothing was spoken of but Paganini's playing; everything in art and fashion was presented à la Paganini. Everyone had to hear him; the poorer musicians sold their clothes to buy a ticket. Sonneteers and acrostic-writers occupied themselves with his name. Serious critics began to smile at the extravagance into which the madness of the moment intrigued them. When some of these panegyrics were translated for Paganini, he said that he could not admire the tact of their composers, since they blinded themselves to the merits of other artists and created for him—through no fault of his own—a number of enemies among the envious. Nevertheless Weidmann, Casper, Giftschütz, Kanne, Hirt, and others published every poem in praise of Paganini that the papers would print. He appeared as a laurel-crowned victor, another Orpheus, a demigod. In the meantime the lithographers were turning out and selling portraits by the hundred; his face appeared in sugar, in chocolate, on cakes; the only hats worn by men of fashion were à la Paganini; no snuff-box could be offered that had not his portrait on the lid; knobs of walking-sticks and buttons and buckles and fans and everything else that could bear his effigy was decorated with it. Rolls and bread were sold in the shape of fiddles, the *Wiener Schnitzel* that shortly before had been à la Catalani or à la something else, was now à la Paganini. The ladies wore their hair à la Paganini. The only one who seemed to remain unperturbed was Paganini. All the popular composers from Strauss downwards produced waltzes à la Paganini—generally based upon themes from the violinist's works—most commonly the bell-rondo. The violin became popular as never before; the heavens literally rained fiddles. The most elegant afternoon tea-cloths were those that showed a picture of the *Redoutensaal* with Paganini before a huge audience; ribbons, cravats, billiard-strokes—all were *à la* Paganini; to a stranger arriving in Vienna during that summer the city was all Paganini—Paganini—Paganini. The cab-drivers no longer spoke of a five-gulden note—it was now a *Paganinerl* because the virtuoso always paid with such a note when he took a fiacre—however long or short the distance. Others say it was because five florins was the commonest price of a ticket to his concerts. A third version is that Paganini was one day walking in Vienna when he was caught in a shower of rain a short distance from his hotel. He hailed a cab. Arrived at his destination he asks the fare. ' How much? '—' Five gulden '—' What? How can you demand five gulden for so short a ride? '—' Paganini asks five gulden and plays on only one string '—' Can you drive your cab on one wheel '?—The fiacrist, who turns out to be an expatriated Italian, is paid his price and given—marvellous to relate—a free ticket for the next concert. He goes, and applauds diligently. The following morning he presents himself before the artist and recites : ' I am a poor man and have four children; I am a countryman of yours; may I name my cab ' The Fiacre of Paganini '?—' Diavolo ', says Nicolo, ' paint on it any name you like.' The legend is engrossed on the cab, and the worthy man becomes as famous as Paganini. Viennese anecdotes of Paganini are innumerable. On one occasion he heard a little boy playing the violin in the streets, and questioning the child he discovered that his fiddling had for object the earning of money for his mother and sisters. Visions of the pink house in Genoa rose up before Paganini. Taking the instrument from the boy's hands he played. The crowd that collected would have delighted the heart of any mountebank. Money was poured into the hat that Paganini took round, and the boy was sent home rejoicing. One more : Shortly before the Paganini craze, the Giraffe had been the mania. One of these animals, then rare in Europe, had been presented to the

Emperor by the ruler of Egypt and immediately everything was *à la* Giraffe. One day Paganini, needing gloves, entered a fashionable shop. Would the gracious gentleman desire gloves *à la* Giraffe? 'No, no, Signora; d'una altra bestia,' replied Paganini; at once came, 'Well, then, *à la* Paganini'?—and they were proudly displayed, the very last word in fashion, the right-hand glove with a tiny bow, and the left-hand with a little violin, embroidered neatly on the backs.

One of the most amazing pieces of genial impudence inspired by Nicolo was the presentation of a farce called 'The False Virtuoso,' palpably based upon Paganini and his manner of performance. Written by one Meisel and provided with an overture and incidental music by Franz Glaser on themes borrowed from Paganini's compositions, the piece was staged on May 22nd, at the *Theatre an der Wien*. The librettist places his hero behind the footlights under the name of Celebrini, but no one—from the newspaper man in the stalls to the errand-boy in the sixpenny gallery—fails to recognize the Genoese. In a small provincial town lives precariously Adam Streicherl, a peripatetic fiddler who, to serve his own ends, decides to impersonate the great man and so heap ridicule upon the musical society of the place, the members of which were impatiently awaiting the arrival of the virtuoso. These worthies, named Goodtone, Sound, Trill, Staccato, Gutbreaker, Tutti, Fiedler, and so on, are not badly drawn. One passage in particular, in which the coming of Celebrini is announced, contains a rollicking skit on Vienna's enthusiasm over Paganini. 'This letter, just received, contains a detailed account of his playing in the capital. Three hundred victims are in hospital suffering from over-enchantment; four hundred—all artists—opened their mouths and ears so wide in astonishment that they cannot close them again, and will have to be operated upon. Over forty critics are seriously affected by inflammation of the brain since writing their reports on him; in short, it is indescribable'. Fiedler is the only one not impressed: ' Oh, it won't be anything so extraordinary; so far as *I* have heard he only plays on a single fiddle, like everybody else. . . .' Eventually Streicherl, disguised as the false virtuoso, appears and is hailed as ' the last word of art, the quintessence of harmony—in short, as the celebrated Celebrini '. The programme announces that ' the whole orchestra will play a solo, which I shall accompany '. But Fiedler has not been idle. He has sent to every fiddle-dealer and string-maker in town, and has bought up every G-string in the place; he has removed the G-string from every violin in the neighbourhood, and has had the one on the concert-giver's instrument stolen. His envy will not allow the masterpiece to be performed. There is much more in the same strain, including the ubiquitous love-element. When the fun is at its height, the real Celebrini appears, and the farce ends with a ridiculously happy curtain. A good burlesque, especially when provided with clever lines, never harms its original, and Paganini's popularity became greater than ever. But he had not come to Vienna for the purpose of providing the satirist with themes or the cafés with anecdotes. He came to give concerts and to earn money. Let us return to business.

On May 11th he gave his sixth concert and the hall was still packed to capacity. Moreover, the Empress, the Archdukes and Archduchesses were present again, and the recital was a brilliant one. This time Paganini went back on his word and played a concerto by Rode (with additions by himself). ' I had often decided ', he told Schottky, ' never to play works by other composers, and had indeed torn up all such music; but in Vienna I was urged to be unfaithful to my intention. It is contrary to my nature to play strange compositions—not that I cannot read anything placed before me. But I wish to accentuate my own peculiarities, a desire for which I should not be blamed, since it seems to be the wish of most of my audiences also '. His G-string item this time was based upon a theme from Rossini's *Moïse,* and it created the usual sensation. The Bianchi sang two numbers, and the success of the whole concert set all Vienna talking again, until the seventh concert put the sixth into the shade. The Emperor and his family had derived so much pleasure from Paganini's art that some sort of recognition was called for, and on May 23rd his Imperial Majesty, in an elegant decree in Italian, bestowed on him the honorary title of 'Virtuoso da Camera': 'His Imperial and Royal Highness is graciously pleased to grant to the artist Nicolo Paganini, in recognition of the rare talent that this master exhibits on the violin . . . of which he has given such admirable examples before the Imperial court, the title of Chamber Virtuoso, free of tax. He wishes . . . in addition to hand to Signor Paganini a gold snuff-box'. How many of these precious snuff-boxes he had collected to date cannot be computed. This one, together with the Imperial decree, was dedicated to 'The celebrated Signor Nicolo Paganini, professor of the violin, Knight of the Golden Spur', and was set with diamonds.

On June 11th Paganini remembers Genoa, and writes Germi a letter full of interesting details. He says 'I have given my ninth concert at the Italian Opera-House here, and scarcely were the posters put up before all the boxes and other seats were sold. So I am forced to stay here all this month and the next, to give five or six recitals. I have written two slow solos on two strings, which produce contrary effects—the one making the audience cry, and the other, with a sacred title, making them all penitent. One can really enjoy music here, and the composers go off to their country-houses when they wish to write . . . I have written a grand sonata for the fourth string, in which I introduce variations on Haydn's "Emperor Hymn", and I shall play it soon. I have heard some new quartets by Beethoven played by the best performers here, who executed them at my house; after which I gave them some pleasure by playing in these works myself'.

The Venetian fly, unfortunately, is still in Paganini's ointment. The mode of the letter suddenly changes from major to minor, and he adds that the Bianchi has been very troublesome again —or still—closing his complaint with: 'I shall really have to send her from me. Owing to my having made so much of her, she has become a veritable pest. Before she leaves me, however,

I shall give a tenth concert at the Italian Opera for her exclusive benefit '. This needs no comment. The benefit concert took place at the *Kärntnertor* theatre and netted three thousand florins; and whatever differences may have marred their domestic happiness, the two artists kept their bargains and Antonia sang for Paganini at his concerts of the 24th, 27th, and 30th of June. On the fifth of the following month Germi is further informed of the happenings in Vienna: ' I should have given my fourteenth recital, had I not been unwell; but I shall give it next week, or a week later, to comply with the pressing invitations of her Majesty, the Archduchess Marie Louise, whom I must visit when I am better. . . . The Bianchi has now been separated from me for some time, and I shall never submit to her again—but I shall tell you the whole story little by little '.

The state of affairs had indeed become deplorable between Paganini and the Bianchi. Her outbursts of temper had lately become more frequent, while she complained that he was very difficult to live with in peace. They quarrelled over money and other things. If Paganini merely wrote a complimentary line in an artist's autograph-album—and the artist happened to be a lady —she tore the album to ribbons in her rage. He could stand it no longer and offered her six hundred *scudi* annually for his freedom, which she accepted. One more quarrel and a visit to the Vienna tribunal settled their differences once and for all. Paganini paid her two thousand *scudi* in one sum, and in return she renounced all her rights to Achillino. Thus ended a romance that should never have been commenced. Two lutes, however good, can never produce harmony unless they are tuned in the same pitch. He allowed her to take with her all the things he had given her—the elegant dresses, the furs, and the diamonds; all the money she could lay her hands on she took without his permission. But he made her return all the music he had written for her; and in the Heyer Collection at Cologne there are a number of manuscripts containing extracts from operas, copied for her use by Paganini.

On July 10th the municipality of Vienna consoled the artist by honouring him with a gold medal, in recognition of his kindness to the poor. This was one occasion of many on which he helped local charities and they should all be remembered when we later find him being accused of never giving his services to the needy. The Viennese address is worth reading: 'The Magistracy of the Imperial and Royal Capital and Residence City of Vienna—overwhelmed with gratitude for the nobility and charity which Herr Nicolaus, Ritter (Knight) von Paganini, Chamber Virtuoso to his Majesty the Emperor, has evinced in favour of the unfortunate Viennese citizens in the almshouses of St. Mark, by means of the valuable proceeds of one of his concerts—have decreed that the great medal of St. Salvator be bestowed upon you. Accept this souvenir of the city of Vienna as a proof of appreciation for your great artistic talents and as a token of gratitude for the benevolent gesture you have made so generously and willingly for the poverty-stricken citizens and for the magistrate who acts as administrator to these poorhouses'. In addition, another fine medal struck in his honour, was engraved by Joseph Lang, and issued in silver and bronze. The motto on it reads: *Periturus sonis non peritura gloria* (' By fleeting sounds, imperishable fame ').

From Bauernfeld—the intimate friend of Schubert—we have an amusing account of how he came to hear Paganini: ' After his eighth concert he had already earned over twenty thousand florins. He had to postpone only one concert because on the day originally fixed for it, a giraffe was shown for the first time in the Zoological Gardens at Schönbrunn, and such an event brought all Vienna on to its feet. After all, to the Viennese, a giraffe would take precedence over a Paganini. I was not able to manage the five florins that this concert-pirate demanded. That Schubert must hear him, is easy to understand; but he insisted that he would not go again without me. He was very cross in real earnest when I refused to take the ticket from him. " Stuff and nonsense—I have heard him once already ', he cried, ' and was angry because you were not there. I tell you, such a fellow will not come a second time. And I have money now like chaff; so come on ". So saying he took me with him. We heard the infernal-heavenly fiddler and were no less charmed by his wonderful adagio than we were astounded by his other diabolical arts. He is also not a little humorous by reason of the awkward bows of his demoniacal figure that resembles a lean black doll on wires '.

When Paganini first intended visiting Vienna it was his plan to ask Beethoven to write a ' Tempest ' piece for him, to which he wished to add a set of concluding variations. Unfortunately Beethoven's death before Paganini's arrival brought this project to nothing. The death of the great symphonist affected Paganini very deeply, and it was some time before he could bring himself to realise that so divinely-gifted a man should have to die at all. In May, like the good Viennese citizens, he went to the *Augarten* concerts, where Beethoven had frequently played. Perhaps, when he was there, he still heard the Kreutzer Sonata—played by its composer and Bridgetower. On one occasion the Symphony in A was being played. Paganini sat immobile; and as the work drew to its close, the tears rolled down his sunken cheeks, and in a hollow voice the cry was forced from him: ' *È Morto* '. Perhaps the memory of Beethoven never received a higher or more sincerely felt sign of homage.

But the idea of a ' Storm '—so dear to that age of popular descriptive music—was not abandoned. In Vienna Paganini had met the violinist and composer Joseph Panny, and in May commissioned him to write an orchestral work of that nature. The score, in the Heyer Museum at Cologne, shows us how monstrous a work this was, its musical worth being in inverse proportion to its bulk. From notes on the manuscript it appears that the piece was ordered on May 25th, and finished on June 14th, Paganini paying two hundred florins for the work, and lending Panny a further two hundred which were never returned. The composition, at the close of which Paganini added a set of G-string variations, was first produced at his farewell concert at Vienna, on July 24th. This last recital in the city that had treated him so well was a very brilliant function. In addition to the ' Storm ', which the press considered ' very poor tone-painting ', though Paganini's variations on the G-string were received with the usual applause, the programme contained the concerto in E-flat and the variations on Haydn's ' Emperor ' hymn, mentioned in Paganini's letter to Germi. The Emperor was himself present to give his ' Imperial and Royal Chamber Virtuoso ' an Imperial send-off, and Paganini was honoured by an ovation that remained with him as a happy memory to the end of his days.

Except for the teacup storms brewed by the Bianchi, Paganini's stay in Vienna had been very happy. He liked the people and they accepted him as a godsend in somewhat dull days—for a giraffe or a Schubert concert did not come as a surprise more than once. Society welcomed him; but it is doubtful if he visited anyone but Metternich. His portrait at this period is drawn by de Laphaleque in a few deft strokes : ' Above the middle height; his constitution weak, and his carriage one of extreme languor. Although retiring, his deportment does not want ease or dignity. Long black curling hair shades his face, and makes the melancholy paleness of his complexion still more remarkable. His nose is prominent, and his long and thin countenance has the aspect of what physicians call the Hippocratic face. His eyes, though small, are sharp, piercing, and full of expression, and his physiognomy, which, without being disagreeable, is not prepossessing at first, and becomes attractive as soon as it is animated. . . . After a concerto, his symptoms are those of a man under an attack of epilepsy; his livid and cold skin is covered with a profuse perspiration, his pulse is scarcely to be felt. . . . The night after a concert he never sleeps, and he continues in an agitation which sometimes lasts two or three days. These facts have been communicated to us by Dr. Bennett, who attended Paganini during his stay in Vienna. It is generally believed that Paganini has fingers of an immense length. This also is an error. His hands are in proportion to his stature, and rather small than otherwise, but very dry; the fingers are well formed, but thin '.

When de Laphaleque wrote and Dr. Bennett practised, neurology and psychology had not yet been so deeply studied; if they had, they might both of them have discovered other reasons for his agitation than merely physical ones. Who knows how often a domestic storm, during which the harassed artist was torn between his love for his child and his contempt for its mother, was the cause of the nervous reactions that followed the strain of a public performance. Paganini's letters to Germi tell more of the brain-storms he suffered during Antonia's fits of frenzy than his audiences or his doctors ever knew.

The strain of a score of important public concerts, besides his private engagements, left Paganini fatigued if not actually ill The army doctor, Marienzeller, who had treated him homeo-pathically, recommended a visit to Carlsbad where he took the cure and gave a couple of concerts. At the end of October he wrote to Germi: 'All was finished with the Bianchi at the Viennese courts, to which I turned to secure the guardianship of my beloved Achillino, who has grown most lovable. . . . On August 1st, the Bianchi departed for Milan, while I left for Carlsbad, where I gave only two concerts, as there were so few visitors in the place '. In the first week of December he received a letter from a Viennese friend who said, ' I have heard that you gave two nice concerts in Carlsbad, and that you now intend, being recovered, to satisfy the yearnings of the inhabitants of Prague '. He had already left for the Bohemian capital.

When Paganini was in Vienna, that city was a centre in close touch with all the capitals of Europe, and the fame of the artist quickly spread. The correspondent of the London *Harmonicon* helped to increase the curiosity of the English by sending his paper a report slightly infected by the Viennese enthusiasm: ' The great novelty and prodigy of the day is one M. Paganini, an Italian, on the violin. He is without con-tradiction not only the finest player on the violin, but no other performer, upon what instrument soever, can be styled his equal: Kalkbrenner, Rode, Romberg, Moscheles, Jew and Gentile, are his inferiors by at least some thousand degrees; they are not fit, as we say in Germany, to reach him water. . . . In a word, he is a necromancer, and bids fair to beat *la Giraffe* ', —which definitely determines Paganini's relative position in the social scheme of the day, in the mind of the man in the street. The contemporary accounts we have read leave us in no doubt as to the place he occupied in the eyes of the experts. He had chosen well when he decided to open his ' grand tour ' at Vienna, for there he had an atmosphere which suited his purpose perfectly, and there also he found an audience notoriously enthusiastic when they were pleased. His first concert on the Danube marked the beginning of the most brilliant five years of his life, and had the Bianchi been other than she was, they might also have been the happiest.

CHAPTER XV

(Nov., 1828—Jan., 1829)

TOWARDS the end of November, 1828, Paganini arrived in Prague—that picturesque and historic city on the Vltava, then still coloured and dominated by the romantic spirit of Dalibor. With the optimism born of his success in Vienna he immediately made arrangements for six concerts, forgetting to take the local conditions into account. His first concert was undoubtedly highly successful; but after this, the size of the audience dwindled, and the last, though he advertised that it was given by general request, was very poorly attended. The *Abendzeitung,* in seeking reasons for the comparatively cool reception accorded the great virtuoso, suggests that the stories of his gay young life in Italy—unnoticed in a great city like Vienna, with its own love of gaiety and gallantry—would be much more likely to influence the narrower minds of a provincial town like Prague. For in the eyes of the German writer, Prague was but a provincial town, however strenuously the Bohemians persisted in regarding their beloved city of the green copper domes as the ' golden ' and royal capital of the ancient kingdom. Alternatively the paper thinks that the ' pride and the parsimony of the Pragers' may have had something to do with the smallness of the audiences. ' Pride ', because they hated to accept what Vienna admired, and loved to applaud what Vienna censured— as Mozart had already discovered. ' Parsimony ', because Paganini had multiplied the usual prices of admission by five. Apart from all this, Bohemia had a fiddle tradition of her own and looked with suspicion, if not dislike, upon a foreigner who ventured to tread upon their national preserve.

But in the university professor, Max Julius Schottky, Paganini found a truly helpful friend, who did more than anyone else to make his stay in Bohemia pleasant. It is from this friend that we obtain a good deal of information on Paganini's personal character, and in Prague we learn to know him more intimately than anywhere else. His real self was generally kept carefully hidden from chance acquaintances, for whose benefit he usually acted a part representing the romantic and sometimes eccentric virtuoso. From the biographer's point of view the few weeks he spent in the Bohemian capital are more valuable than any other period, for they bring us as close to Paganini's personality as anyone ever came. In Naples, Venice, Parma, and Lucca we met the philandering Don Juan; in Milan, Vienna, Paris, and London the artist is presented to us; but in Prague we are admitted into the presence of the man Paganini —the father, the friend, the good, genial, respectable fellow.

Paganini's first appearance before the public there—on December 1st—was very successful. Curiosity had brought a great gathering together and, as usual with those who heard him, they were conquered. As in Vienna, so also in Prague, we shall do well to depend upon the writings of eye-witnesses for our information concerning the effect produced by Paganini —for no one is in a better position to judge and tell us what really happened. Professor Müller of the *Prager Unter-haltungsblätter* says, ' Expectation in Prague was so often dis-appointed by the accidents of ill-health under which the Cavaliere suffered, that in the end all hope had been abandoned of ever hearing him. On this account the effect of an announce-ment that he was about to give a concert was all the more electrifying. The five-fold raising of the theatre prices had for its only result the filling of the house, because the charm of novelty had also been increased five-fold. Paganini surpassed the most reckless of expectation . . . and the public could scarcely restrain their outburst of enthusiasm after the first two movements of the first concerto had been played. . . .' Then follows the highly-coloured and romantic picture, the fervent effervescence of superlatives over the wizard's technical perfection and emotional appeal, with which we are already thoroughly familiar. His long series of successes is beginning to become monotonous and the supply of fresh complimentary adjectives and adverbs is failing.

Paganini's programmes were long ones; indeed, he told Schottky, 'I play more music at my *accademie* than is the case with many other artists; but I do so with pleasure, and would do even more, were it not to impose too great a strain upon my physical powers—for I suffer very much with my chest and abdomen, as is especially noticeable to-day, when I have scarcely recovered from my last long illness. I have undergone three operations'—this is news to us—'and I believe I have, like Mutius Scaevola, conquered pain. Indeed, I am in need of rest very urgently, because the doctors feared that I might overstrain my nerves and run the risk of permanent blindness in the left eye. That danger is, however, now happily passed'. We see again, as we saw so many times in Italy from 1808 onwards, under what handicaps Paganini worked; and a far greater cause for amazement than that provided by his supernatural powers on his instrument, is the facile and nonchalant manner in which he brought off his most astounding feats while suffering so much physical pain.

There will be no need for us to follow Paganini through all his concerts in Prague. The programmes and the applause followed the routine to which we are accustomed. In announcing his last appearance he shows us how closely Panny's ' Storm ' adhered to the usual plan of the then admired ' programme ' music : ' The Cavaliere Paganini, virtuoso to his Majesty the Emperor of Austria, will have the honour of giving another concert, which will be the last, on Saturday, 20 December, by universal request. Among other compositions he will play ' *The Tempest,*' a dramatic sonata for the grand (*i.e.* full) orchestra, with solos and variations for the violin by Paganini, using the fourth string only : 1. The Approach of the Storm; 2. Commencement of the Tempest; 3. The Prayer; 4. The Fury of the Ocean; 5. The Hurricane; 6. Confusion at its Height; 7. The Return of Calm; 8. Lively Expression of Joy'. To our more sophisticated sense this sort of thing seems just as charlatanic as the animal imitations that pleased Paganini's earlier audiences; but in Beethoven's day, and for a considerable time afterwards, such ' descriptive ' music was very popular, and the great symphonist himself was not entirely innocent of these —to us— childish performances.

There will always exist a certain number of superior persons who, impatient, if not envious, at the enthusiasm aroused in their more easily pleased contemporaries, seek to overthrow the idol of the moment with the crudest form of sarcasm and the most pitiable display of ignorance. Generally such perverse iconoclasts are themselves crushed by the falling idol; sometimes, as in Paganini's case, the idol refuses to be overthrown, to the utter discomfiture of the windmill-tilting knight. Schottky with mock concern says that before Paganini's last concert had been given in Prague, ' a dark and sinister rumour was spread to the effect that an art critic of that city, with the noble self-assurance of his own sufficiency, had mounted his Rosinante and was preparing to do battle with Paganini to the death. . . . The day on which the violinist was to give his farewell recital was also to be a day as black as Erebus for Paganini; a day when his artistic reputation was to be buried for ever'. In plain English, an anonymous Bohemian critic published in the Hamburg *Literarische Blätter der Börsen-Halle* an article in which he proposed to put Paganini into his rightful place. It reads as follows :

' Proclamation '.

' Oh, foolish world; oh, marvellous taste of the enthusiastic Viennese. Never have I fallen so suddenly from my heaven as through this—virtuoso. I cannot understand how people who have heard Romberg, Rode, Spohr, Lafont, *etc.,* can lend their ears for a single moment to such Harlequinades as these. I attended one of his concerts, and never again will he see me at another. He possesses great facility in the left hand, which can be attained by practice, without possessing talent, genius, spirit, feeling, or understanding—it is a purely mechanical facility. The principal features that are repeated indefinitely, are an unbearable squeaking near the bridge—which is no well-regulated tone at all, but only a chirping of sparrows—and then. at the end of each variation, a rapid pizzicato with the left hand, consisting of six notes; a something that every fiddler, if he desires to learn so useless a thing, can acquire with half-a-year's practice. His compositions (and he plays only his own, which he has probably performed two thousand times in the last fifteen years) are beneath all criticism. The so-called *Campanella,* over which the Viennese almost went insane—what is it? The following: In the orchestra someone strikes a small bell twice, *pik, pik.* He up there, takes an harmonic on the E-string and moves his bow from the lower part upward, so that the result exhibits a very distant resemblance to the tone of the bell; but which, after all, only sounds like two harmonics on the violin. This solitary pair of notes, which almost every violinist here imitates—this is the whole ' Bell-Rondo '. His bowing is the most miserable conceivable; there is not a single musician here to whom it would ever occur to break his own violin in despair (as has been said was done in Vienna), but they laugh at him and at the Viennese. Of expression, soul, interpretation of slow movements—the climactical points of a concert—there is no suspicion. It must be admitted that there are here also a few people who allow themselves to be dazzled by his reputation, and who beguile themselves into the belief that all he does must be beautiful. Yes; there is even a rumour that one emotional lady actually wept; but since no one else shed tears, no one believes in her. There was some talk of his giving six concerts. Now he sings a different song . . . I am convinced that in the north they will know how to honour him as he deserves. His facility in a few useless and unpleasant artificialities will be acknow-ledged, and after that—*Basta* '.

The croaking raven of Prague—if he existed—was wrong. Berlin and Hamburg were sufficiently lacking in taste and knowledge to go as frantic over Paganini's playing as Vienna did—but that is another story. I said, ' if he existed '; for the article is so unutterably foolish in the thorough-going manner in which it decries Paganini's talents, that the suspicion must be created that it was written by a friend of the virtuoso in order to provoke discussion and increase his publicity. He ran no risk of the experiment recoiling and damaging his reputation; no one would believe that Paganini could possibly be as bad as the article claims. Schottky had the pleasant task of translating this precious ' proclamation ' for Paganini's benefit, ' but he—who can credit it?—made no comment other than to smile and shrug his shoulders indifferently—so sorely did he suffer under the weight and keenness of this sword, so little was he annihilated by them '. If Paganini had any knowledge of the article's authorship he was a good actor too. Heaven alone knows what possessed the writer of the effusion—whoever he was—to force him to spread so much hate on paper; but by the time his colleagues of the press and the counter-proclamationists were finished with him, he was nine-tenths ridiculed to death.

When Paganini wrote his paragraph of vindication against the slanders that were rife, he did not succeed in stopping the many mouths of the hydra. Schottky drew his attention to a few of the rumours. ' Diavolo ', said Paganini, ' these are cursed things; do not these people know that I have never been married? ' And to refute them he begged Schottky to write his biography and tell the truth. The professor did his best; but his only sources of information were his own acquaintance with Paganini (which means that he was prejudiced in his favour), the newspaper reports of the day (which only noticed his public concerts or repeated rumours and anecdotes), and the materials supplied to him by Paganini himself. The booklet was published in 1830, and though it abounds in errors, lacunae, and hero-worship, it remained for at least twenty years the only work that was passably trustworthy. To assist in his campaign against the libels, he asked Schottky to give publicity to a letter he had received from his mother during the summer, thinking that this would acquit him at least of the charges of miserliness and neglect of his family :

' My dearest Son,
At last, after waiting about seven months since sending you my letter to Milan, I had the consolation of receiving one from

you, dated the ninth instant, through the agency of Signor Agnino, which brought me great joy, for I learned from it that you are in good health, and that you intend—after your journeys to Paris and London—to come to Genoa in order to embrace me again. I assure you that I pray to God every day to keep me as well in health as you, so that our wishes may be realised.

The dream has come true, and what God promised me has come to pass : Your name is great, and your art, with God's help, has given you a comfortable living. Loved and esteemed by your countrymen, enjoy at length the repose that your health demands, in the arms of your friends.

I had great pleasure in receiving the portrait which you enclosed in your letter, and I have read all the details concerning you in our paper; you can easily believe that such news must give a mother extreme joy. My dear son, I desire nothing more than to receive your communications; for with that prospect I should live longer, and allow myself to hope for the pleasure of pressing you to my heart once more.

We are all keeping well, and in the name of your relatives I thank you for the sums you have sent. See to it, and do your best, that your name remain immortal. Take care against the treacherous climate of those great cities, and remember that you have a mother who loves you from the depths of her heart—who asks for nothing better than your health and your happiness, and who will never cease to beg the great God to keep you safe. I beg you to embrace your amiable companion in my name, and give a kiss to little Achille.

Love me as you are dear to me.

Always your affectionate mother,
TERESA PAGANINI.

The letter is dated from Genoa, July 21st, 1828, and shows that no news of the differences between Paganini and the Bianchi had yet reached his mother.

Achillino was now nearly three and a half years old, grown into a bright and lovable little fellow. That his father spoiled him goes without saying; but then Nicolo had no other outlet for his love, and the boy was his only real joy, besides being, as he often said, his only reason for continuing to work. No one was allowed to wash and dress the child, and Nicolo looked after him with the care and the devotion of a mother. He went nowhere without him, and every childish whim of Achillino's was a law to Paganini. In Prague a number of Italians foregathered to dine and chat, and Paganini was often of their number. Schottky tells us a good deal of Paganini's private life—if existence in hotel apartments can be called that —and one story in particular places him and his son clearly before us. Paganini had been invited to dine with his Italian friends, and one of them, calling for the virtuoso at his hotel, provides us with a good account of Paganini in ' negligée ' : ' I visited Paganini in his lodgings '—it is our old friend Giovanni Gordigiani, of the ' Ferrara asses ' anecdote, speaking —' for the purpose of inviting him to dinner. Everything in his room was in the usual disorder : here lay a violin, there another ; one violin-case was on the bed, a second was partially hidden beneath a heap of his son's toys. Music, money, cap, letters, watches, and boots were mixed in colourful confusion. The chairs, tables, and even the bed, were moved from their proper places. He himself sat in the midst of this chaos. His black silk night-cap still adorned his sable hair ; a yellow stock was carelessly wound around his neck, and a long chocolate-coloured jacket hung disconsolately from his shoulders. On his knee he had Achillino, his little four-year-old-son—on this occasion in very bad humour because he had just been compelled to submit to having his hands washed. How much love and patience is exhibited by this man. The child is often restless, but Paganini never loses his equilibrium ; he prefers to tell those present, " the poor child is bored ; I don't know what to do, for I am quite exhausted by playing with him. The whole morning I have been fencing with him ; I have carried him hither and thither, made chocolate for him ; and now I am at a loss as to what else I can do " '. Schottky adds an aside : ' It was screamingly funny to see Paganini in his slippers, fencing with his son who barely reached his knees. At last Achillino threatened his father with his sabre and gradually forced him backwards. Nicolo cried, " Enough, enough ; I am already wounded " ; but the youngster was not content until his tall antagonist fell " dead "

PAGANINI

*Sketched by Sir Edwin Landseer from memory after a
London concert.*

across the bed '. Gordigiani continued : ' Paganini asks, " What time is it? "—Midday.—" Are we to eat Risotto? "—Yes; in the company of some new arrivals from home.—" Who are they? "—One is a Neapolitan who plays the mandoline, the other a poet.—" Good, charming; music and poetry can to-day shake hands in sisterly fashion ". Paganini had by now completed Achillino's toilet, but he himself was still in the most disordered negligée. Now he began the most difficult part of his own toilet. Where were his cravat, his boots, and his coat to be found? Everything was hidden; and by whom?—By Achillino. The child was highly delighted when his father strode about the room with long paces, throwing questing glances from side to side. And at the question, " Where have you put my things? " the little rogue pretended to be astonished and dumb; he shrugged his shoulders, turned his head, and implied that he knew nothing. After a long search the boots were discovered, hidden under the pillows; the cravat was found in one of the boots; the coat in a trunk, and the vest in a table-drawer. As Paganini found each article, he donned it in triumph, took a huge pinch of snuff, and renewed his search with great fervour, accompanied everywhere by the little one who was tremendously pleased whenever his father looked in a spot where nothing was hidden. At last we were ready to go. Paganini locked the room-door, but left his rings, watches, money, and—what surprised me most—his precious violins, lying unprotected on the tables and chairs. He worried about nothing. It is fortunate for him that none but honest people inhabit the hotel where he lodges. The day was cold and our friend put on a huge fur coat, and since he feared Achillino might take a chill, he carried the child, completely covered, under his coat. The boy, to obtain fresh air, pushed his head from out of its voluminous folds. It was a lovely spring day in the arms of winter. Paganini's long strides soon covered the distance that separated us from Francesco's house. On arrival he was quite out of breath, for the child, though young, was heavy enough '. Paganini seems to have enjoyed himself in the company of his compatriots, who sang and played and ate a real Italian dinner. 'Paganini did justice to the Risotto, and to all the other dishes he could masticate; but he was compelled to allow the daintiest morsels to pass him, as they were too hard for him'. After the meal there was more music, and finally Paganini, in a thoroughly good humour, reeled off one anecdote after the other, recounting some of the episodes in his early career with which we are already acquainted. He further 'proved that he was well instructed in the history of his country, and gave us a list of all the celebrated men that Genoa had produced'. In the evening the party played *Tresette* for farthings while Gordigiani entertained Achillino. 'At nine o'clock we accompanied Paganini back to his hotel . . . and so the day ended'. If we are to form a just opinion of Paganini the man, we must see him as he was during that day; unconcerned with his appearance, untroubled by his public. In such circumstances we find him a fond father and a genial companion. For a man accused of avarice and miserliness, he was exceedingly careless about his possessions. We saw him leave his valuables lying loose in his bedroom; he even left his cash-box in his travelling-carriage, which was stabled in the courtyard of the hotel. Herr Hübsch, the landlord of the 'Black Horse' in Prague often advised him to lock up his money and be more careful generally with his valuables. But, according to Schottky, 'the artist did not mend his ways, and on this occasion he had no reason for regret. But hotels like the "Black Horse" were not to be found everywhere'.

Achillino himself deserves a few moments of our time. Schottky describes him as a very interesting child 'with brown falcon's eyes and long hair parted in the centre'. He exhibited a good deal of talent and keen powers of observation, learning German very rapidly and on many occasions serving his father as interpreter. We are asked to believe that he was altogether very attractive, sang 'very correctly' and attacked his notes faultlessly—a gift of pitch that he already possessed at the age of two. When Paganini was asked whether he would train the boy as a musician, the indulgent father replied, 'Oh, why not?

If his desire to learn increases, I shall teach him with pleasure. I love him very dearly and am almost jealous of him. Should I lose him, I would be lost myself, for I find it quite impossible to separate myself from him. And when I awake at night, my first thought is of him '. Gordigiani wrote to Schottky to the effect that Paganini's love for the child was ' not only that of a father ', but that he ' brought up the boy with a mother's tenderness, care, and patience '. If Achillino returned from his lessons a little later than usual, Paganini would be almost bereft of reason by his anxiety. Naturally, the boy ' was always surrounded by toys of all kinds ', and he drew ' quite bearable sounds from a violin, even managing a melody '—which is not too bad for a child of three and a half years. Paganini had ultra-modern ideas on the subject of infant-education, and never forced his son to learn anything that did not attract him ; but he encouraged every form of study that the boy appeared to like. Such indulgent treatment may have spoiled Achillino terribly ; but it seemed to have had no evil after effects upon his future character. Fortunately, slanderous gossip in later days could find nothing reproachful to say of Achille, and writers who use the word ' ingratitude ' in this connexion are merely guessing. Paganini lived and worked for his son's future comfort, and he achieved his object. Writing to Germi in December he says : ' . . . in two or three years I shall have two million *scudi* '—he becomes heroic—' my fame demands it '—then funny—' But what can I do with so much money? Do you like fireworks? '—and finally he remembers—' But no ; I have a son, and I pray that heaven will keep him safe for me '. Certainly little Achillino, even at this early age, rewarded his devoted father, for the latter wrote to a friend that his son was his only consolation and his greatest joy.

His health in Prague was not particularly good, though his old complaints were not to blame this time. Suffering from an abscess or a bad tooth, he had it removed. The operation was performed so badly that inflammation of the gums set in and, probably owing to his generally septic condition, all the teeth in his lower jaw were sacrificed. It was on this account that he was compelled to forego the choicest tit-bits at the Italian dinner-party described by Gordigiani. Naturally, the continued indulgence in soft foods threw his digestive apparatus out of gear, and the dyspepsia that resulted further complicated his intestinal trouble. In addition, a new enemy appeared—either now or a little earlier—in the form of a laryngeal inflammation which developed later into tuberculosis of the larynx that, a little over eleven years afterwards, was the immediate cause of his death. He is said to have derived much benefit from the homeo-pathic treatment popularized by Dr. Hahnemann, but from this moment onwards he was hardly ever completely free from some form of indisposition or other. That he was able to continue his work of delighting and astounding thousands of critical people all over Europe, in the face of so many physical obstacles and so much suffering, says more for his will-power and tenacity of purpose than volumes of praise could reward.

The state of Paganini's health at the time of his concerts in Prague, together with its psychological effects, now determined his personal appearance and presented him to the world as a subject upon whom the caricaturist was soon to get busy. Even Professor Schottky, surely prejudiced in his favour, could not refrain from alluding to the peculiarities of his talented friend's features. Returning from the second concert, he noted down his impressions of the artist while they were still fresh in his mind, and they probably give us as accurate a portrait as was possible at this period of his life: ' It is true that at the first glance his appearance is discouraging rather than attractive. Some jokers were heard to say that he was the living likeness of Old Nick himself; no one in the depths of deadly despair could enter more bowed than he; while others compared him with the distorted portrait of a fallen angel—and much more in the same strain. All this is, of course, exaggerated enough; and yet Paganini does present a remarkable appearance—that is, in the theatre under the full glare of the illumination and at a little distance, which circumstances prevent his features from standing out clearly. He is so thin that no one could scarcely be thinner with decency; and with it he has a pale, yellow, complexion, a large curved nose, and bony fingers. He looks as if he were hardly held together under his clothes, and when he bows his acknowledgements his body moves in so extraordinary a manner that one fears to see his legs part from his trunk at any moment, and the whole frame fall together as a heap of bones. When playing, his right foot is well advanced, and with it he beats time when the music becomes more animated, in a manner that borders on the comic. At the same time his face does not lose any of its death-like immobility—except when thunders of applause shift it into his peculiar smile, and his eyes flash, not without good humour, in all directions . . . At the present moment, when he is scarcely recovered from a dangerous illness, he could be mistaken for one of the poorest of starving beggars, did one not know that he often earns two or three thousand florins, silver, or more, at a single concert. In some aspects he appears as a caricature of himself, as a shape that reminds us of Callot's figures, or of Dr. Syntax in the distorted English pictures. Nevertheless, these peculiarities make of him an original, reminiscent of the spiritual and of all that is antithetical to the everyday . . . . Paganini steps before us as the incarnation of technical perfection and, at the same time, he is all emotionalism. On this account it would have been a real error if Nature had given him more flesh '. At this period the long hair that so fascinated the ladies of Vienna, was considerably reduced in luxuriance.

The only information we have concerning Paganini's education comes from his own lips as preserved by Schottky : ' I also love and honour the sciences, and have studied them a little ; but certainly not so deeply that I can speak of learnedness in the way you German gentlemen can. I am, in these things, only a weak amateur, but my present association with learned men gives me the greatest possible pleasure. Heaven apparently did not wish me to enjoy this privilege in my early youth '. We have seen how well he behaved and how pleasant a conversa-

165

tionalist he was in Italy, His friends in Prague found him no less attractive. He was discovered to be exceedingly pleasant in the social circle; often quite jovial; his expressions were well chosen and neatly applied; and a few of his remarks are epigrammatic. We do not need Schottky's assurance that Paganini understood to perfection the art of making himself agreeable in feminine society; but since the blow he received at the Bianchi's hands, he does not seem to have interested himself in any fresh ' first real passions '. When relating an anecdote, he would begin quietly, gradually warm up, and allow his enthusiasm to increase as the story developed. The accounts that make of him a morose and taciturn being, belong to a later period when his throat trouble had developed sufficiently to make conversation difficult and painful. The director of the Prague theatre, when the professor asked him for his opinion of Paganini from the business-man's point of view, wrote: ' I will always value his memory and I should have the greatest satisfaction and joy if any words of mine could add to his fame. The Chevalier Paganini should be looked upon as a thoroughly honourable man of business; and he is far easier to get on with than is sometimes imagined—though how this doubt arose I cannot say '. This was written on January 12th, 1829, apparently three or four days before Paganini left Prague. On the 16th of the previous December he wrote an extract from a Rondo in Schottky's autograph-album, addressed ' All 'amico Sigr. Prof. Schottky, Praga, li 16 Dec., 1828 ', and at the same time gave his written permission for the publication of the biography that the professor had in hand.

Round about the middle of January, 1829, Paganini set out again on his travels in the direction of Saxony, leaving behind him a number of new friends.

CHAPTER XVI

THE INVASION OF GERMANY
(1829)

WHEN Paganini passed through the beautiful frontier country
known as 'Saxon Switzerland' on his way from Bohemia to
Dresden, he found, in the German states that were four decades
later to be welded into an empire, an atmosphere ideal for
his purposes. As in Austria, the reactions of the post-war epoch
were favourable to the acceptance of such a figure and such an
art as Paganini's. The romanticism of the time was tinged
with adventure; and the quaint, the mysterious, the bizarre,
and the supernatural, still excited an interest born of curiosity
and limited by fear. Any degrading influences set in motion
by these mental tendencies were held in check by the example
set by the many petty courts still under the artistic spell of
Frederick the Great; and what was encouraged by *Serenissimus*
one day was copied by the baronage the next. Honest Herr
Biedermeier could do no less than lay down his two thalers to
hear the man applauded by the leaders of artistic fashion—
if only out of respect for the still lingering feudal traditions.
Simple Michel was of course content to open his mouth in
amazement and swear that the devil had a hand in it, because
he could do no other than imitate his 'betters'. Luckily for
Paganini, he crossed the frontier when the German states had
time for him and were in the mood to be astonished. Here
rather than in Bohemia he found his Viennese audiences again.

The court of Dresden, famous musically by reason of its
magnificent Opera and its exceptional orchestra, still followed
the traditions sanctified by the example of the great Frederick

and his beloved sister the Margravine of Baireuth. Paganini belonged to the generation that profited by the fruit of their planting. Without waiting for the judgment of the profession or the press, the King and Queen of Saxony had Nicolo at court, and before an audience almost exclusively composed of connoisseurs he played himself into the affections of the Germans. For the pleasure he gave this music-loving court he received a hundred royal ducats enclosed in a valuable—snuff-box. With such a beginning his progress with a loyal public was easy. His concert of January 23rd, 1829, was a triumph in every sense of the word. The theatre, converted into a concert-hall, was packed; the popular operatic stars, the Signore Pallazesi and Chiasetti, provided with their art a perfect foil for the individualistic style of Paganini; and the takings were twelve hundred and fifty thalers. If we add to all this the enthusiastic applause of the large audience and the praise of the press, we have the reasons for Paganini's satisfaction at his first experience on German soil. The *Merkur* of Dresden, in the course of a long and detailed report, says: 'This artist stands as a solitary and extraordinary phenomenon in the realm of music; and as such he should be recognized and honoured. But far be it from all young artists to make an attempt at imitation, or to try to tread in his daring footsteps. Whoever appears as a courageous master in the true classic style may found a school, and he should be chosen as a model. But he who, ruling in the kingdom of fantasy and poetic moods, can permit himself every-thing because he succeeds in everything; he to whom the most unheard-of difficulties are as child's play; who can produce from the most bizarre ideas the happiest of results by the charm and grace of his manner, and can place them by the side of the noble and the elevated—*his* path should not be tried, for it is the lone dangerous path of a comet. What can result when an imitation of such a genius is attempted, was seen in the equally famous violinist, Alexander Boucher. He also possessed great geniality; but how far below Paganini did he stand! He wished to *appear* what Paganini *is*. That is why his art was charlatanism, while Paganini's is the spirit of true genius expressed with daring. It may honestly be affirmed that no virtuoso on any instrument has ever been so genuinely *humorous* as Paganini; and none other has ever understood how to unite this with the pert expression of coquetry, the teasing mood, the sound of deep sorrow, and the most agonizing heartache, in such a way that the sum of all appears with no disturbing transitions as a great whole. With justice he may be designated as a Shakespeare among artists '.

Paganini, much as he enjoyed the thunder of enthusiastic applause called forth by astonishment, was not proud of it. What raised his head to the stars was the praise of men who— like the writer in the *Merkur*—gave reasons for their applause. He left Dresden a prouder man than usual. This being the case, he was in no mood, when he arrived in Leipzig, to be dictated to by business-men who had planned to take advantage of a rare occasion. Everything was prepared for a successful appearance in this important musical centre, and the press had placed Paganini in an excellent light: ' February 12th was the auspicious day on which he arrived. On the 16th, we are to hear him. Everyone is charmed by his humanity, geniality, and fairness. He allowed himself to be persuaded into reducing the price of the tickets from four thalers to two so that less wealthy people could also admire his wonders. The shameful libel that Paganini is avaricious is thus exploded '. At the same time we may wonder if the genial writer did not have his tongue in his cheek while he was writing this. The reduction of the price from twelve shillings to six does not seem to be a very convincing proof of his complete innocence; for the sale of two thousand tickets at six shillings is not too bad an evening's work. But the advertised concert did not take place, and the charge of avarice was directed at the directors of the theatre. The latter, hoping to make all their hay during one short spell of sunshine, imposed a very high fee for the use of the building, insisted upon the artist engaging the whole of the powerful orchestra, instead of the half he needed, and prescribed the vocalist he was to employ into the bargain. The object of the directors was laudable enough; they were anxious that the funds of the Subscription Concerts should profit by their deal with Paganini. Surprising as it may seem, the Genoese, always quick to resent such invasions of his rights, was in a conciliatory mood. He agreed to pay a triple fee for the orchestra—although the members had expressed their willingness to perform at the ordinary rates in exchange for the privilege of hearing Paganini play—and he showed himself ready to tolerate the singer nominated; but he resolutely refused to engage the orchestra at its full strength—which was of course quite reasonable. The directors, believing they could force him to accept all their conditions, refused to give way on the last point. They were mistaken in their man. It was true that there was at that time no other auditorium suitable or large enough for his performance; but they overlooked the fact that Paganini had another alternative—that of not playing at all. He merely said, ' Amazing that others should wish to dictate to me how many violins I need for my concert '—and drove off. Leipzig had to wait another eight months before a fresh opportunity of hearing him presented itself. In the meantime the good Leipzigers were compelled to content themselves with anecdotes of the great artist. Here is an example from the ' Hebe ': ' In one of the larger cities where Paganini was to give several concerts, a young and affected fop was boasting at the Table d'Hote that he knew the artist intimately and had great influence with him. Unluckily for the boaster, Paganini himself was also sitting at dinner. The vaunting manner of the mincing fool annoyed him and he decided to teach him a lesson. Rising and stepping behind the young man's chair he slapped him cheerily and none too lightly on the shoulder, crying, " Good-day, my dear friend ". Startled and indignant the braggart turned, and seeing a totally strange face before him, demanded angrily, " Sir, who are you, and how do you come to permit yourself this intimacy with me? "—" I am Paganini ", said he, amid laughter that extinguished the boaster '.

Meyerbeer, who had given many proofs of a great affection for Paganini, and an equally great love for his art when in Italy, was now in Berlin; and the violinist was very fortunate to have so influential an advance agent in the Prussian capital. The great composer had prepared the King, the court, and society generally for the wonders they would hear from Paganini, and clinched this argument with the aphorism: ' Where our powers of thought end, there Paganini commences '. The virtuoso had intimated that owing to the precarious state of his health he was forced to take advantage of such moments for his concerts when his ' sufferings declared a temporary armistice ', and Frederick William III., as the worthy successor— from the artist's point of view—to Frederick the Great, placed the latter's magnificent opera-house at the Italian's disposal. Spontini had for the past nine years been the general director of the royal music, and since he made common cause with Meyerbeer in Paganini's favour, the enmity of the anti-Spontini party was aroused against the violinist. Writing to Germi he said that in frosty Berlin he had found for the first time a theatre-directorate, artists, and others, who behaved helpfully and considerately, a circumstance that called forth his gratitude no less than his surprise. The antagonism of the clique opposing the Spontini coterie did not worry him unduly, for he had met musico-political enemies of this kind before. He depended upon his talents, and once more he converted those who had come to scoff into wildly applauding friends before he had played them half-a-dozen lines.

On March 4th, 1829, Paganini gave his first concert in Berlin, and so potent was the effect of his magic that the scientifically-minded and sober Prussians were changed quite unnaturally into enthusiastic Viennese. Paganini, surveying the excited scene from behind the curtain, said quietly with his inscrutable smile, ' I am once more in Vienna; these are the same sounds of applause as at Vienna ', So great was his success that he immediately abandoned his earlier plan of travelling directly to London, and decided to make an extended tour of Germany first. It was over two years before he eventually reached England.

The writers for the Berlin press were unanimous in their verdict after Paganini's first appearance. It is difficult to choose a representative report that tells us something new of his performance from the mass of hyperbolic extravagances. Rellstab, as is to be expected from a man of his fame, experience, and standing, provides us with what is perhaps the most dependable account, because he at least did not become quite incoherent with excitement: ' . . . There was a state of exaltation the like of which I have seldom seen in a theatre, and never in a concert-hall. But now the sympathy of the audience increased; the Adagio of his concerto was so straightforward that any student could have played it without difficulty—it was nothing more than a simple plaintive air . . . . But never in my life have I heard such weeping. It was as if the lacerated heart of this suffering mortal were bursting with its sorrow . . . . I never knew that music contained such sounds. He spoke, he wept, he sang, and yet—compared with this Adagio—all virtuosity is as nothing . . . and (at the end of the *Moïse* variations) . . . when Paganini reproduced the melody at the end in harmonics, it was as if he stood alone in the vast auditorium; all who sat there held their breath as if afraid to rob the player of air. But when the concluding trill came, a burst of jubilation broke loose and it seemed as if all the earlier applause had never existed, so little could it be compared with this. The ladies leaned over the balustrade of the gallery to show they were applauding; the men stood on the chairs the better to see him and call to him; I have never seen a Berlin audience so; and this was the effect of simple melodies, simply performed. Yesterday I heard him play ' Nel cor più non mi sento ' with variations, at the end of the programme without accompaniment, as well as four-part music; but to-day I no longer believe it. The general impression that he—including his personal appearance—made upon me, is not a very gratifying one. All great violinists are something—have a style—can be followed; yet the mighty Spohr, the sweet

Polledro, the fiery Lipinski, the elegant Lafont, only won my admiration. Paganini is not himself; he is rather the incarnation of desire, of scorn, of madness, and burning pain; now this, now that; the tones he produces are merely his instruments . . . Sometimes he scrapes and scratches quite unexpectedly as if ashamed at having just rendered too great a homage to mildness and nobility; and the instant you prepare to turn away in disapproval, he has recaptured your soul with a golden thread, and threatens to drag it out of your body. His compositions are the fruits of a wild and unquiet life, and it is as if a gigantic personality were engulfed in them. After the first piece, a fur cloak was brought him in which he wrapped himself, pale as death, drying the perspiration from his forehead, literally sinking into a chair'. Another writer adds: ' Paganini and his violin are one and the same person. His external appearance already shows that he desires nothing more from the world than what he can obtain through his instrument '.

At the second concert on March 13th, over two thousand tickets were sold at two thalers each; and although the audience had found fresh energies for applauding him, all that the newspapers could say was: ' I say that . . . no one can understand Paganini's performances, and I cannot explain them '. The phrase ' Two Thalers-'—six shillings—in Berlin soon became synonymous with the *Paganinerl* of Vienna. This, and the growing craze for the lion of the moment—in addition, perhaps, to Paganini's known reluctance to distribute free tickets—may have been the inspiration for the little squib let off by the popular humorist, Moritz Gottlieb Saphir, a journalist with a European reputation. As a guide to the bourgeois amusements of the day the joke has its uses:

' Paganini, Two Thalers, and I! '
' Dear reader,—Can you credit an editor with sufficient weakness to spend two thalers for a concert? Only consider, dear sympathetic reader, how much money must be spent if I, poor editor, were compelled to buy tickets for all the concerts, art-exhibitions, and harlequinades that take place. Just for fun, let

us make a short list : For Grand Concerts, 2 thalers; for other music, 1 thaler, 20 silver groschens; ventriloquist Schremser, 20 sgr.; the reciter Sturm, 15 sgr.; the great Giantess, 7½ sgr.; concert in Faust's Winter Garden, 2½ sgr.; readings, 20 sgr.; the trumpeter in Adler's hall, 5 sgr.; Enslen's drawing-room voyage, 10 sgr.; diorama, 15 sgr.; altogether, 7 thalers, 15 sgr. So you see, dear reader, nearly 8 thalers weekly for art and pleasure. No! Ask something reasonable. No! I shall not pay 2 thalers for a concert, even if the great Christopher descended from heaven and played a concerto, not only on *one* string, but on no string at all. Two thalers! . . . . So you see, honoured, sympathetic reader; the editor has better uses for his two thalers than to spend them on Paganini's concert; and Herr Paganini has also a better use for his tickets than to give them away. We are both right; he on one side (*Saite,* spelled this way, meaning also ' string ') and I on many sides '.

The atmosphere was all geniality, and Paganini quickly acclimatized himself to the social conditions of the city, even if he did not take kindly to the climate of this northern latitude. He wrote home : ' I am enjoying myself very much, especially at the Opera, the value of which you cannot appreciate without having witnessed it. Meyerbeer and Spontini have been very kind to me and have helped me in every imaginable way '. He also adds that he is writing a set of variations on the theme of ' Heil dir im Siegerkranz ' (' God save the King ') as a compliment to and a surprise for the King of Prussia. At the beginning of March, too, he writes to Schottky, in French : ' It is time that I let you have my news, and it is not all bad news. I am suffering a little with my eyes and that is the trouble which incommodes me most at the moment. You will have read the Dresden papers. I found this town all that is agreeable, and the kindness of the royal family completed the pleasure of my stay there. I was also told in Dresden that you had published an article promising my biography; since then I have heard nothing. My curiosity is whetted. The kinsman I told you of, rejoined me at Dresden, and is also impatient. Let me see some part of your work. My honour is entrusted into your hands. How happy I am to have found an avenger whose name alone is enough to crush the calumnies spoken of me. Your probity and talents will be the despair of my enemies, and you will be able to congratulate yourself upon having performed a very generous action '.

During March Paganini was introduced to the Mendelssohns, and on more than one occasion he was Abraham's welcome guest in the peaceful, dignified, and friendly house on the *Leipzigerstrasse*, just before Felix left for England.

In April he gave two concerts for charity. Of the proceeds of the first, on the 6th, he devoted one-half to the poor; the second, on the 29th, produced the sum of two thousand thalers, all of which was given to the fund in aid of the sufferers from the abnormal tide-floods in East Prussia and especially at Danzig. This was his ninth concert in Berlin and yet every seat in the great opera-house of Frederick II. was sold. The King was present and duly ' surprised ' with the ' God save the King ' variations, as well as astounded by the ' Witches' Dance ' set written sixteen years earlier at Milan. So far had Berlin gone the way of Vienna that a newspaper of May 13th, said: ' Paganini is the central point of Berlin life at the moment; the topic of all daily conversation in higher and lower circles, the catch-word for fashion and fancy-goods, the subject for the journals, the theme for the poets. Only an overwhelming natural phenomenon and national calamity like the flooding of the coasts of East and West Prussia can divert the attention of the public partially to another subject '.

The correspondence between Zelter and Goethe contains a few very interesting remarks on Paganini's Berlin appearances, especially valuable when we remember how conservative Carl Friedrich Zelter was. Before he had heard the Genoese he wrote to the great poet: ' Paganini is driving men and women insane with his cursed fiddling . . . The true misfortune of his coming lies in the fact that he ruins all our young orchestral violinists '. Here certainly was a danger; for the example of such a performer naturally inspired many a student to imitation, with the result that the orchestra lost a useful member while the world did not gain another Paganini in his stead. But Zelter changes his tune when he hears the magician : ' Last Tuesday (April 28) Paganini visited me at the Academy and witnessed our production. On the following day I at last heard him. What that man can do is extraordinary, and it must be admitted that the effect of his playing is a very desirable one, though quite incomprehensible to the other virtuosi. His manner is more than music without being higher music . . . The hundred arts of his bow and fingers, which are all carefully thought out and studied, follow one another in tasteful sequence and prove him to be a real composer. In any case he is a complete master of his instrument in the highest degree . . . '—which is high praise coming from a Zelter. On May 14th, he writes yet again to Goethe : ' Yesterday I heard Paganini again. The man is a true rarity : he is the violin itself. One takes fright, one laughs, one is reduced to despair over the most hazardous tricks of technique . . . and charm and spirit are not lacking either '.

For this, his last and tenth concert in Berlin, the King placed the opera-house at his disposal free of charge, and in addition addressed the following autograph letter to him in French : ' I have resolved, before you leave my capital, to give you a proof of the satisfaction I have had when assisting at your concerts. Nature has endowed you with a rare talent that you have fostered in an original spirit. The notes you entice from your strings come direct from the soul and call into being the most unusual emotions in your audience. I have bestowed upon you the honorary title of *Conzertmeister,* and give you permission to use it '. Being a successor of the parsimonious Frederick William I, the King did not enclose the flattering letter in a jewelled snuff-box. Perhaps he was too overwhelmed by 'unusual emotions ' to think of it. Paganini probably appreciated the free use of the opera-house rather more highly than still another snuff-box in his growing collection. By this time even the papers gave up the task of thinking out new ways of expressing the old amazement, and the critic on one of them evaded his duty by saying: 'The concert is over, and I am to write the criticism; but where shall I find words to describe the indescribable?' The great Rellstab, after ten concerts, gives it up in an anecdote: 'At a party—one member of which was a notorious miser—a collection was being made for charity. The collector, through inadvertence, approached the miser a second time. "Sir, I have already given", said he, to which the collector replied, "Pardon me; I did not see it, but I believe it". A witty neighbour remarked under his breath, alluding to the man's miserliness, "I saw it, but did not believe it". So is it with Paganini. Those who leave the concert-hall say: "They who have not heard his performance, cannot believe it". The present writer thinks, "I have heard it, and still cannot believe it"'.

Some time after leaving Berlin, Paganini wrote to Prince Radziwill, begging him to use his influence with the King so that a title of nobility or, at least, an order of some sort might be bestowed upon him. He assures the prince that the desire is not prompted by vanity, but rather by the knowledge that such a distinction would carry great weight with those who were still disseminating false rumours concerning him, and help in putting an end to the slanders that were clouding his happiness. The petition was not successful.

At about the middle of May, Paganini set out for Warsaw whither he had been invited to grace the festivities held on the occasion of the Czar Nicholas's coronation as King of Poland. The journey by road was a long and difficult one, and Paganini probably made more than one stay en route. Nine days separated his last concert in Berlin from his first appearance in Warsaw, and he was able to travel east by easy stages. He certainly spent at least one day at Frankfort-on-the-Oder, where he was the guest of the art-loving wife of General Zielynski. He gave one concert there, which was better arranged than might have been expected, considering the short time at his disposal for making the necessary arrangements. Nevertheless, he excited the greatest enthusiasm. He did not arrive in the Polish capital until the 22nd of the month, and though very weary after his long and jolting journey, he was ready for his first concert on the following evening.

In Warsaw, as in so many other places, Paganini came to give one or two concerts, and stayed to give ten. His success was once more complete. The nobility, the musicians, the music-loving professional-classes, all crowded in until the theatre could hold no more. The Emperor of all the Russias presented him with a diamond ring and the box-office took nearly nineteen hundred Prussian thalers at the first concert alone. But the most interesting feature of these Polish concerts was the presence of Chopin in the audience, though the violinist never dreamed that this pale young man of twenty would soon be enjoying a celebrity as great as his own. It is quite possible that Chopin had already attended one or more of Paganini's Berlin concerts, for he was at this moment only home on holiday. The impressions made upon the receptive pianist by so overwhelming a personality were deep and lasting; and to the end of his life Chopin spoke with enthusiasm of Paganini's playing in Warsaw.

Tempting offers encouraging him to continue his journey farther east and north came to Paganini from Moscow and St. Petersburg; but much as he had always desired to visit the northern capital, his health forbade a tour so far afield. Reluctantly he remembered that he had made several promises to his German friends, and he abandoned the Russian objective. Writing to Germi on May 30th, 1829, he says: 'On my way back to Berlin I shall give some concerts at Breslau. In my twelfth concert at Berlin I gave the public some intimation that I should return, and I have promised to do so on the 20th of next month, so that I may be there for the wedding of the King's son . . . . Later on I shall write you more about Spontini who loves me very much, and about Meyerbeer, who has treated me with the greatest kindness. He is at the moment terribly afflicted by the death of his second son, having already lost his first-born also'. Well, Paganini kept his promise about

Breslau; but concerts kept him busy in Warsaw until well over the Prussian royal wedding. Indeed, there is no evidence that he returned to Berlin at all—or at least to play there. His tenth and last concert in Warsaw took place on July 14th, and so great was his drawing power that the hall was once more completely filled.

The coronation had also brought Lipinski back to his post at the leader's desk of the royal orchestra, and after eleven years the two great violinists met again. Memories of the happy days in Piacenza were dug up and the two probably had very much to tell each other. Lipinski was still a very great artist; but Paganini had become greater. Nevertheless, there was room in Warsaw for both, and Lipinski gave a concert during Paganini's stay. But the papers, probably influenced by the stupid agitation of an Italian singing-master named Soliva, instituted a discussion on the relative merits of the two artists, not omitting a few personal digs at Paganini. From this circumstance many writers have imagined that Lipinski and Paganini had now become enemies and were busily trying to play each other down. Nothing could be farther from the truth, and the two men were both too big to descend to folly of this magnitude. Lipinski, indeed, publicly disclaimed all part in the newspaper war, said that he would never think of comparing himself with Paganini since their lines of development tended in such diverse directions, and took no other share in the squabble. As the two principals remained friends, there was no further use in fighting, and hostilities accordingly ceased. It may be noted in passing that Lipinski had dedicated his Op. 10—published a couple of years earlier—to Paganini.

During the evening of July 19th, Paganini left Warsaw after two busy and happy months. His departure had not been marked by any unusual scenes of leave-taking, and the musicians of the city, who for several weeks had shown him the deepest respect and the most helpful friendship, were all conspicuous by their absence. Paganini settled himself comfortably and philosophically in the corner of his carriage, preparatory to dozing the first few leagues away, when the vehicle came to a sudden stop at the gates of a garden belonging to a villa at some distance from the city walls. There the principal artists and local dignitaries of Warsaw, to the number of about sixty, had ambushed the virtuoso. They requested him to alight and permit them to wish him God-speed in a glass of wine. Nothing loth—even if it went to the length of a few glasses—and more deeply touched by this delicate proof of their esteem than he dared admit, he joined the party and quickly discovered that he was the guest of honour at a carefully planned farewell reunion. Dr. Elsner, the Rector of the conservatoire, spoke a few words of sincere appreciation, and in the name of his colleagues handed Paganini a gold snuff-box bearing the inscription in Italian: 'To the Chevalier Nicolo Paganini, from admirers of his talent. Warsaw, 19 July, 1829'. The recipient was so deeply moved by this genuine proof of affection that words failed him, and he thanked the donors by silently pressing the box to his lips. With good wishes and farewells the party accompanied him back to his carriage and he resumed his journey to Breslau.

Paganini did not enter this important Silesian town until July 24th, but by the following evening all arrangements had been made for his first concert, and three days later he gave a second one at which he played one of his own concertos, the *Moïse* variations, and 'Nel cor più non mi sento'. In addition, the C-Minor Symphony of Beethoven was performed, the movements being separated and played between the soloist's items. These two concerts were given in the great hall of the University; but the senate, disapproving of the noisy applause, refused to extend their permission, and the third concert had perforce to be given in the theatre.

It is interesting to note—and it is significant—that he did not forget his old friends. From Breslau he wrote on July 31st to Onorio de Vito, the violinist who had played the test-quartet with him when he arrived in Naples for the first time. The note contains nothing that we do not know already—that he had been called to Warsaw for the coronation and that he had given ten concerts there. He adds again: ' I am returning to Berlin, having promised the public to do so '. His tour so far had been very successful; his health, though not very good, was not bad enough to stop his work; and, in addition, he was well on the way towards the second million which ' his fame demanded '. He did, indeed, say that ' Berlin, Vienna, and Warsaw had brought him in so much money that he need never have taken a violin in his hand again '.

He does not appear to have played in Berlin as he intended— in fact, he would hardly have had the leisure to do so—for in a few days' time we find him in Frankfort-on-the-Main, having made the enormous journey by road from the Vistula to the Rhineland.

CHAPTER XVII

APOLLO TRIUMPHANT
(Aug.—Dec., 1829)

THERE was an atmosphere about nineteenth-century Frankfort-on-the-Main that proved very alluring to the foreigner. The very air seemed charged with geniality, and while the city was a prosperous commercial centre, it preserved the quiet dignity of a University-town. When Paganini arrived at about the middle of August, 1829, he experienced the same absence of strangeness as he had done when, on his flight from Florence, he first entered Milan. In Frankfort he at once felt at home, happy, and comfortable. Appreciating its advantageous geographical position, he made of it a centre for quite a long time, and from this moment until he left Germany for good, he was continually returning to the birthplace of Goethe as to his home. The explanation is probably to be found in his having discovered lodgings that appealed to his taste, for it is certain that he often left little Achillino with his landlady when he made short professional journeys to neighbouring towns. Remembering how meticulously careful he was about everything concerning his Achilles, we may be sure that the people to whom he would entrust his child were such as had gained his full confidence—a distinction that was enjoyed by very few who came in contact with the suspicious Italian.

Soon after his arrival, and within a comparatively short space of time, he gave six concerts, and increased his reputation immensely by making many friends who later did much to uphold his good name. Frankfort's status as a highly critical musical centre goes a long way towards proving a complete absence of anything approaching charlatanism in his performance. With violin-experts like Carl Guhr watching him closely, he had little chance of succeeding except by purely legitimate means. Financially, too, he did very well, for Frankfort then housed—as it did for long afterwards—a wealthy and art-loving population. No one could fill the great theatre dedicated to 'Dem Wahren Schönen Guten' six times over at two Prussian thalers a head, and be the poorer for it—even though the arrangements agreed to gave one-third of the takings to the theatre-management,' and 'only' two-thirds to the artist. The press, though sober in manner, was just as enthusiastic in tone as it was in Vienna and Berlin. *The Theater-Zeitung* said: 'As soon as he placed his violin under his chin and his bow on the strings, a higher spirit seemed to take possession of him. His features became animated, his eyes lit up, and his movements, as far as they affected his performance, became assured and definite. In his expression an inner conflict seemed mirrored; the most unspeakable of pain, the most ardent of longing, the cruellest jest, even the most cutting scorn, became discernible— all in sum reminding one inevitably of Hoffmann's *Kreisler*'. He gave the sixth of this set of concerts on September 11th and at its close was greeted with an ovation that surprised even Paganini. Called before the curtain innumerable times, the orchestra finally joined in the applause with a triumphal fanfare on the brass and drums. The excitement in the building was indescribable. So overwhelmed was Paganini that he felt called upon to return public thanks, and in the *Frankfurter Oberpostamts Zeitung* he wrote on September 26:

'The undersigned, permeated with feelings of the deepest gratitude for the friendly and honourable reception accorded him in Frankfort, can scarcely suppress the wish that he be not compelled to say farewell to a public whose kind approbation will always remain one of his most precious memories. It is the artist's greatest pride to realize that he has been received by receptive connoisseurs with so much enthusiasm, and it shows him that his efforts have not been made in vain. This joyous conviction has been forced upon the undersigned with increasing weight at each of the six concerts he has been privileged to give in the presence of Frankfort's noble inhabitants. These lines can express his thanks only very inadequately; but he may not omit to indicate at least, by these means—while acknowledging an almost unpayable debt—his deep gratitude before departing.

NICOLO PAGANINI '.

While making Frankfort his headquarters he undertook several short tours in the vicinity. Thus he visited Darmstadt, where he made 2400 florins at one concert, a sum increased by a subscription of a hundred ' Carolins ' from the Grand Duke and another twenty from Prince Emil. Representatives of concert-organizations from Mayence and Mannheim waited upon him to make arrangements for recitals. Schottky tells us that Paganini had been asked to give a concert at Düsseldorf, but that he refused to go unless the sum of three hundred *Friedrichs d'Or* were guaranteed. For this again he has been accused of being inartistically mercenary. Why he should be condemned on a charge of avarice whenever he mentions his fee, while every other public performer is permitted to name his price without losing caste, must remain a psychological mystery. We shall see later on what kind of reception the good folk of Düsseldorf had prepared for him, and how slight was the effect of spiteful gossip upon the actions of people possessing a common sense of justice. In the meantime Paganini had an old score to settle with Leipzig, and he settled it as only a great artist should. He forgot his experiences there earlier in the year, and punished the inhabitants of the linden city by making them applaud him until their arms ached.

During his stay in Frankfort, Paganini took part in the cele-brations connected with Goethe's eightieth birthday and attended the dinner given in honour of the occasion. Whether the performance of scenes from that master's *Faust* the evening before, on the very boards trodden by the violinist, had materialized ' the Spirit that denies ', or whether the property-master had inadvertently left behind the gentleman with the cock's feather when he packed up the rest of the gear, we shall

184

never know. But it seems to be well enough established by the evidence of trustworthy persons that in the year of grace, 1829, Paganini and Mephistopheles arrived in Leipzig together. These mediaevalists were probably ignorant of the teachings of Martin Luther who persisted in his conviction that the devil hated music; but perhaps Luther was mistaken—or possibly, in conformity with those teachings, Paganini was no musician. We in England have not taken Old Nick seriously for quite a long time: even Ben Jonson already considered the poor devil a poor fool who in turpitude could scarcely keep pace with mankind. But in Leipzig with her authentic memories of Auerbach's cellar and the sprightly traveller from Rippach, conditions were very different. In this enlightened university-town the father of lies could still find a comfortable asylum in the nineteenth century, safe from the indifference of a material world. This may seem too deliciously exciting to be true; but—well, here is the account of an eye-witness: 'In Leipzig at the *Hotel de Pologne* there lived a lady; her hair was beautiful, her eyes like the unfathomable heavens over a limitless ocean, a suspicion of melancholy on her brow, a sweet yet wan smile on her cheeks and lips. I had seen her but once, and that was enough to make me see her always and seek her everywhere. In the evening Paganini was to give his penultimate concert; there she would surely be. I sit on the stage and allow my questing glances to travel over the boxes; in vain—I do not find her. Paganini appears. How he played!—Should I even try to describe it? He touches the sad G-string and charms from it the most ravishing sounds. They find their way into every heart, and this time with an all-conquering power such as I have never experienced before. At this instant I feel close behind me the soft breath of an expiring sigh; I turn quickly and see my beautiful Unknown sitting there, pale as a marble statue, apparently unaware of the glistening tears that bedew her cheeks. Surprise forces from me an involuntary cry which, coming at a moment of tense silence, is clearly heard. Even Paganini, standing barely two paces away, turns and looks in my direction. Immediately a peculiar smile, the

like of which I have never seen, flits over his face. It appears
to be intended for something or someone other than the lady
or me. I follow the direction of his smiling glance and see—
who can imagine my amazement?—dressed in an English cloak,
and close to my lovely enigma, my unpleasant acquaintance of
Elbingerode, to whom the violinist had smiled so strangely. The
two are thus unquestionably in league. *Now* I can recognize
that unearthly smile; now I can understand all the memories
of past meetings that danced before my mind's eye. In short,
everyone has guessed the solution to the mystery—a solution
they should have discovered long ago: Paganini and Satan
stand in the closest relationship—if indeed they are not identical.
I say it should have been discovered long since, if only by his
playing. My astonishment causes me to lose sight of the lady
for a moment. Who, then, can picture my horror when, turning
again, I see her neighbour pressing her hand tightly, while she
grows visibly paler and paler. As I sit petrified by terror,
thunders of applause shake the building; Paganini is finished;
the interval in the programme is reached. Everyone rises; so
also the lady and her companion. I follow them as he leads
her out of the hall. At the entrance stands a carriage to which
are harnessed a pair of coal-black steeds. The lady enters
followed by her sinister escort, and the carriage rolls away, the
horses snorting while fiery flashes dart from their wild eyes.
In the strangest agitation I return to the concert, and now I
comprehend everything in Paganini's playing. The performance over, I prepare to leave by the door through which the
mysterious couple had passed, and am rooted to the spot in
amazement: for where an hour ago they had driven off, *there
was now not sufficient space for a carriage to stand*'.

When Paganini reached Leipzig at the beginning of October,
he made the acquaintance of one Friedrich Carl Julius Schütz
who was kind enough to publish a booklet in the following
year, which is as useful in our researches into the artist's activity
during the fortnight he spent there, as was Schottky's work in
our consideration of the Prague period. According to Schütz,

the stage-manager Remie, with the authority of the *intendant,* Court-Marshal von Lüttichau, Baronet, concluded an agreement with Paganini for three concerts to be given in the theatre at the usual prices tripled. What redounds to the eternal glory of the management is the fact that the whole of the takings were to be handed to the artist as a token of esteem, the house and the orchestra being placed at his disposal free of all charge; a noble gesture that must reinstate Leipzig in her proper place in our estimation. The first of these concerts took place on October 5th, with the assistance of the opera-singers Mesdames Franchetti and Ubrich and the Demoiselles Meisselbach, Löwe, and Hanff. The programme contained his E-flat concerto, his *Cantabile* 'with double-stops', his 'military' sonata on the G-string, the variations on 'Nel cor più non mi sento', as well as a rondo by Kreutzer. The second concert followed on the ninth of the month with the B-flat concerto— 'the singing sadness of which overshadowed our spirits with a brooding melancholy which even the bell-rondo did not dispel' —the *Moïse* variations, and a set on a Mozart theme. The third recital, on the twelfth, brought to a hearing a rarer work of his, the 'Cantabile Spianato et Polacca Brillante', and a movement from a concerto by Rode. We see that he is still occasionally playing works by composers other than himself. Though he disliked doing this, he probably felt it necessary to prove that the secret of his phenomenal success did not lie wholly in his compositions. The third concert concluded with some variations upon a Neapolitan canzonetta, 'Oh, mamma, mamma cara', which became very popular with his audiences. One newspaper report, following the third concert, should suffice to represent all the others: 'Paganini may be serious or light-hearted in the extraordinary handling of his instrument, but he remains a human and versatile master, sometimes a little exaggerated, perhaps, but never one-sided: a performer whose work must appeal to this one or that, according to the more limited taste of the individual'. For the rest, the reports present the usual enthusiastic outbursts of verbosity. On the 14th, he made an excursion to Halle and gave a concert there; but the only information vouchsafed us is that although he charged the customary two thalers for a ticket, he took only five hundred thalers away with him. But what the audience lacked in size, it made up for in fervour, and Paganini was probably quite satisfied with the manner in which he disposed of what would otherwise have been a wasted evening.

The three concerts arranged for Leipzig, on the other hand, did not satisfy the demands of the music-lovers there, and a fourth was organized for October 15th, which allowed the audience to hear, among other familiar items, the 'Witches' Dance' variations. Schütz tells us that 'although, as we have already noted, the prices were raised threefold so that "the gods"—to which the price of admission was half a thaler— became a noble seat, the multitudes that clamoured for admittance were so great that on each of the four occasions they collected four hours before the time of the concert, and ten rows of chairs had to be placed on the stage itself. The enthusiasm of all four audiences was indescribable. In spite of the congestion in the auditorium a death-like silence fell over the house as if everyone feared a single note might be lost, except when a particularly brilliant passage surprised the audience into a burst of involuntary applause, which was the louder because of the restraint previously placed upon it. Several times Paganini was compelled to wait until the applause —which drowned even the full orchestra—had subsided'. We also have it from Schütz that Paganini's business-manager at that time was one Herr Curiol, a keen man of affairs whose acquaintance he had made somewhere in south Germany. He was engaged chiefly on account of his intimate knowledge of the conditions in north Germany, a part of the country still entirely unknown to Paganini.

Accounts of his personal appearance and habits are always welcome; for with so many erroneous notions concerning him firmly fixed in our minds, it will require more than the word of one contemporary to convince us that Paganini was no more

188

diabolic than the next best man with an outstanding personality. The portrait painted by the writer in the Leipzig *Musikalische Zeitung* (1829, No. 42), has an air of verisimilitude about it : ' His external appearance, in our eyes, exhibits nothing repellent or fearsome, but rather much that is actually attractive. He looks, it is true, pale and ill; but in no appreciable sense gloomy—and only when spiritually not excited does the least trace of the latter show in his expression. His dark eyes give evidence of something very affable in his character; in conversation he is very vivacious, though controlled by manly restraint; in manners he is courtly and polite, without concerning himself unduly about his formal outward appearance. His behaviour is marked by an untroubled frankness and a certain modesty, combined with a seriousness and a consciousness of his own considerable abilities, that should belong to the consituation of every proper man. His gait when he appeared publicly in Leipzig was in no sense undecided, as seems to have been noticed in other places, but rather firm and rapid, like that of a man anxious to avoid being late . . . Before commencing each of his pieces he appears to pause for a few minutes to collect his thoughts, after which he proves himself, from the very first stroke, to be a true virtuoso as he should be; not as a mere wizard, and still less as a charlatan, but as lord of an instrument that he can command as he will. He can transport his listeners through the whole gamut of human emotions—now joyous and playful, now moving and noble; sometimes carrying them with him in lively movement, sometimes astonishing them with the unexpected; so that one is compelled to wonder more often than not, how it is possible to produce such effects, and in such perfection '. His courtly manners were the joint products of the training he had received at the hands of the Marchese di Negro, of Dida, of the court-chamberlains at Lucca and Florence, and by observing men like Monti and Foscolo, Romano and Pini, Byron and Metternich.

Before Paganini had given his fourth concert in Leipzig a deputation from Magdeburg called upon him with the request to play in that town. Terms were arranged and Paganini committed himself to two appearances. One of these took place while a violent thunderstorm was raging and the newspaper report gave a graphic account of the effect produced. The usual highly-coloured description of his miracles followed and it appears that between October 17th, and 24th, he gave not two, but three concerts. During the week he also paid a flying visit to Halberstadt and gave a concert there on the 20th of the month. The following day he wrote in the autograph-album of the cathedral-organist and conductor of the choral society of Halberstadt, a line of chords and the souvenir: ' L'Egregio Sigr. Maestro Ferdinand Baake è pregato di ricordarsi del suo amico Nicolò Paganini. Halberstadt li 21. Ott. 1829 '. The page is preserved in the Heyer Museum at Cologne.

Paganini's next objective was Dessau, and the date originally determined for his appearance there was October 23rd. The third Magdeburg concert, however, caused the postponement of the Dessau performance, the *Abendzeitung* commenting as follows: ' On October 23rd we were to have been awakened from our slumbers; this day was to have been a day of joy. Paganini was expected—but he failed to appear. The court-councillor P . . . travelled to Magdeburg to beg the Chevalier to bring his art to Dessau also, guaranteeing a minimum profit of a hundred *Friedrichs d'Or* in the name of our Duke. Herr P . . . spoke with Paganini's travelling companion and manager, the ex-lieutenant and theatre-director, Herr Curiol. The latter assured our representative that the prince of violinists could, should, and would give a concert here on the 23rd. In consequence the greatest expectation was aroused, people had collected from the whole neighbourhood, and all awaited the evening with impatience. Paganini did not come, but in his stead news arrived at four o'clock to the effect that he had been pressed to give another recital at Magdeburg, and so could not appear here until the 26th. On this date Paganini did at last appear and gave his concert in the theatre. The great building was scarcely large enough to admit the mass who desired to hear him. The Duke and the whole of the princely family were present. Shall I add anything concerning Paganini's playing?' The reporters in the smaller towns were already quite bereft of words suitable to such occasions, and this one in Dessau contented himself by saying that Herr Curiol had informed him ' that Paganini's health was now noticeably better, and that travelling about seemed to be doing him good. May Apollo and the nine muses preserve this unusual man for many years'. But the representative of the Leipzig *Komet* in Dessau had not yet exhausted his vocabulary, and he added a few fresh details to our portrait of Paganini at this period : ' Never in my life have I been able to forget my surroundings so completely : the sea of brightly-dressed listeners vanished, and my eyes remained riveted on none but him. There stands the tall, lean figure in an old-fashioned dress-suit, his bow held high, and his right foot planted well in front of his body with its knee bent '—just as Landseer sketched him in London—' nothing but bones and spirit in clothes that seemed too loose for him. Only so much flesh as is absolutely essential for the concentration of his fires and the holding-together of his half-dissolved body. Framed by his long black hair and curly side-whiskers, his long pale face is in repose. The immobile stony earnestness of his features are in striking contrast with the sparkling vivacity of his dark eyes. His fine high forehead betrays nobility and sensitiveness, the curved nose indicates courage just as his tightly-closed lips speak of cunning, obstinacy, and irony. In his cold and serious features lay intense suffering and a wonderful mixture of the tragic and the comic—even of good nature and diablerie at the same time. If features that bear the authentic stamp of geniality can be termed beautiful, then can this head be called a handsome one—a head that must attract and arouse the liveliest sympathy at the first glance '.

Without the assurance of Herr Curiol we can already see in the very regularity of his concerts that Paganini's health had improved. From his earliest youth he had been fond of movement, and strongly disliked staying long in any one place. The applause of great audiences was as the breath of life to him, and from now onward, until his departure from England for the last time, his tour became a veritable triumphal progress. From Dessau he moved to Weimar where Goethe heard him on October 30th. Appearing at the Court Theatre he attracted an overcrowded house, he played and the ' applause roared through the building like ocean waves '; and the next morning he was on his way to Erfurt where he performed the same evening— October 31st. The month of November was a pretty busy one for Paganini, concerts following each other with no longer interval between them than that occupied in travelling from town to town. Speaking roughly, it may be said that he spent most of the month in Bavaria. Approaching Nuremberg by a zig-zag route touching Gotha, Rudolstadt, Coburg, Regensburg, and Bamberg, he gave a concert in each of these art-loving communities. Small, comparatively, though the populations of these towns may have been, the audiences were large out of all proportion, and their social and artistic importance by no means negligible to a man like Paganini. But we need not be detained by accounts of his performances there, or by an analysis of the effects he produced : for the applause was but an echo of that from the larger cities, and the local press, seizing ravenously upon so unusual a phenomenon, ' wrote up ' Paganini until he appeared as a being of non-terrestrial provenance. One newspaper editor, with a Newtonesque turn of mind, calculated that the artist had made a clear profit of eighteen thousand florins in seventeen days.

The city of the Mastersingers, with its mediaeval streak of romanticism, extended a rapturous welcome to the fascinating virtuoso who belonged to the world and who was nevertheless not of it. *Hesperus* writes : ' The highly-honoured artist, Cavaliere Nicolo Paganini, has also transported everyone here in Nuremberg at two concerts on the ninth and twelfth of November . . . In Paganini we find everything united; can it therefore be surprising that he celebrates triumphs every day ? And successes such as he enjoys here can only be called triumphs; here where we are usually not at all extravagant with applause. It was very pleasant to see that the musical conqueror was visibly pleased with the effect he produced, and still more pleasant to receive his thanks for the assistance afforded him by the excellent performance of the orchestra. He was especially grateful for the attention paid him socially by several lovers of the art during his sojourn among us. Everything conspired to convert our ancient and artistic city into a memory which the new Orpheus can hold dear . . . . The two concerts produced nearly 2200 florins gross and over sixteen hundred florins net . . . with bad weather into the bargain '. They did not do things by halves in Nuremberg. Several societies were formed to see that Paganini's reception was worthy of the man. ' The artistic Herr Dr. Campe, who took upon himself, and at his own expense, the preparation of the programmes for the second concert, produced a document of such typographical beauty that Paganini will assuredly not have seen its equal '. The artist's ' modest and considerate bearing, and the gratitude he expressed in our public press when he left Nuremberg ', proved that whenever this virtuoso was approached and treated in a manner befitting him, he knew how to show his appreciation. The impression he created was such ' that many evilly-intended rumours concerning him were completely disproved '.

Reaching the Bavarian capital, Paganini attained his artistic apotheosis in Germany—especially significant when we remember how critical Munich was in all matters connected with virtuosity in art. The *Münchener Politische Zeitung,* being a very influential organ, permitted itself the liberty of rapping the music-loving inhabitants severely over the knuckles for suffering a few stalls and a couple of boxes to remain unoccupied at Paganini's second concert (the first having been given on November 17th): ' Yesterday, November 21st, Paganini gave his second concert at the Royal Court and National Theatre. It is true that the prices of admission were increased; but then the artistic value of the performer was also much greater than that of others, and a few gulden more or less should not have been regarded with such trembling. When we consider how much money is squandered in play, for luxury and fashion, bonnes bouches, *etc.,* we cannot think that any well-to-do part of a potential audience was kept away on the ground of economy. . . .' After sneering at the ' supposed love of art ' in Munich, the writer continues : ' But Paganini recognized in his enthusiastic reception and the stormy applause of yesterday and the day before yesterday, his appreciative audience. The universally admired artist again played only pieces of his own composition, and *without any music before him ; viz.,* a concerto in B-Minor (with bell obbligato), a sonata on Rossini's " prayer of Moses " with variations on the G-string, and finally an *Adagio Cantabile Spianato* and variations on the canzonetta " Oh, Mamma, mamma cara " '—a familiar programme. ' His art is as indescribable as is the mood into which he charmed us. Whoever desires to give an adequate account of it, cannot possibly say the last word ; and by means of mere exclamations nothing new, still less anything exhaustive, can be said. Paganini must remain unforgettable even to those who have heard him but once '.

Between Paganini's second and third Munich concerts, he was invited to play before the widowed queen of Bavaria at the castle of Tegernsee. Schottky's account is interesting in so far as it illustrates the geniality and gracious condescension of the rulers in the German states. ' While Paganini was playing, a subdued murmuring could be heard near the concert-hall, and her Majesty, sending one to seek the cause, learned that about a hundred country-people were curiously anxious to hear the violinist, and begged that the door might be left open so that they could enjoy the performance from without. The kindly princess immediately ordered these people to be admitted. They entered the salon and proved themselves worthy of her gracious act by behaving respectably and quietly '.

The censure of the *Politische Zeitung* produced the desired effect, for the third concert on November 25th had to be given with all the doors open, since the house could not have contained the enormous crowd of visitors who sought admission unless the corridors had also been filled. The royal family of Bavaria, Prince Carl, and a brilliant assemblage of dukes and duchesses were present, and the scene was one of great splendour If you, gentle, sympathetic, and honoured reader imagine that the high-water mark of enthusiasm was reached in Berlin or Vienna, you are mistaken. Wait until you have heard what happened at Munich after Paganini's last concert there : ' The programme showed that Paganini would appear three times during the evening. But as he desired to give his public the pleasure of hearing him four times, he changed his programme at the last moment '. All the items were ' received jubilantly . . . the " Witches' Dance," considering the manner in which it was performed, being the last word in originality. When at the close of the concert he had been thundered forth yet again, the whole of the *parterre* rose in order to do honour to the master of masters in a worthy manner. From on high thousands of leaflets containing a poem in honour of the artist fluttered down. The conductor, Herr Stuntz, amid the deafening acclamation of the closely-packed house, placed a magnificent wreath of laurels upon the brow of the hero of the evening. This unexpected, though thoroughly deserved, distinction, so surprised Paganini that he shed tears loosed by his deep emotion, and he embraced and kissed conductor Stuntz and the director Moralt. The general effect of this scene leaves the most perfect account of it far behind. In the stalls the reflection of his tears could be seen in a thousand eyes '.

To the imagination of the Müncheners Paganini appeared as a man with ' a pale face and fairly long black hair; lean; of natural and modest bearing; dressed in the simplest of clothes '. The *Abendzeitung* sent him off on his travels to delight other thousands with : ' Paganini is gone; yet he will always live as a memory in our eyes and ears. And if he were to return quite soon—this Orpheus of our own times—we should once more put our hands into our pockets and pay the price of his magic '. On November 28th and 30th he gave two concerts at Augsburg, drawing from the press the encomiums we have been reading for over a year. The Augsburg papers record with pride that he presented several lucky people with free tickets, so that ' the reproach of miserliness cannot be placed upon him here '. To relieve the monotony of an unbroken paean of praise, one dissentient voice—reminiscent of the anonymous critic of Prague—was raised in Augsburg; but its owner was left crying alone in the wilderness, while the good Augsburgers anointed their tingling hands.

Paganini was beginning to feel the effects of nerve-strain when he reached Stuttgart during the night of December 2nd—3rd. He arrived at the Suabian capital at three in the morning after a chapter of accidents that included the overturning of his carriage. He was feeling very unwell, for the experience of being turned out on to a rutty road in the darkness of a cold December night is not one likely to improve the condition of a man with Paganini's constitution. But the concert had been arranged, and the violinist, although he had made up his mind not to appear, attended a rehearsal at ten o'clock. He hurried to the performance which commenced at six, and confessed that he bungled his playing very badly. For the first time in his career a concert of Paganini's failed to produce its usual effect. Perhaps the devil that controlled his hands was shaken out of him by the carriage-accident. He was more himself when he played before the King of Würtemberg and his court on the fifth of the month; but he was still far from well. On December 7th he gave his third concert at Stuttgart, and this time Paganini was quite himself again, the local paper saying : ' With Paganini a new epoch in the history of violin-playing suddenly begins. He leaves all his predecessors far behind him; he stands, like a brilliant meteor, before the whole of Europe as a unique artist, to compel admiration and amazement '. The Heyer Collection at Cologne possesses the manuscript of ' Il Carneval di Venezia ' —the variations on the Neapolitan canzonetta, ' Oh, Mamma, mamma '—which he played again at this concert, the programme of which is also preserved in the same museum. Travelling north, Paganini spent a couple of days at Carlsruhe whence he addressed a letter to Germi. He tells his friend that he played at the theatre on the 10th, takings to the extent of ' 150 *Louis d'Or* being guaranteed by his Highness the Grand Duke (of Baden) '. He refers to his coronation at Munich and to the kindness of the royal widow at Tegernsee (the relict of King Maximilian Joseph). He then returned direct to Frankfort, his body weary to breaking-point, his bank-books showing many new entries, and his heart full of longing to see his beloved Achillino again. He deserved and needed a long rest. All he allowed himself was less than a single week. His second million was not yet nearly complete.

CHAPTER XVIII

BARON PAGANINI
(Dec., 1829—Feb., 1831)

WHEN Paganini returned to Frankfort at the middle of December, 1829, the *Morgenblatt* summed up his German tour of the autumn in the words : ' Paganini, with his art, enjoys an important name in the world's history. Had he been born, with that art, two or three thousand years ago, the same would have been said of him—and certainly with more justification—as was written in the fables of Orpheus '. The Christmas number of the Munich journal *Flora* tells its readers that the Chevalier Paganini, returned from his triumphal progress through Germany, was warmly welcomed back to Frankfort by proven friends. He has allowed himself a few days of repose which no one will begrudge him, after having given thirty concerts in rapid succession '. The directors of the ' Museum ' concerts had long been anxious to honour Paganini with an invitation to play for the society, and to be honoured by his acceptance. Very diplomatically, and with a certain amount of doubt, the plan was suggested to the virtuoso who, to the committee's great surprise, agreed at once. He was perhaps more flattered by a request to play before that important and influential body of musicians than by the praises of Kings. *Flora* faithfully reports the sequel : ' At the meeting of December 18th, after our spirits had been properly attuned to a receptive mood by the dignified singing of our flourishing choral section, Paganini appeared accompanied by applause that gradually increased in intensity as the audience realised the surprise that had been prepared for them '. The scene that followed can now be well left to the imagination. The artist was then ceremoniously handed the documents creating him an honorary member of the Museum Society. Always overcome by emotion on occasions of this kind, Paganini turned to the audience and, holding the roll of papers high above his head, he made known by signs how gratified he was to be permitted to join their exclusive circle. According to eye-witnesses he was in the happiest of spirits. After a pause he ' played himself in ' and the proceedings terminated. Rarely had a meeting of that august body been so animated and excited ; never had a recipient of the honour that it was in their power to bestow, been so childishly pleased to have it publicly accorded him. It is to be feared that there was in Paganini a strain of the pot-hunter, and he loved collecting honorary titles and distinctions. Most of all he longed for an hereditary title of nobility—not so much for the reasons he gave Prince Radziwill as to have something to bequeath to Achillino that would permit the little fellow to commence in the social scale where his talented father stopped.

At the end of January, 1830, he writes a note to Germi that shows us a Paganini who is becoming a little more particular in the choice of environment. Hitherto, when he was not stopping with friends or admirers, he did not much mind where he lodged or what sort of room he had. Association during the past couple of years with people to whom pre-eminence in art also meant a certain social status, was making him more selective and fastidious ; he must stay in the hotels patronised by members of high society : ' On Wednesday I shall give a concert in the theatre, to satisfy the ladies who are anxious to hear me before I leave for Paris. I shall set out at the beginning of next month. . . . Perhaps you had better write me at the Hotel des Princes, rue de Richelieu, 109. All the best folk go there. The Meyerbeer family will be there also. I am told that all the Parisian papers are saying very nice things about me '. But he was not yet to satisfy the curiosity of Paris. In the first place, Achille, now almost five years old, contracted one of the usual infantile complaints, and Nicolo, being the father he was, could not tear himself away from Frankfort until the child was quite recovered.

Watching at his son's bedside and writing new compositions kept him occupied until Easter, and in addition he made a number of public appearances at Frankfort between February 14th and April 26th. Robert Schumann was then at Heidelberg and, as was customary, made an Easter excursion to the Main. Possibly he was especially attracted by Paganini whom he had not yet heard. Several writers say that he had already attended a concert of the violinist's during his Italian journey of 1829; but, as we have seen, Paganini was not in Italy during the whole of that year. That the Genoese should make a deep impression upon the still very unstable Schumann goes without saying, and his performance of the twenty-four violin *Caprices* sowed in the mind of the coming pianist the seeds that were soon to produce his clever transcriptions of these brilliant studies. Subsequently Paganini re-appears as one of the ' characters ' in Schumann's ninth work—the *Carnaval*. In his Diary the student jotted : ' Easter Sunday. . . . In the evening Paganini . . . was it not ecstatic? ' and later on he added, after a fanciful account of the fiddler's tone-production, ' Paganini is the turning-point in the history of virtuosity '—a profound truth, as his own and Liszt's performances were soon to prove.

Relieved of his anxiety on Achille's behalf, another set of circumstances developed to prevent his promised visit to Paris. Political events were moving rapidly in France, and soon the revolution of the summer made the capital hardly the place for foreign musicians. There was nothing for Paganini to do but postpone the journey once again and arrange a further tour in Germany. He accordingly set out early in May for a progress through the Rhineland; but we have next to no detailed information on his movements, and of dependable biographical material there is little more than a newspaper report here, or a diary-entry there. He played at Coblenz on the twelfth, at Bonn two days later, at Cologne on the 16th, and at Düsseldorf on the 19th; yet only a couple of references remain to us concerning these appearances. Herr Hartmann, the leader of the orchestra at Cologne, relates a story to the effect that Paganini, when rehearsing, was kind enough to fill the snuff-box of an elderly member of the band with ' real Parisian snuff ', which the foolish musician surreptitiously threw away, fearing it might hold some satanic spell. The superstitious old gentleman may have been a survival of that part of the eighteenth-century world which was left untouched by the ' rule of Reason '; but the anecdote shows clearly that the basic idea of the Leipzig devil was still firmly rooted in some quarters. At Düsseldorf an organised triumph, similar to the receptions arranged at Stuttgart and Munich, was prepared for Paganini. Half-a-dozen virgins of honour from the best families in town were sought and—there being so few Paganinis in the world—found. And on the stage these paragons of virtue and beauty once more placed upon the artist's head the wreath of a conqueror. The next day he gave the first of two concerts at Elberfeld (May 20th and 22nd).

On the 25th of the month Spohr and Paganini met again at Cassel. The German, though he admired the Italian's perfect intonation and technical facility, could praise the atmosphere of his compositions, and his manner of performing them, no more now than he could do in Venice. But Spohr was hospitable, and in the *Autobiography* we read: ' As his coming coincided with Whitsun I invited him to lunch on the second day, at Wilhelmshöhe; he was very gay, even expansive '. Paganini did his best to draw his host out; to make him commit himself to a definite criticism on the performance he had heard at the theatre. Spohr, however, was a polished gentleman who hated hurting the feelings of any artist, and he eluded the snare. The two got on very well together, spending a happy day; and only Spohr's journal was ever told the secret verdict—that in spite of his many excellences, Paganini broke too many time-honoured rules and departed too frequently from classic traditions. Still, as we saw before, we may not judge Paganini too harshly on the strength of Spohr's finding, for the latter—then court-conductor—was never especially distinguished for his powers of disinterested criticism. In his eyes even Beethoven was guilty of writing monotonous movements lacking in taste. The material results of the first concert at Cassel did not come up to Paganini's expectations, for in a note which he wrote to Spohr on the following day, he complained that the takings did not amount to even half of the fifteen hundred thalers guaranteed when he was engaged to play, and he therefore desired the conductor to cancel the second concert, arranged for the 30th —the natives apparently ' not being interested in foreign artists '. He adds that he would much appreciate ' some sort of souvenir from her Royal Highness ' if she could be persuaded to confer such an honour upon him. He is still tuft-hunting. The second concert, in spite of Paganini's request, *did* take place on May 30th, for Spohr mentioned it; but whether the pecuniary results were better than before, we do not know. Between his two appearances in Cassel, Paganini gave a concert at Göttingen on the 28th of the month.

The first week of June found him at Hanover, where he played in the court theatre on the 3rd and 6th, though we have no details of his programmes. Here he made the acquaintance of George Harrys, a gentleman who looked after the English interests at the Hanoverian court. What brought about the intimate friendship that existed between these two men has not been discovered; and all we know is that this polished and diplomatic *attaché* joined the violinist as his travelling-companion and business-agent. There is ample evidence to show that the admiration of Harrys for Paganini amounted to hero-worship. Whether the old German pilot, Curiol, was then dropped overboard we do not know. Throughout the remainder of the tour in Germany, the Englishman had un-equalled opportunities for observing the virtuoso, and a good deal of what we know of Paganini's habits while on tour, was obtained from the booklet Harrys published later in the same year—*Paganini in seinem Reisewagen* (' Paganini in his Travelling-Carriage ', 1830). It was Harrys who suggested that Paganini write a vocal work in honour of William the Fourth's accession to the throne as King of Hanover on June 26th. With an eye to the King's gratitude when he should meet that genial personage in London, the violinist immediately agreed, and produced the ' Chant Patriotique, Composé à l'occasion de l'avènement en Trône de sa Majesté Britannique et roi d'Hanovre Guillaume IV. Musique de Nicolo Paganini. Paroles de George Harrys '. The original manuscript is preserved in the Kestner Museum at Hanover, and the work was published there in 1830. A composition for a solo voice, chorus, and pianoforte, the ' Chant Patriotique ' is one of the only two vocal pieces composed by Paganini—the other being the ' Ghiribizzo Vocale ' (Heyer, Cologne, No. 899). His engagements filled at Hanover, he left for Hamburg, breaking his journey to play at Celle on June 8th.

At the great seaport we are once more fortunate in having a description of our ' wandering Orpheus ' from the pen of a keen student of human nature and judge of character—the poet Heinrich Heine. But this particular poet exaggerated that aspect of Paganini which fed the imagination of the mystic, the gossip, and the scandalmonger. After all, it is not a poet's business to enquire too closely for material truth so much as it is his vocation to present a picturesque and intriguing figure to his readers : ' Only in crude, black and fugitive strokes can those supernatural features be limned—features that seem to belong rather to the sulphurous realm of shadows than to the sunny world of living things. . . . He wore a dark grey coat which, reaching to his feet, gave the impression of great height to his figure. His long black hair fell in twisted curls about his shoulders and formed a dark frame round a pale, corpse-like face, on which trouble, genius, and hell had graved their indelible marks. By his side tripped a short, comfortable, figure, quaintly prosaic, with a pink puckered face, a little light grey coat with steel buttons, darting irresistibly friendly glances in all directions, at the same time looking up with worried shyness at the gloomy figure that moved meditatively and seriously at his side. It seemed as if we had before us the picture of Retzsch, in which Faust and Wagner promenade outside of the gates of

Leipzig. . . . The deaf painter (Lyser) commented upon the two figures in his own mad way, and directed my attention to the broad, measured, paces of Paganini: "Is it not," said he, "as if he still carried the iron cross-bar between his legs? He has accustomed himself to this gait, and it will remain with him for ever. Do you not see also, how contemptuously ironic is his downward glance at his companion, when the latter bores him with his prosaic questions? But he cannot dispense with him; a blood-sealed contract binds him to this servant, who is none other than Satan himself. It is true that the ignorant people believe this companion to be the comedy-writer and anecdotist Harrys from Hanover, whom Paganini had picked up on his travels to see to the financial business of his concerts. The common people do not know that the devil has merely borrowed the outward shape of Herr George Harrys, and that the poor soul of this unfortunate man is in the meantime shut up in a box with other lumber at Hanover, until the devil gives it back its envelope of flesh, and decides to accompany his master through the world in a more worthy shape—say, as a black poodle." If Paganini appeared to me in broad daylight under the green trees of the Hamburg Jungfernstieg as sufficiently uncanny and romantic, how much more must his creepy and bizarre appearance surprise me when I see him at his concert in the evening. The Hamburg theatre was the scene of this concert, and the art-loving public had arrived in such numbers and so early, that I could scarcely snatch a seat near the orchestra. Every eye was directed on to the stage. My neighbour, a fur-dealer, removed his dirty plugs of cotton-wool from his ears, the better to suck in the priceless notes he was soon to hear—notes which cost two thalers to approach. At length a dark form appears on the stage, looking as if it had risen from the underworld. This was Paganini in his black gala-clothes: his black coat and vest of a terrible cut, such as is probably dictated by the hellish etiquette of Proserpine's court; his black trousers flapping disconsolately against his bony legs. His long arms seemed lengthened by the violin he carried in one hand, and the bow in the other—both perpendicular and almost touching the ground, as he trotted out his ungainly acknowledgements before the public. In the angular contortions of his body there was a wooden horror, and at the same time, something stupidly animalistic, that involuntarily called forth our laughter; but his face which, in the garish illumination of the orchestra, seemed still more corpse-like in its pallor, contained an expression so pleading, so idiotically humble, that a horrible sympathy crushed the desire to laugh it out of existence. Did he learn these obeisances from an automaton or from a dog? Is this pleading glance that of a being stricken with a fatal disease, or hides there behind it the scorn of a cunning miser? Is this a living being who wishes to delight his audience at the moment of his dissolution in the art-arena with his last quivering gasp, like a dying gladiator? Or is it a corpse that has risen from the grave—a vampyr with a violin, who would suck, if not the blood from our hearts, at least the money from our pockets?'

'Such questions crossed our minds while Paganini went through his interminable bending and bowing. But all such thoughts had perforce to vanish instantly, at the moment in which the marvellous master placed his violin under his chin and began to play. . . .' Lyser's drawing of Paganini, more caricature than portrait, matches Heine's words like an echo.

Paganini arrived in Hamburg on June 10th, and gave three concerts on the 12th, the 16th, and the 19th, leaving on the 23rd of the month. He appeared in Bremen on the 25th and the 28th. From this moment his movements again become vague and he cannot be followed with any accuracy.

It was during this summer of 1830 that the Westphalian court raised Paganini to the peerage with the titles of Baron and Commander. His dearest wish was at last fulfilled. The French and English papers probably obtained their information at second or third hand, and by the time it reached their printing-establishments the rumour went that Paganini was *buying* a title. What truth, if any, there was in this suggestion, no one can say; but it was a report that Paganini did not deny.

The barony was not an important one in the eyes of the old nobility, and society looked upon its bestowal as indulgently as it regarded the papal knighthood. The honours looked well on Paganini's visiting-cards and no one suffered through the childish pleasure taken by the great violinist in these external decorations. The most important feature to Paganini's way of thinking was that the barony was hereditary in favour of the first-born male issue; Achillino would be a baron; Paganini would die happy. In the meantime he could sun himself in its glory and call himself, as he does on his pale mauve, gilt-edged, carte-de-visite, ' Le Baron Nicolo Paganini, Commandeur de plusiers Ordres '.

At this point he seems to have taken a short holiday, though there can be no certainty in the chronology; and to the end of the year we have only three or four dependable dates. He went to Frankfort, was seen at Nassau, took the ' cure ' at Ems, played there on August 24th, and at Wiesbaden on the 26th. Four days later he was at Baden-Baden, for he sends Germi a letter dated from this pleasant spa.

And the letter is very interesting. Since Antonia Bianchi packed up her finery, her jewels, and Paganini's money, and left Vienna for Milan, our Don Juan had had no love-affairs, no more ' first real passions '. In Prague he had been very ill; fully occupied in washing and dressing and spoiling Achillino; in associating with his Italian friends there and with Schottky. During his German tours he had been too busy to think of such trivialities, or the German girls estimated his cheerful flirtation at its just value. He was now relaxing, and Eros, finding idle hands and wishing to jest with a suffering invalid of forty-eight, let fly a couple of light shafts at once to see the effect. The young scapegrace probably did not wait to learn the result; but Paganini told Germi all about it: ' I approve all you have done on my behalf. I have instructed Eskely to remit you 51,305 lire. After all this, a quiet retreat and happiness will come to me as a grateful solace, where we can enjoy our musical duets and quartets, and eat our *ravioli*. . . . I often feel in me the poetic frenzy which urges me to marry. At Frankfort I asked in marriage the hand of a sweet girl, the daughter of a merchant, not actually wealthy, but quite well-to-do. Then, reflecting firstly that she was too young for me, and too pretty; and secondly that she might not love me; and lastly that she had no soul for music, and would thus be dedicating herself to me with a false object in view, I doubted the wisdom of the plan '. He may have discovered these objections after he had met a more mature charmer—this time a lady who had married a baron three years earlier. A husband is, after all, only a trivial objection, and as the baroness had not married for love, Paganini felt no scruples about falling in love with her. She came from Nuremberg to hear him play, and actually had the audacity to ask her husband to take her to a second concert. This time Paganini spoke with her, discovered that she was hopelessly in love with him, and decided in his own mind that she would die if fate kept them apart. He tells Germi that she has a fine figure, is very fond of music, and can sing; she is well-educated, and he considered that the twenty-four letters he has had from her are worth printing, for they give proof of feelings far deeper than those which Eloise ever had for Abelard. He became so childish over these epistles that he offered to send them to Germi, fondly imagining that that worldly man of law would immediately recommend him to abduct the lady. He is quite sure that she would make him a perfect wife and Achillino an ideal mother. He stayed incognito at a village inn, posing as ' the King of Prussia's architect '—an Elysium where the indiscreet baroness paid him visits, heavily veiled. It was all deliciously romantic and so impossible. He sends Germi a specimen of her poetry —some sentimental verses inspired by himself, ' though no longer good-looking '—and adds that the baroness has actually asked her father to institute divorce proceedings so that she might be free to marry him. He sends his love to his mother and brother. What the outcome of this tender episode was, we do not know. The Herr Baron probably gave his pretty and silly young wife a mild lecture and took her to the Harz or the Riesengebirge for a change of scene. Paganini, not too deeply wounded to go on living, most likely burnt the letters of the educated and musical Hélène, and set about his preparations for a journey farther afield. How long he took life easily at different spas cannot be determined. Early in November he was back in Frankfort, the correspondent of the *Harmonicon* writing to London: ' Paganini is still with us. . . . All the world here has been to see the performance of an actor from the Breslau theatre, who mimics the Italian virtuoso to a wonder. Paganini himself, instead of attempting to cut the poor mimic's throat, as most of your sensitive artistes would have done, had the good taste, not to say good sense, to attend one of these performances, and join in the general laugh with the best grace in the world '.

The rest he had enjoyed in the south German watering-places and the very few public appearances he made during the autumn and winter—which he most likely spent in Frankfort—must have set him up sufficiently to give him the courage to cross the frontier. Early in February 1831, he travelled to Strasbourg and gave two concerts in the theatre—on the 14th and the 17th. He discovered that the French audiences he found there could be as enthusiastic as any he had enraptured in Italy, Austria, and Germany—in spite of the fact that his first recital was marred by a severe attack of his old intestinal malady. Anders says that the trouble was caused by an accident brought about by his nervous irritability, but that it ' rather enhanced the prestige of his incomparable bow ', being in keeping with the ' effect produced by his expression and the inspiration which dominated it '. At the end of his German tour the press of all Europe was ringing with his praises. Reports on his concerts were reprinted everywhere, and all the capitals of Europe were asking when they would be privileged to hear him. St. Petersburg, Stockholm, Copenhagen, Lisbon, Madrid—all speculated upon the direction his next journey would take. In his uncertainty Paganini remembered a letter, now some two years old, which he had received from the villa on the Lake of Como, now occupied by Major Fontano Pino. The letter set him thinking, for it ran as follows:

'If you now feel better—as we all hope—then go at once to Paris in order to surprise, terrify, and annihilate those professors who deny the existence of a Paganini. In this connexion I will tell you a little story. A few days ago a Frenchman, just arrived from Paris, visited me. The conversation turned upon the immortal Paganini, and hear what I had to learn from this animal (*bestia*). He told me that in one of the Parisian journals your arrival in, and departure from, that city were announced simultaneously. The paper expressed itself as follows: " The much-belauded Paganini had been in hiding in the French capital for eight days in order to hear the best of our violinists; and when he had convinced himself of their superiority, he left us immediately, fearing to enter into competition with them." Oh, the cursed asses (*ciuci maledetti*). Hurry, my friend, and convince these unbelievers of your incomparable merit; this one laurel-leaf is still wanting in your crown. La Pasta, who is also on the Lake where she has bought a house, asks me to send you her greetings. Farewell, dear friend; write as often as you can, and keep in your affections your devoted friend,

FONTANO PINO '.

Paganini could make and change his plans with great rapidity. On February 19th, 1831, his horses' heads were turned to the west, and he crossed the Vosges. Paris and London lay before him. He was entering upon the last nine years of his life; and into those nine years were crowded more honours and suffering, more glory and misery, more rewards and disillusionments and misunderstanding, than have perhaps fallen to the lot of any man for whom Fame's clarions have blared forth in triumph. Such destinies have been imagined often enough in fiction; in history they have been exceedingly rare.

CHAPTER XIX

MAKING the necessary allowance for differences in national temperament, it may be said that the political events of the past year had the same effect upon all the countries of Europe. In France the results of the Parisian revolution of 1830 were accepted throughout the country, and Louis-Philippe I, replacing Charles X, became the ' citizen-king '. The younger branch of the Bourbons took the place of the elder—and that was all as far as the ordinary citizen was concerned. The population of the larger cities, sighing with relief because peace of a sort was once more established, eagerly sought all forms of entertainment, and welcomed what came to them from without. But in spite of this, the path of the foreign artist was not made too smooth for him. Paris was burdened with the consciousness of a status to uphold, and her leaders in the field of art set up a standard to suit their taste on the one hand, and safeguard the interests of the native musicians on the other. Audiences generally, spoiled by the excellence of the artists who flocked thither for their final *cachet,* called for novelty in Paris as they did in Vienna and Berlin; the professionals and the critics, jealous of their reputation as the deciding tribunal of artistic appeal, felt that superlative merit was essential before they could acclaim a newcomer as an artist worthy of their voices. The struggle of romanticism against the confining barriers of what was then called classicism in all the arts, was in full swing.

In such a movement Paganini should surely figure as a high priest. Innovations such as would never have succeeded before, were now welcomed; and on this account alone, a form of art like that exploited by the Genoese violinist should have been certain of success. But, Paganini, though safe in the knowledge that he possessed in his magnetic personality and in the daring of his manner and methods in performance something that went beyond the limitation of nationality, of schools, and of fashion, still felt a little nervous as to the reception he could expect. From now onwards Paganini was always handicapped when he first appeared before any new audience : rumour, running like wildfire in advance of him, credited his performance with attributes veritably miraculous, and his public expected to see miracles performed before their eyes at every concert. Had Paganini not his unique personality to help him out, he must have failed, perfect though his technical equipment was. In Paris and in London he discovered how often a man's reputation for good can be greater than his performance, and in Paris also he was compelled to fight against a reputation for evil that was greater than he deserved. His twenty-four *Caprices* were known to the musicians of Paris. They had been studied, tried, and given up as inexplicable enigmas. The violinists, at least, looked forward with curiosity to the coming of the man who had had the audacity to write such things and, if report did not lie, had also the ability to play them in such wise that they meant something.

Nor were the flies that batten on the garbage-heaps idle : the stories of Paganini's murders, rapes, and imprisonment went the rounds once more, this time in a highly-coloured dress full of French imagery. His portrait greeted him from the shop-windows. But not the flattering pictures of Vienna or Milan with the noble head surmounted by a wreath of bays held up by flying cherubs. Here he is portrayed in a prison-cell, playing his violin for dear life, intent upon mastering the difficulty in hand before his last string breaks. He took the air and saw an idle crowd gazing into a print-seller's windows. Joining them he found himself looking intently at himself in such a picture. He was livid with rage, not only at the injustice done him, but also at France's flagrant violation of the laws of hospitality. What seemed worst in his mind was the sickening fact that the crowd recognized him as the original of the picture. He made up his mind to speak to his friend Fétis about it; something must be done to stop these libels. But at the moment he had other things to think of; primarily, his first appearance before these people—these *ciuci maledetti* who would not believe that Paganini the violinist even existed.

He arrived in Paris on February 24th and, as he had intimated to Germi a year ago, he went to the Hotel des Princes, 109, rue de Richelieu. He did not hide himself; quite the contrary. On the evening of his arrival he went to the Italian opera and applauded the Malibran as Desdemona. The following evening he was one of the guests at a party given by Eugène Troupenas, the wealthy and genial music-publisher. Here life began again for him. He met his old friend Rossini—an intimate in the Troupenas household—and exchanged happy reminiscences of Roman carnivals; he became acquainted with the young and elegant Charles de Bériot who followed with his eyes every movement of the fêted prima donna of the night before, because he intended to marry her; he met again the stupendous bass Lablache, with whom he was soon to be associated in London; and he was introduced to many other musicians of the calibre of Rubini and Tamburini, whom he was also to meet again in England. This was a new world; these were international celebrities; Paganini was among his peers in all the different branches of the musical art. And being in an atmosphere that pleased him, he did what was very rare—he played to the guests. Of course, it needed the delicate raillery of the experienced Malibran to perform this miracle—but she succeeded. Seizing upon the air she had just sung he varied it, developed it—in short, did all that a clever musician can do with a theme when he is playing before people who understand. On the 27th of the month he went to the Conservatoire, as a visitor, to hear Beethoven's C-Minor symphony—for Beethoven was now as sure a bait for Paganini as ever. He had time on his hands while hunting for a suitable hall for his own concerts, and he spent it in sight-seeing with Achillino in the glorious sunshine of a French spring, in attending concerts, in going to the opera.

On March 2nd his old teacher Ferdinando Paër—how far back the memory connected with that name took him when he associated it with far-distant Parma!—introduced him into the Palais Royal where the *roi-citoyen* held his court. Unfortunately he was compelled to ask Paër to make his excuses to the King; he could not play as an attack of his old cough prevented him from presenting himself before his Majesty. On May 5th he had not yet secured a hall. At length he was able to arrange terms with Dr. Véron, the recently-appointed director of the Opéra. It is quite possible that he delayed making other reservations in the hope of booking this magnificent edifice for the exhibition of his talents. On the 8th the *Courrier des Théâtres* announced that 'to-morrow the celebrated Paganini will be heard. There will be an extraordinary performance in celebration of this solemnity. A ballet will bring the spectacle to a close. *Soirée de gourmets*'. The terms arranged were generous enough. The prices of admission were to be raised to threefold the usual charges; concerts were to be given on Wednesdays and Sundays; the artist was to receive two-thirds of the takings for the Wednesday performances, and the whole of the Sunday proceeds less three thousand francs. On Wednesday, March 9th, 1831, Paganini made the first of his peculiar bows before the Parisian audience.

If we can imagine the enthusiasm of Vienna, Berlin, and Munich combined, and grafted on to a temperament of Latin growth, we may be able to form a faint idea of the scene that followed his playing of the E-flat concerto. Some there were who had seen the music and decided that it was unplayable; some were incredulous for no reason at all; some had spoken with travellers who had heard this indescribable monster of the tonal art and were prepared for anything. The excitement was intense; those who attempted to describe it regretted the absence of a language rich enough for the task. The Escudier brothers—protégés of Troupenas—did their best : ' Paganini was heard for the first time in Paris in the Salle de l'Opéra. The élite of the aristocracy, the flower of the amateurs, all the artists, all the dandys (*sic*), all the women of fashion, all the foreigners of distinction—all made this their rendez-vous. At the first sounds from his instrument the silence became so profound that the most sensitive ear could not hear the slightest noise, the lightest breath. Seeing his prodigious facility . . . the spectators were struck with astonishment and a kind of giddiness. But their stupefaction was turned to enthusiasm when the great artist dazzled all present with the wealth of his melodic inspiration. It was truly the revelation of a new world; it was art in its most varied and striking manifestations. Ironic and scoffing like the Don Juan of Byron, capricious and fantastic like an hallucination of Hoffmann, melancholy and dreamy like a meditation of Lamartine, fiery and impetuous like an imprecation of Dante, soft and tender like a melody by Schubert, the violin of Paganini laughs, sighs, threatens, blasphemes, and prays in turn. In such wise did Paganini appear before us at his first concert. His success exceeded the wildest expectation . . . And the connoisseurs present shared the opinion of the public'. What was there left for the other papers to say? The *Revue de Paris* followed the German method: ' Paganini does not play the violin; he is an artist in the widest sense of the word—one who creates, who invents his instrument, his manner, his effects, and everything down to the very difficulties which he conquers. He has taken everything outside of the accepted domain of the art. No comparison is possible between him and all who have gone before '. The celebrated Castil-Blaze in the *Journal des Débats* escapes by turning facetious: ' Tartini in his dream heard a demon play a diabolic sonata; this demon was surely Paganini. But no; the imp of Tartini with his double-trills, his bizarre modulations, his rapid arpeggi, was nothing but an elementary scholar compared with the virtuoso we now possess in our midst —a timid little devil, even innocent . . . The trumpet of Fame is only a miserable whistle with which to celebrate the high deeds of this marvellous violinist '. One more account is worth recording—that of Ludwig von Boerne: ' It was a heavenly and a diabolical enthusiasm; I have never seen or heard its like in my life. This nation is mad and all go mad with them. They listened so intently that they forgot to breathe, and the necessary beating of their hearts disturbed them and made them angry. When he stepped on to the stage, and before he had played a note, he was welcomed with a thunderous jubilation. This deadly enemy of the dance must be seen to be believed, in the awkwardness of his body. He sways like a drunkard. His own feet seem to be in his way . . . . an absolute lout to look at . . . but . . . he played divinely. He did not please me nearly so much in Frankfort . . . so much for environment '.

Among all the famous poets, novelists, painters, composers, and executants who attended this concert, one young man of twenty must be especially mentioned. It was Franz Liszt. To the young, slight disappointments and trivial disillusionments sometimes seem very tragic. In Liszt's case the world appeared destitute of joy, holding out no hope; the monastery beckoned to him sadly as the only asylum left to his wounded soul; a place where neither the instability of human love nor the cynical fickleness of fame could harm him. At this, perhaps the most solemn and decisive moment of his life, Paganini rises above his clouded horizon and sweeps Paris off its feet before his dreamy eyes. But Liszt was not concerned with the changeful enthusiasm of the French; his pain was too deep-seated to be dulled by a pitying smile at the uncontrolled rapture of other people. The effect of Paganini's playing upon him was quite different. In the first place it awoke him from his pessimistic lethargy; in the second, it sent the Hungarian blood coursing through his veins to a rhythm that kept pace with his heart-beat and yet inspired a blessed sense of freedom; in the third, it set his mind working along lines that needed only such a suggestion to be followed. Here before his eyes was an artist who had the courage actually to express himself with the freedom that others only preached. Should the proud Magyar despond before the valour of a Genoese? What an Italian could do on the violin

was surely possible to an Hungarian on the pianoforte. Solemnly
the young man promised himself that he would not relax in his
efforts until he had wrested from his instrument the secret that
the industrious violinist had dragged from his. Liszt was under
no illusions as to the provenance of Paganini's facile perfection :
it came, he well knew, from labour and pain—the price of really
important achievement; and that he realized how literally the
soul had to pass through the fires of purgatory before it conquered the difficulties that beset its passage, is shown in the
words he wrote to a friend : ' Réné, what a man ! What a
fiddler, what an artist ! Heavens ! What suffering and misery,
what tortures dwell in those four strings ! ' Whether Paganini's
influence upon Liszt extended to the field of technical detail,
and became as great and as effective as some recent writers
claim, is debatable. No one has the means of proving what
Liszt would have become without the appearance of Paganini.
It is more than likely that he would still have been Franz Liszt
—nationalistic, romantic, descriptive, and brilliantly technical—
a pianistic Paganini, not so much influenced by his Italian
encouragement as impelled to action and urged to develop his
own potentialities by the playing of this phenomenal violinist.

Paganini's influence upon those violinists of his day who were
attracted by his peculiar style, was greater, though the results
were less noticeable. Of exact imitation there could be no
question; the personality of Paganini belonged to no one else.
To rival his technical finish seemed an ambition more easily
attainable; here also none matched him on all points. Only in
tendency did Paganini influence the violinists of his time and
of the years to come. A school of brilliant technicians came
into being—belonging to no particular nation, but having its
followers wherever the necessary physical and temperamental
conditions showed themselves. If Paganini's technical manner
and instrumental methods were not exactly equalled, they did
at least open the eyes of the more advanced exponents of his
art to the possibilities of the instrument. Many were the players
who converged upon Paris to hear him and possibly learn from

him. Perhaps more deeply than any other, the Norwegian Ole Bull was impressed by Paganini's performance, and in many ways the ideals, objects, and methods of the two were identical. In spirit Bull's virtuosity was closer to Paganini's than was that of Sivori who had enjoyed personal instruction from his countryman. Heinrich Wilhelm Ernst was another of the outstanding exponents of violin-technics to be attracted by the scintillating brilliance of the Italian. Between the ages of sixteen and eighteen his wanderings often brought him into contact with Paganini, and he frequently followed the older artist from place to place in order to observe his methods. These were men of unusual talent and aptitude, less known to the world at large only because the electrifying appearance of Paganini placed them in the second rank in the public esteem. There was more in Paganini's playing than the mere exhibition and exploitation of a transcendent technique; and on this account his performance has never been equalled. At the same time he would be a very rash man who ventured to suggest that without Paganini there would have been no Sivori, no Bull, no Ernst—as hazardous a statement as to claim that without Paganini there would have been no Liszt. The players of the old school in Paris as elsewhere, simply accepted Paganini as a forecast of a future that no effort of their own could stave off. Habeneck, it is true, attempted to master the *Caprices,* but was beaten by them. The invaluable Baillot said to the Malibran: ' Ah, Madame, it is miraculous, inconceivable; do not speak to me about it—there is in his playing that which drives one to distraction '.

Paganini's second concert in Paris followed on Sunday, March 13th. For this occasion he had reserved a new work—a concerto in D—which he had written somewhere in Germany, saying at the time, ' Lo voglio sverginare à Parigi '. To this he added such familiar items as the bell-rondo and the *Moïse* variations, besides vocal numbers sung by four popular operatic stars—the tenor Adolphe Nourrit, the bass Nicolas Prosper Levasseur, Dabadie, and Mademoiselle Dorus. Castil-Blaze

217

summed up the opinion of musical Paris on the new concerto
when he wrote in the *Journal des Débats:* ' Paganini is without
doubt very learned, and his compositions for and discoveries on
his instrument prove it. He has shown his respect for our
musical taste by composing a concerto expressly for this country,
a work that is not to be played anywhere else. It once more
provides evidence of his marvellous gift of divination—a gift
that brought home to him the knowledge that our musical taste
favours the noble, the elegant, the passionate, and the charming.
. . . This work in D exhibits a most original form and contains
several highly picturesque effects . . . . The skilful handling of
his instrument and the magic of Paganini's playing astound us
more at each hearing '. There will be no need to mention
separately each of the eleven concerts he gave during this
season; it will suffice to record that he earned over 165,000
francs. His most successful Parisian appearance was that of
Sunday, March 20th, when his takings amounted to almost
22,000 francs. Of his artistic triumph no more need be said
than that the French press, like the German, exhausted itself
in its efforts to describe the first two or three concerts, and
was then reduced to saying—*tout court* : ' Paganini played as
usual '. A temporary rift appeared in the excellent relations
between Paganini and his French public when the officers of
the Garde National took over the opera-house for their charity-
ball. The organizers invited Paganini to play during the
evening for a deserving cause, never suspecting that he would
refuse. But refuse he did. Rightly or wrongly, Paganini always
objected to exercising his benevolence to order. We have
already seen how often he devoted the proceeds of concerts to
charity when the impulse to do so came from himself; we saw
how much money he earned for such purposes in Germany.
But this did not place him in any better light in the eyes of the
Parisians. In vain did he point out that he lost a considerable
sum by transferring his concert of the same day to a smaller
building; equally vainly did *Le Moniteur* draw public attention
to the fact that Paganini had made an independent donation of

three thousand francs to the fund for the relief of the poor. A large section of the press seized upon him, pilloried him in print in the good old Gallic way, and designated their idol of yesterday as a mean and uncharitable miser. The squall blew itself out for the time being; but it was the first warning of a storm that was later to rage about the ears of the unfortunate artist. The worst that can be said of Paganini in this respect is that he was erratic in his generosity—sometimes giving his services and his substance unasked; at others—and especially when expected to give—he refused the smallest alms. This peculiarity, probably traceable to his inherent pride and obstinacy, was the cause of much bitterness a little later on; and we shall have to return to it when the *Journal des Débats* in France, and the *Harmonicon* in England, attacked him in the cruellest and most unjust manner possible—good journalism, perhaps, but ethically one of the darkest stains upon the reputations of those papers. Though feeling very hurt by the attitude taken up by these and a few other papers, he nevertheless carried out his own plan of giving a concert for charity, and to this end he devoted his share of the proceeds from his tenth concert, on April 17th, to the poor—a donation of 6105 francs and a respectable sum in those days. His farewell concert in the first Parisian series took place on the 24th of the same month.

About halfway through the season, on April 6th, Paganini wrote to Germi: ' It is impossible to give you any idea of my triumph here in Paris. Laporte, the impressario for the London theatre, has come over here expressly to look after me. I have promised by a contract signed yesterday, to begin my concerts there on the first of the coming month, and to give at least eight in six weeks '. Most of the information given in this short extract was later to prove incorrect. It is true that the astute Laporte, fearing to lose so great an attraction to a possible rival manager, hurried to Paris to make sure of Paganini. But both were to suffer much heartburning before the great violinist faced his London audience a full month later than Paganini

expected.   On the other hand, the number of public appearances he was to make on English soil far exceeded the minimum
contracted for.

The time for his departure from Paris was fast approaching,
and Paganini, knowing by bitter experience how rapidly the
poison of slander spread, thought the moment had arrived when
he must enlist the aid of the press in his attempt to prove the
falsity of the rumours that connected his name with stories of
callous murder and shameful imprisonment.   He unburdened
himself to Fétis, and this fine musicologue, in the generousness
of his heart, composed an open letter to the editor of the *Revue
Musicale* from material supplied by Paganini.   This letter,
partly based upon trustworthy matter and partly upon incorrect
information—though largely reprinted—did little to stem the
tide of gossip.   The shallow minds of the greater part of the
human race are ever illogical enough to prefer a sensational
legend to a sober truth.   Paganini should have needed no other
defence than that provided by the chronology of his life.   Fétis's
effort on his friend's behalf ran as follows, in the first translation
of 1852 :

'Sir,—So many proofs of kindness have been showered upon
me by the French public, so much encouraging approbation has
been bestowed upon me, that I cannot avoid believing in the
fame which is said to have preceded me, and assuming that my
performance did not fall short of my reputation.   But if any
doubt of that kind existed in my mind, it would be removed by
the eagerness evinced in your artists to produce my likeness, and
by the great number of portraits of Paganini—faithful resem-
blances or not—which cover the walls of your city.   But, Sir, it
is not only simple portraits that speculators of that nature stop
at ; for, while walking yesterday on the Boulevard des Italiens,
I saw in a shop, where engravings are sold, a lithograph representing *Paganini in prison.* Oh, I exclaimed, here are some honest
folks who, after the fashion of Basil, make a profit out of certain
calumnies which have pursued me for the last fifteen years.
However, I examined laughingly this mystification, with all the
details that the imagination of the artist had conjured up, when
I perceived that a large number of persons had congregated

round me, each of whom, confronting my face with that of the young man represented in the lithograph, verified the change that had taken place in my person since my detention. I then comprehended that it was looked on in a serious light by those you call, I believe, *Cockneys,* and I saw the speculation was a good one. It struck me that, as everybody must live, I might furnish the artists, who are kind enough to consider me worthy of their attention, with some anecdotes—stories from which they could derive subjects of similar *facetiae* to the one in question. It is to apprise them of this, that I claim from your kindness the insertion of this letter in your *Revue Musicale* '.

' They have represented me in prison—but they are ignorant of the cause of my incarceration; however, they know as much of that as I do myself, and those who concocted the anecdote. There are many histories in reference to this, which would supply them with as many subjects for their pencils; as, for example, it is stated that, having found a rival in my mistress's apartment, I stabbed him honourably in the back, while he was unable to defend himself. Others assert that, in the madness of jealousy, I slew my mistress; but they do not state how I effected my bloody purpose. Some assert I used a dagger— others that, desirous of witnessing her agony, I used poison. Each has settled it in accordance with his own fancy. Why should not lithographers have the same privilege? I will relate what occurred to me at *Padua,* nearly fifteen years since. I had played at a concert with great success. The next day, seated at the *Table d'Hôte,* I was the sixtieth; my entrance into the room passed unobserved. One of the guests spoke of the great effect I had produced the previous evening. His neighbour concurred in all that was said, and added, " There is nothing surprising in Paganini's performance—he acquired his talent while confined in a dungeon during eight years, having only his violin to soften the rigours of his confinement. He was condemned for having coward-like stabbed one of my friends, who was his rival ". As you may imagine, everyone dilated upon the enormity of my crime. I then addressed myself to the person who was so well acquainted with my history, and requested to know when and where this had taken place. Every eye was directed towards me. Judge the surprise when they recognized the principal actor in this tragical history. The narrator was embarrassed. It was no longer his friend who had been assassinated—he heard—it had been affirmed—he believed—but it was not improbable that he had been deceived. This is how an artist's reputation is trifled with, because indolent people will never comprehend that one may study at liberty as well as under lock and key'.

'A still more ridiculous report, at Vienna, tested the credulity of some enthusiasts. I played the variations entitled *Le Streghe*, and they produced some effect. One individual, who was represented to me as of a sallow complexion, melancholy air, and bright eye, affirmed that he saw nothing surprising in my performance, for he had distinctly seen, while I was playing my variations, the devil at my elbow directing my arm and guiding my bow. My resemblance to him was a proof of my origin. He was clothed in red, had horns on his head, and carried his tail between his legs. After so minute a description you will understand, Sir, it was impossible to doubt the fact—hence, many concluded they had discovered the secret of what they termed wonderful feats'.

'My mind was disturbed for a long time by these reports, and I sought every means to prove their absurdity. I remarked that from the age of fourteen I had continued to give concerts, consequently was always before the public, that I had been engaged as leader of the orchestra and musical director to the court of Lucca; that if it were true I had been detained eight years in prison, for having assassinated my mistress or my rival, it must have taken place before my appearance in public; that I must have had a mistress and a rival at seven years of age. At Vienna I appealed to the ambassador of my country, who declared he had known me for upwards of twenty years as an honest man, and I succeeded in setting the calumny aside temporarily; but there are always some remains, and I was not surprised to find them here. How to act, Sir? I see nothing but resignation, and submit to the malignity which exerts itself at my expense. I deem it, however, a duty before I conclude, to communicate to you an anecdote which gave rise to the injurious reports propagated against me. A violinist of the name of Duranowski, who was at Milan in 1798, connected himself with two persons of disreputable character, and was induced to accompany them to a village where they purposed assassinating the priest, who was reported to be very rich. Fortunately, the heart of one failed him at the moment of the dreadful deed, and he immediately denounced his accomplices. The gendarmerie were soon on the spot, and took Duranowski and his companion prisoners at the moment they arrived at the priest's house. They were condemned to the galleys for twenty years, and thrown into a dungeon; but General Menou, after he had become Governor of Milan, restored—after two years detention—Duranowski to liberty. Will you credit it? Upon this groundwork they have constructed my history. It was necessary that the name of the violinist should end in *i*; it was Paganini; the assassination became that of my mistress or my rival; and I it was who was sent to prison—with this exception: that as I was to discover there a new school for the violin, the irons were not adjusted upon me, so that my arms might be at perfect liberty. Since these reports are persisted in, against all probability, I must of necessity bear them with resignation. One hope remains: it is, that after my death, calumny will abandon its prey, and that those who have so cruelly avenged my triumphs, will leave my ashes at rest'.

'Receive, etc.,'

'PAGANINI'.

Even his last pious hope was not to be realized; for over half a century after his death, his ashes were not suffered to rest in peace.

By the end of April, 1831, Paganini had filled all his engagements in Paris and was free to travel once more. Though he told Germi that he had agreed to commence his English season on May 1st, it is obvious that he could not reach London by that date. Probably correspondence had been passing between him and Laporte postponing his arrival. On April 28th he addressed a flattering letter of thanks to Habeneck for his assistance as conductor of the orchestra, adding that 'only in Paris did I find the best orchestra in Europe—one that presented my music in the way I imagined it should sound—an orchestra that knew how to accompany me perfectly'. Having dispatched this note, he left Paris. That he must have made new arrangements with Laporte is clear from the leisurely manner in which he travelled. He stopped at Boulogne and Calais to give concerts early in May.

Paganini, halfway through his forty-ninth year, stood at last on the shore of the English Channel facing north, holding his son by the hand. Risking an accusation of sentimentality we should pause here for a moment and try to realize what this man had achieved. In an era when safe and speedy travel depended upon the condition of roads and horses, Paganini traversed Europe from Warsaw to Paris, from Palermo to Calais. Handicapped by persistent ill-health and hindered by follies and weaknesses he managed to give hundreds of concerts that aroused an enthusiasm unprecedented in the history of music. He had collected decorations, titles, and other honours; he had amassed a fortune, most of which was safely invested by the faithful Germi. He had some justification for looking across the sunlit waves of the Channel with pride and a sense of high expectation. His joy in his conquests should not be greeted so readily with a sneer at his vanity. After all, his successes on the concert-platform were his only present sources of happiness. He had his duty to perform to his son, and but for him he was alone in the world. To his sisters he was merely a source of income. His mother was ageing in distant Genoa; only heaven knew how much longer she would be able to dictate letters to her Nicolo. Perhaps these circumstances explain why Paganini was so overbearingly elated when the crowd applauded, and so often melancholy with a painful sense of loneliness when condemned to his own society. Setting sail for England his lips curled into his inscrutable smile; over there in that peculiar island his second million was to be completed. Achillino besides being a baron, would also be rich.

CHAPTER XX

PAGANINI arrived in London round about the middle of May. 1831, and at once found himself the centre of a whirlpool of excitement. Discussions and arguments with his manager. Laporte, visits to friends and possible supporters, battles with the ubiquitous slanderers, parry and riposte with the editors of newspapers haggling to obtain the cheapest terms at which the public whose interests they pretended to protect could hear this enigmatical performer, kept him fully occupied. Instead of meeting a warm welcome at the heart of the British Empire, he found himself forced to fight every inch of the way into popular favour. If only he could have played first and argued afterwards, things would have been much easier for him. Accustomed as the musical world of London was to pay high fees to the great operatic singers—by reason of the laws govern-ing supply and demand—an instrumental artist possessing the same degree of virtuosity was something new. Press and public hardly knew how to value him; and to escape from this dilemma they chose the easier way by crying in a loud voice that Paganini or his manager was charging for too much for admis-sion. Storm-clouds gathered until the Zeus of Printing-house Square unloosed his thunder-bolts against this foreign corsair. ' Foreign ': this was the word that always seemed to lie cross-wise in the throat of an English press that was then still labouring heavily under the burden of an insular ' top nation ' complex.

He reached the capital preceded by the speedy post-horses of scandal and the glamourous expresses of Satan. London was still reclining blissfully on the Cytherean couch bequeathed by the Regency; adventure in the ante-chamber and the thrill of the unknown in the dressing-room was the breath of life to the lettered libertine, while the 'lady of fashion'—often brilliantly intellectual—was Georgian enough to take a risk. Paganini might add a new sensation to those already wearing out. Was anyone really shocked at what fame said of him? It is very much to be doubted. The memory of the Georges, and in particular of the 'naughty little Mahomet', was a cherished one in the English mind, for it cheated the idlers with a false impression of freedom. The wise and virtuous lady who was to become Queen Victoria was only twelve years old; the moral vacuum-cleaner which she brought to bear on Court and Society was still an unsuspected possibility; much might yet be done on behalf of Dionysus, Aphrodite, and the Satyrs. In spite of his many amours and his frequent flirtations in high places, Paganini could hold up his head in London, claim to be considered a gentleman, and demand the right to exercise his almost hypnotic influence upon the social drone, the literary giant, and the music-lover. Indeed, the 'lady of title'—that elusive and sharp-witted butterfly of the age—could even expect a legitimate flutter of excitement by mobbing this daemonic Don Juan in the streets of the metropolis and running him to earth in the Piazza of Covent Garden with an autograph-album and an invitation to visit her lord, to beguile her tedium with stories of his foreign adventures, and to frighten her deliciously with the romantic uncertainty of his behaviour. Thackeray was right as well as cynical when he said that 'there was no stronger satire on the proud English society of that day, than that they admired George IV'—and the spirit that bred this admiration was not yet dead. Paganini came, made one or two concessions, and conquered.

In order fully to understand the atmosphere into which the Genoese brought his new art, we must go back a few months, and see how far London differed from the Continental capitals. Towards the end of June, 1830, George IV., paying the price of a reckless life, withdrew to the 'Cottage' on Virginia Water to nurse his gout of the stomach, the ossification of his heart, his dropsy, his bile, his asthma, and his pulmonary inflammation with Curaçoa, brandy, and other remedies highly approved by the medical faculty. Unfortunately, what reduced the suffering caused by some of his many diseases, aggravated the others. But the Marchioness of Conyngham eased his last hours with her beloved presence, and while she bore his ancient bones pleasant company she kept her calculating eye fixed upon his jewel-boxes. And at three in the morning of June 26th, while his sorrowing courtiers were drawing the corks from a fresh relay of bottles, George the Magnificent slipped out of the world smelling horribly of spirits. Lady Conyngham made sure that he was really dead, packed her trunks, absent-mindedly dropped his treasures into her valise and vanished. Later on she was compelled to yield up certain jewelled decorations; but no one ever knew how many of her royal lover's possessions she retained. Into a court filled with card-cheats, drunkards, courtesans, and libertines, the insignificant brother of the late King was introduced as William IV.

As Duke of Clarence the new King had lived the life of most other noblemen of his day. He was guilty of the usual follies and frivolities; but he remained in the background, moved in a very limited circle, and was ignored by the world of fashion. He did, however, possess a good-natured disposition, and exhibit a natural affection for his immediate dependents; he was at least promising, even if his intellectual gifts were not especially noticeable. He was content to live at Bushey with Mrs. Jordan and enjoy the company of his many illegitimate children. The death of Princess Charlotte and later on that of the Duke of York, made him heir to the crown, and William suddenly became a figure of national importance. The invaluable *Journal* of Charles Cavendish Greville tells us that 'never was elevation like that of King William IV. His life had been hitherto passed in obscurity and neglect, in miserable poverty, surrounded by a numerous progeny of bastards, without consideration or friends, and he was ridiculous from his grotesque ways and little meddling curiosity. Nobody ever invited him to their house or thought it necessary to honour him with any mark of attention or respect; and so he went on for above forty years . . . King George had not been dead three days before everyone discovered that he was no loss, and King William a great gain '. Certainly at the funeral of George IV the members of the court ' were all as merry as grigs '. William posed as a hearty, good, and democratic fellow, and the *Magazine of Fashions* actually said of him that ' he has all the members of his family, as a family, about him, and " harmony and affection " is his favourite toast '. All the same, his reign began stormily. The country was unsettled; the agrarian riots were assuming dangerous proportions; ' Captain Swing ' and the incendiaries were destructively active, and rioting broke out over the question of parliamentary reform. The Duke of Wellington as Prime Minister strenuously opposed the Reform Bill while the King, showing far better sense than was expected of him by his subjects, favoured its progress. Nevertheless, both Duke and Sovereign were the targets for the peltings of the honest populace : for every stone that went through the windows of Apsley House, another was aimed at the royal family. One missile, according to Greville, ' shivered a window of the King's coach and fell in Prince George of Cumberland's lap '. The same diarist goes on to say that ' the state of the country is still dreadful . . . London is like the capital of a country desolated by cruel war, or foreign invasion, and we are always looking for reports of battles, burnings, and other disorders . . . A feverish anxiety about the future universally prevails, for no man can foresee what course events will take '. The condition of the middle and lower classes was far from brilliant. No wonder that the writers in some of the papers, when referring to the prices asked by Paganini for admission to his concerts, became almost inarticulate with rage that so much should be demanded for pleasure while so many thousands starved. It seems never to have occurred to most of these bright journalists

228

that those who did not feel justified in meeting his exorbitant demands were free to stay away from Paganini's performances. As a topic for conversation the artist came as a godsend. The rioting had ceased, and the King, feeling more secure, threatened to create a sufficient number of new peers, of his own way of thinking, to ensure the passage of the Bill that aroused so much feeling. This subject removed from the headlines, brought less important happenings into prominence. The Duchess of Kent and the Princess Victoria had been to Covent Garden to witness a performance of *Zemire and Azor* by Spohr, Paganini's acquaintance of Venice and Cassel. Paganini himself was coming. And then there was a coronation to look forward to. A temporary calm had settled down upon the troubled capital, and the great violinist arrived in a city which must have reminded him, in the meaner streets at least, of the harbour quarter of his birthplace. How London appeared to a foreigner at that date is well shown in the words of Baron d'Haussez : ' One is often tempted to ask, not if there is a police in London (for its agents in a blue uniform with a numbered collar, scattered everywhere by night and day, would make that question unnecessary), but what the police does, so little notice being taken of its details, so great its apparent negligence in order to avoid seeming unduly interfering. It is certain that the activity of the police is not visible in the cleanliness of the streets, nor in the indication of their names (for their names are absent at the end of the majority), nor in the passing to and fro of the carriages which are drawn up *pêle mêle* at the entrances of all the public places . . . . It often happens, in consequence of this confusion, that vehicles of all kinds become locked together, and this occasions an exchange of abuse and blows. Nor is the meddling of the police here noticeable with regard to animals, which, in being driven from one end of the town to the other on market days, often cause obstructions and frequently even serious accidents. A certain class of woman, also, in spite of the English modesty, exercise their shameless calling in a most brazen manner, unchecked by the police . . . .

In England, trifles like these are not regarded, and interference is limited to matters of more importance. On the other hand, there are few capitals where robberies are less frequent, where thieves are so soon discovered and punished . . . . ' But though Paganini may have found London well governed, he also found it very noisy. The milkwoman with her untimely call, the watchman, vendors of news sheets, the chimney-sweep, the fish merchant, the dustman, hundreds of hawkers from sellers of cats' meat to brooms, yelled and rang bells unhindered. Even the postman rang a bell. The iron-tyred wheels of every vehicle rattled over the squared granite, and old London must have been a nerve-racking place in spite of the absence of the internal combustion engine. The lower classes were ignorant, badly housed, and lax in their code of mental and bodily cleanliness; they often beat their wives and sometimes sold them by auction. The middle classes stayed in their godly over-ornamented homes, were not overburdened with a superfluity of brains, but usually exhibited an inherent commonsense. There were about a hundred omnibuses plying on the streets in 1831, and the population of London was in the neighbourhood of a million and a half. With all its shortcomings it must have been a lively enough place, with its Nassau balloon, its Wellington, its O'Connells, and its rising Disraeli.

All classes were very well catered for in the matter of entertainment. No fewer than fifteen theatres stood at their disposal: The King's Theatre, or Italian Opera, the Drury-Lane Theatre, the Covent Garden Theatre, the Haymarket, the English Opera, or Lyceum Theatre, the Adelphi, the Olympic, Astley's, the Surrey, the Coburg in Waterloo Road, soon after renamed the Victoria, Sadler's Wells, the City of London in Shoreditch, the Queen's in Tottenham Street, the Pavilion in Whitechapel, and the Garrick in Leman Street, Aldgate. The most aristocratic house was the King's Theatre—the only one to possess stalls, which were usually taken for the whole season, as were also the boxes; its performances commenced at eight o'clock and the admission to the Pit was 8s. 6d. At Drury Lane and at Covent Garden the curtain rose at seven and the prices were much lower: Boxes, seven shillings; Pit, 3s. 6d.; Lower Gallery, two shillings; Upper Gallery, one shilling, and all vacant seats in the house were half-price at nine o'clock. The Haymarket Theatre, though commencing its performances at seven, was rarely emptied before one o'clock; and for six hours of shelter, not to speak of high-class entertainment, the management charged only five shillings for the boxes, three shillings for the pit, and two shillings and one shilling for the two galleries respectively. Naturally, prices were higher at the Italian Opera during the Grand Season when international celebrities appeared. Musical Londoners were often offered the choice of two companies—one German and one Italian—and in the spectacles provided by the latter they were able to enjoy the art of such virtuosi as Lablache, Rubini, Garcia, Tamburini, Grisi, Malibran, and La Pasta. An interesting little paragraph in *The Times* throws a significant sidelight upon the status of the operatic artist in the eighteen-thirties, and we are more surprised than ever that the press should have objected so strenuously to Paganini's prices; for the list shows that there were many great vocalists, while there was only one Paganini:

'Opera Charges'

'The following sums are paid *nightly* to the performers at the King's Theatre: Pasta, £200, Taglioni, £120, Rubini, £100, Tamburini, £100, Donzelli, £50, Zuchelli, £50. Madame Pasta will receive £3500 for the season; and the amount payable to the principal characters alone, on the rising of the curtain, is above one thousand pounds'.

A perfect galaxy of talent shone in the musical and dramatic firmament of the metropolis. There were such actors, actresses, and dancers as Paul Bedford, J. B. Buckstone, T. P. Cooke, W. Farren, Charles J. Kean, C. Kemble, W. C. Macready, John Parry, B. Webster, Mrs. Glover, Fanny Kemble, Ellen Tree, Madame Vestris, and many others as popular in their day. Mrs. Siddons died in the year Paganini arrived; Edmund Kean followed her two years later. Among the musicians active we encounter figures like Balfe and Barnett, Benedict and Sterndale Bennett, Bishop and Costa, Cramer and Moscheles, Sir George Smart and William Vincent Wallace; while the resident singers were headed by such artists as John Braham, Phillips, Madame Allan, Anna Bishop, Clara Novello, Adelaide Kemble, and Miss Paton. Letters and pictorial art were adorned by an imposing array of writers and painters whose names have become household words—too numerous to mention—a great age peopled by men of the calibre of George Borrow, Lytton, Ingoldsby, Campbell, Dickens, Hood, Landor, Lever, Lingard, Southey, and Wordsworth; Constable, Landseer, Maclise, Mulready, Turner, Cruikshank, Tenniel, and their peers.

Such was the world that looked with wonder and amusement, with distrust and even distaste, and finally with admiration, upon Nicolo Paganini.

When his first poster appeared announcing his opening concert for May 28th, London opened its eyes widely and, speechless with amazement, its mouth also; for at the foot of the bill could be read these fantastic figures : ' *Prices of Boxes:* Pit Tier, 8 Guineas; Ground Tier, 10 Gns.; One Pair, 9 Gns.; Two Pair, 6 Gns.; Three Pair, 4 Gns.; Stalls, 2 Gns.; Orchestra, $1\frac{1}{2}$ Guinea; Admission to the Pit, 1 Guinea; Ditto to the Gallery, Half-a-Guinea '. The first to recover the power of speech was *The Times;* and the issue for May 19th appeared with its protest :

' *Laporte and Paganini* '

' Laporte's presumption in doubling the prices of admission to the King's Theatre on the first night of Paganini's performance, is one of those extravagances which could only have entered the head of a foreigner, who had beforehand arrived at the happy conviction, moreover, of the infinite gullibility of the English nation. To understand this more clearly, it is necessary to bear in mind, that the whole theatre is on this occasion set apart, not for a dramatic performance, but for a concert merely, and that it will hold, if filled at the ordinary prices, at least

£1500 in money. The expense to be sustained is considerably less than on an ordinary night. There is no chorus, no *corps dramatique*, nor *corps de ballet*, to be engaged. Nothing is wanted but an orchestra, the whole attention centring in fact in the single talent of Paganini, which, without doubt, having the concurrent testimony of all Europe, is of no common kind. But is he justified, or Laporte for him, in levying this enormous tax on those who may desire to form their own opinion of him by hearing his performance on the violin? We have had instances enough before in this country of extravagant pretension on the part of Opera singers, dancers, and others; yet none of them, in the full zenith of their popularity, and with far stronger reasons on their side, ever ventured on such an outrageous proceeding as this . . . The prices at the King's Theatre are already higher than any others in Europe. They secure, as they are, the most brilliant recompense that can possibly await individual talent. We may allow, perhaps, to very rare eminence in a public performer, that he shall occasionally count his hundreds for a single night; but this scheme, should the public swallow the bait, may possibly secure his thousands to Paganini: he may appropriate as much in that one night as former managers have assigned to our Billingtons and Catalini's for a whole season. There can be nothing in his art, a mere instrumental performer, so great a prodigy, as to deserve such a price. The frequenters of the King's Theatre are frivolous enough, perhaps, many of them, to take their estimate of Paganini's concert by the rate of admission which is demanded to it, but the common sense of the great majority of them will, we are persuaded, furnish the best remedy for such extortion, by causing them to absent themselves till Laporte and his foreign idol are brought to their senses'.

The *New Monthly Magazine* in a sarcastic paragraph suggests flippantly that Paganini was probably not aware that ' our prices were always double prices ', while an evening paper with a mathematically-minded staff discovered that ' the King's Theatre, at the prices demanded by the Italian violinist, would hold the enormous sum of £3980 . . . a sum which, if properly invested, would give to Signor Paganini and his heirs, *etc.*, for ever the income of an Italian gentleman '. Laporte, panic-stricken, wrote that he heard with deep regret that *The Times* should throw upon him the blame for the advance in the prices, adding that a ' feeling of delicacy ' prevented him from going into details. A letter from ' A Friend of Native Talent ' added its quota by saying that the English were far too prone to paying so much money to foreigners. Indeed, the word ' foreigner ' still seems to have been the red rag of the argument. The public were permitted to pay five shillings to hear John Braham while so many of their poorer countrymen starved, but it was ' monstrous ' to pay ten to hear an artist who in his way was unique. The *Athenaeum* in the dignified manner of White's Club blesses the efforts of *The Times* : ' We have been well pleased to observe that the press has been raising its voice against the monstrous impositions proposed to be effected in this performer's name ; we shall add ours, and entreat the public not to submit to them '. *The Times* of May 21st, while noting Laporte's ' delicacy ', still blames that impressario, if not as the prime instigator in advancing the prices, at least as a very interested agent :

' Paganini, having frequently received on the Continent, the compliment of double prices, naturally expected the same thing here, without making much enquiry, perhaps, what those prices were, or about the actual produce of that theatre when completely filled. He was probably, also, never informed how unusual it is to appropriate the whole of that theatre to a concert merely, and what uncommon attraction was requisite to fill it, even at the ordinary prices. It is but courtesy to a foreigner, and a man of eminent professional talent, as Paganini undoubtedly is, to state these circumstances on his behalf '.

A terse remark in the same issue gives with silent satisfaction the information that ' Paganini has deemed it necessary to postpone his concert '. The issue of the 23rd contains a very sarcastic article on the loss that England would sustain if Paganini—as he threatened—were to depart without playing at all. The opportunity was seized to gird at the high fees demanded and obtained by many great artists—especially at Catalani's five thousand pounds for a single season. *The Times* then gives its readers the 'Substance of the articles between Signor Paganini and M. Laporte' and comes to the conclusion that though Paganini is 'fond of high prices—and who is not? —Laporte was quite willing to second his efforts to obtain them . . . The agreement stipulates on the part of Laporte, that he is to take one-third of the gross receipts; that Paganini is in all cases to guarantee to him £290 sterling per night; that if the receipts should fall short of that sum, Paganini is to make it good; that Laporte is to have fourteen boxes and thirty-three admissions to the best seats of the house during each night of the performance; that these performances are to be for eight nights up to the 20th of June; that Paganini is not to play elsewhere for money; and that the prices of admission, and all minor arrangements, are to be settled between M. Laporte for himself, and Signor Torri, or some other person, for Paganini. It is plain, from an examination of these terms, that M. Laporte had a secure monopoly of the best days of the violinist'. Paganini, thoroughly disgusted at what he considered the impertinent interference of the press with the liberty of the subject, decided not to play. Knowing his constitution as we do, and being aware of the effect that a public wrangle of this kind could have upon him, we may accept the reason he gives. On the other hand he may have been simply too obstinate to give way. On May 27th, therefore, he addressed a note to the papers:

'Sir,—Finding myself too unwell, I request you will respectfully inform the public that the Concert announced for to-morrow will not take place.
Your obedient servant,
NICOLO PAGANINI'.

Wiser counsels prevailed the same day, and Paganini, realizing that half a loaf was better than no bread, climbed down in as dignified a manner as he could. The *Athenaeum*—always the complete gentleman—did not cry 'Victoria', but merely carried this paragraph in its issue of the 28th:

'*King's Theatre*'

'We have no wish to keep up excitement beyond the occasion, and shall therefore only announce that Paganini will appear at the Opera House, early in June, *at the old prices*'.

The editor, however, could not resist the italics. The *Brighton Gazette* gleefully rubbed its hands together and noted in its vulgar provincial way that 'There has been a delightful row in London about the high prices demanded for Paganini's concert, which were, in honest truth, scandalous enough . . . . The blame of the transaction may probably be divided, in about equal portions, between Paganini and Laporte'. The fiddler was soon to present Brighton with a 'row' of its own.

Paganini's first concert was ultimately fixed for June 3rd, and the diplomatic Italian, probably feeling that he ought to say 'good dog' before attempting to stroke the animal, sent a conciliatory letter to the editor of *The Times* on June 2nd:

'Sir,—Oblige me by inserting in your next paper the following letter, which I pray you to translate literally :—

'The evening of my first concert at the King's Theatre is now so near, that I feel the duty of announcing it myself to implore the favour of the English nation, which honours the arts as much as I respect it.

'Accustomed in all the nations of the Continent to double the ordinary prices of the theatres where I have given my concerts, and little instructed in the customs of this capital, in which I present myself for the first time, I did believe that I could do the same : but, informed by many of the journals that the prices already established here are higher than those on the Continent, and having myself seen that the observation was just, I second willingly the desire of the public, the esteem and good will of which I ambition as my first recompense'.

'Nicolo Paganini'.

He had passed through an exceedingly trying fortnight and was very relieved to find himself out of his quandary with an unscathed skin. The publicity given him by the discussions made of him a marked man whenever he showed himself in the streets. People followed him, crowded before him and behind him, so that often he could not move at all; they spoke to him in English of which he understood not one syllable; they even touched his clothes and pinched his arms to make sure that he was real. After having appeared in England at more than thirty concerts he wrote home that these public demonstrations were continued, sometimes annoying and sometimes pleasing him. He was never sure whether they were called forth by interest or merely bred of rudeness. Certainly there was no excuse for the preliminary notice in *The Examiner,* a paper that had evidently never heard of that delicacy known to *The Times* as ' courtesy to a foreigner ':

> ' There cannot be a more inoffensive creature. His sole propensity is to gain money by his art, and his passion to lose it at the gambling-table. Paganini's bow is almost as wonderful as his bow—the crawfish would attempt something like it were he on the stage, but not so well '.

This, innocent reader, was considered funny in the England of 1831. The quips of Heine and von Boerne were at least artistic.

While awaiting the date of his first public appearance, Paganini probably filled some of the private engagements we know he had booked, and gave a few well-paid lessons to wealthy amateurs of both sexes. He certainly called upon a number of persons to whom he bore letters of recommendation from friends in France and Italy; and among these visits was one that he paid at the house of Ignaz Moscheles. This renowned pianist's father-in-law, Mr. Emden, had on the Continent once treated Paganini with kindness, and had been the means of securing a lucrative engagement for the violinist. Paganini was always grateful for such signs of interest. Moscheles himself wrote an account of their meeting in London : ' On his first visit to us, his gratitude found vent in such expressions as are known only to an Italian vocabulary . . . and he took down from the mantelpiece a miniature portrait of his benefactor, covered it with kisses, and addressed it with the most high-flown epithets '. It is also a tradition in the family of Messrs. Hart that Paganini often used to drop in at the famous shop in Wardour Street to chat about fiddles with the founder of the firm.

By the time that Paganini first played behind the footlights of the King's Theatre in the Haymarket, he had learned much about the temperament and the psychology of his hosts. He discovered that such a welcome as he had received need not presage continued ill-feeling. To do full justice to our outspoken press, it must be admitted that having gained its point it forgot—as far as concerns the important majority of its organs—all past animosity, and the performance of Paganini was awarded praise as enthusiastic as any he had been given on the Continent. He found out eventually that even if the English liked to have their little joke at a newcomer's expense, they were always ready to pay handsomely for the privilege.

CHAPTER XXI

THE FIRST ENGLISH TOUR
(June, 1831—March, 1832)

WHEN the newspapers spoke of Paganini as 'a mere instrumental performer' at the end of May, they little suspected how completely they would be compelled to change their opinions when they came to report his first London performance of June 3rd. The most elevated planes of musical virtuosity were peopled by the operatic singers with their astonishing *fioriture;* the instrumental soloist still stood far in the rear in the popular mind. When instrumental music generally freed itself from vocal influences in the seventeenth century, a new era opened for the violin, and a succession of great masters brought its technics up to the standard of Paganini's best contemporaries. Then, suddenly, the Genoese appeared and left his fellows far behind him. He came to London, and to the speechless amazement of everyone, substituted his tiny instrument for the voice. What he could do on it, being strange like the Giraffe, could not be believed so easily. The Philharmonic Orchestra under Costa opened the programme with Beethoven's symphony in D, and Lablache followed with the *Largo al Factotum;* only such attractions could have succeeded in keeping the impatience of the audience passably in check until Paganini appeared to play his concerto in D. His performance was succeeded by pandemonium. Although only two of the boxes were occupied, the rest of the house was packed, and the scene that ensued almost defied description. We who have accompanied Paganini through Italy and have heard the applause of Vienna, Berlin, and Paris, can form some idea of the effect he produced in London, where the wildest flights of imagination came nowhere near his realities. His programme, not new to us, naturally exhibited his daring on the G-string, obtaining for him the familiar soubriquet of ' the one-string fiddler ', and he showed his skill in the usual set of bravoura variations. The professionals on the stage made no attempt at criticism; no search was made for faults or weaknesses. Like their colleagues on the platform of the *Redoutensaal* they admitted that here indeed was ' so great a prodigy ' that comparison with him was impossible. John Cramer, with a great sigh of relief, said, ' Thank Heaven, I am not a violin player ', while Mori, during the interval, held his instrument aloft and offered it to the first comer for eighteenpence. The newspaper reports on this first London concert, quite apart from the amazing manner in which they differed in tone from the preliminary journalism, are exceedingly interesting and instructive in other respects, for they show us far more convincingly the trend of thought, the plane of taste, and the social and artistic conditions under which a great performer worked in those days, than could any speculations of a present-day writer. *The Times,* completely converted, led the London press in offering the Italian violinist handsome reparation for past doubts :

' Nothing can be more difficult than to describe Paganini's performance on the violin, so as to make the effect of it intelligible to those who have never heard him. Hence, and it is but justice to say so much of this extraordinary man, all the anticipations formed of him, however highly coloured, have fallen short of the reality. He is not only the finest player perhaps that has ever existed on that instrument, but he forms a class by himself, and produces effects which he has been the first to discover, and in which few, if any, imitators will be able to follow him. The difficulty and complexity of the passages played by Paganini are truly wonderful, and the ease with which he conquers them is perfect. They do not, however, form that which is most to be admired in him. His genius is displayed in a far greater degree in his slow movements, in which he develops, as it may without exaggeration be said, every shade and gradation of feeling. His violin in such passages seems to be a part of himself, and to become that medium in which he can best portray the workings of his mind. If the instrument could be said to speak and to feel, it does so in his hands . . . . The enthusiasm which his performances excited last night among the audience, certainly surpassed anything of the kind within these walls . . . At the end of every performance, and especially after the last, the applause, cheers, and waving of handkerchiefs and hats, altogether presented a most extraordinary scene . . . The grouping on the stage when Paganini played his concluding piece was extremely striking. All the veterans of the orchestra, Spagnoletti, Dragonetti, Lindley, and others, had placed themselves so as to watch his performance to the best advantage, and they marked strongly by their countenances the lively impression it made upon them. They were not the least fervent in their applause of what they of course were the best able to form a judgment '.

A couple of days later *The Times*, feeling it had not done justice to Paganini, asked a well-known amateur, one Mr. Gardner, of Leicester, to favour the public with his impressions; and if we may accept him as representative of the vast crowds that thronged to hear the Italian, his account will be worth our attention :

'At the hazard of my ribs, I placed myself at the Opera two hours and a half before the concert began : presently the crowd of musicians and violinists filled the Colonnade to suffocation . . . . A breathless silence, and every eye was watching the action of this extraordinary violinist; and as he glided from the side-scenes to the front of the stage, an involuntary cheering burst from every part of the house, many rising from their seats to view the spectre during the thunder of this unprecedented cheering—his gaunt and extraordinary appearance being more like that of a devotee about to suffer martyrdom than one to delight you with his art. With the tip of his bow he sent off the orchestra in a grand military movement with a force and vivacity as surprising as it was new. At the termination of this introduction he commenced with a soft streaming note of celestial quality, and with three or four whips of his bow elicited points of sound that mounted to the third heaven and as bright as the stars . . . It was curious to watch the faces of Lindley, Dragonetti, and the other great players, who took up places on the platform to command a good view of him during his performance—they all seem to have agreed that the like had never been heard before, and that in addition to his marvellous eccentricities and novel effects, he had transcended the highest level of legitimate art that had ever been reached . . . . Though he retired amidst a confusion of huzzas and bravos that completely drowned the full orchestra, yet he was called for to receive the homage of the audience; and was so apparently affected, that he would have dropped had he not been supported by Laporte and Costa'.

The last remark is disconcerting; it reminds us of what we saw on the Continent, and speaks volumes on the subject of his health generally and the state of his nervous system. But what is most important from the point of view of the Paganini-apologist is Mr. Gardner's closing remark: 'There was no trick in his playing; it was all fair, scientific execution, opening to us a new order of sounds, the highest of which ascended two octaves above C in alt'. *The Athenaeum* feared that 'the arrival of this magician was enough to make the greater part of the fiddling tribe commit suicide. Never was there a more rapturous reception; it was a most musical house, and enthusiasm was the order of the night'. The writer pleads lack of space and promised a fuller account later on. When it came it confessed that 'we have not the *ingenium par materiae* properly to describe him. He stands alone; and it is quite as desponding a task to explain his peculiarities of superior-ship to other violinists, as it would be to picture the grandeur of the Falls of Niagara to one whose notions of the " thunder of the waters " never extended beyond the tide-fall of the Thames at old London Bridge'. The reporter of this concert was probably the celebrated Henry Chorley and he seems to have penetrated deeper into the soul of Paganini than did most of his colleagues. ' Sorrow is the characteristic of his style and music ', he says, ' and although some French author has said that *La melancholie est toujours friande,* it certainly never was half so delicious as

242

it appears in this strange being's performance. He literally imparts an animal sensibility to his instrument, and at moments makes it wail and moan with all the truth and expression of conscious physical suffering '. But even a Chorley was not free from that low form of humour so prevalent in those days: ' A fanciful writer has observed that the cause of the melancholy that prevails in the Irish melodies is that the harps whence they have had their origin were generally made of Yew-tree; we should like to know of what wood Paganini's violin is composed. A punning friend at our elbow says it must be *Satan*-wood; abominable! ' He makes amends by saying that there is no trickery in Paganini's performance and ' the sooner our violinists learn some of his tricks the better—for then they will play in time and tune, with expression and power '. The closing sentences are characteristic of Chorley's honesty: ' Last year we ventured to back de Beriot against him; we here retract. De Beriot is a sweet, chaste player—but Paganini is a solitary man in his art. There is a relation between an unit and a million—none between him and his fellow men '. Paganini caused a sensation among the musicians at his first concert by playing the whole of his programme ' without a reading-desk ', which gave ' an air of improvising to his performance which we hope to see imitated, if any one be found hardy enough to undertake a violin solo for the next seven years '. Paganini was probably the first virtuoso to play from memory in England. His first performance in London was an occasion when we may safely follow the example of the *Brighton Gazette*: ' We may believe the papers this time; for *they all agree* '.

A few dissentient voices were raised, it is true; but they were mainly those of persons ignorant of the instrument's technics. Sir Thomas Moore said that ' Paganini abuses his powers; he *could* play divinely, and *does* so sometimes for a minute or two; but then come his tricks and surprises, his bow in convulsions, and his enharmonics (*sic*) like the mewlings of an expiring cat ' It was the novelty of his effects and not their inartistic nature that so bewildered the laity, and their verdict fully justifies Goethe's 'We are accustomed to find men sneer at what they do not understand'. George Hogarth, the music critic, disliked Paganini's technical innovations too, but he said that 'it was not by these tricks, but in spite of them, that he gained the suffrages of those who were charmed by his truly great qualities'. *The Harmonicon,* though occasionally forced grudgingly to admit the artist's unusual powers, never quite forgave Paganini for surprising its experts; and whenever an opportunity for poking fun at the Italian presented itself, this paper was sure to seize it. That a musical journal should have been guilty of such a paragraph as the following is difficult for us to understand in these days of more enlightened journalism:

> 'To effect so much on a single string as Signor Paganini does, is truly wonderful; nevertheless any good player can extract much more from two than he produces from one, and two are always to be had. But, say the panegyrists, the silver string gives such delicious tones. Then employ two silver strings, we reply. Would any man out of Bedlam hop from Hyde Park Corner to St. Paul's upon one leg, if he had a couple to walk on? Certainly not—unless, indeed, he could get a thousand pounds, or so, by each journey. If Paganini really produces so much effect on his single string, *a fortiori* he would draw forth much more from two. Why not, therefore, employ them?—Because he is waxing exceedingly wealthy by playing on one only'.

We may wonder, however, whether the writer of this argument —or was it meant to be a joke?—had read Saphir's 'Paganini, Two Thalers and I'.

Paganini's playing had the same effect upon Leigh Hunt, who was present on June 3rd, as it had upon the poets of his native land, of Germany and of Austria. The Englishman felt inspired and impelled to add his metrical homage in a long composition of which the following is a sample:

> 'So played of late to every passing thought
> With finest change (might I but half as well
> So write!) the pale magician of the bow,
> Who brought from Italy the tales made true

Of Grecian lyres, and on his sphery hand,
Loading the air with dumb expectancy,
Suspended, ere it fell, a nation's breath.
He smote; and clinging to the serious chords
With godlike ravishment, drew forth a breath
So deep, so strong, so fervid, thick with love—
Blissful, yet laden as with twenty prayers,
That Juno yearned with no diviner soul,
To the first burthen of the lips of Jove.
Th' exceeding mystery of the loveliness
Sadden'd delight; and with his mournful look—
Dreary and gaunt, hanging his pallid face
'Twixt his dark flowing locks, he almost seemed
Too feeble, or, to melancholy eyes,
One that has parted with his soul for pride,
And in the sable secret lived forlorn '.

. . . .

On June 10th Paganini gave his second concert in London,
and so powerful was the influence of the press, that, as *The
Times* says, 'the house was completely filled in every part',
the artist's profits being in the neighbourhood of twelve hundred
pounds.   Signor and Madame Rubini, besides Curioni and
Santini, provided the vocal relief in the programme which
included the *Campanella* rondo with the bell-accompaniment
played by the celebrated bass, Lablache.   *The Examiner,* in
its notice, finds one or two new words to say in perfectly sane
criticism : 'Wonderful alike in the strongest bursts of power,
and in the softest and sweetest touches, air-drawn and evanescent
as the voices of distant birds'; and provides us with a perfect
answer to those whose envy or ignorance caused them to
designate Paganini as a charlatan : 'The triumph of mechanical
skill, astonishing as it is in itself, is the smallest part of the
wonder.   The real magic is not the novelty of the feat, but the
surprising beauty of the effect. . . . None of the phenomena of
his execution appears to be exhibited for the sake of their own
display : they appear as means, not ends. . . It is this transcendent beauty and effect, that hushes his crowded audiences into
an attention more profound than we ever witnessed in this

usually gossiping theatre. The stillness was so deep, on the night of his concert, that a single piece of wax, dropping from the side of a candle on the stage, had an effect absolutely startling'. *The Examiner's* man describes Paganini as having ' a narrow and pale face, bearing traces of long and habitual ill-health; a figure that would be uncouth if copied : manners that would be grotesque if imitated—but both agreeable, and even graceful, from their natural and unaffected simplicity'. His third concert followed three days later and brought him in a further thousand pounds.

By the middle of June Paganini dominated London as he had done several continental cities during the past two years. Even the Italian Opera receded into the shade cast by his brilliance, and the great operatic stars seemed to twinkle a little less brightly. *The Athenaeum,* under the heading ' King's Theatre ', can only report : ' We have nothing particularly new to say of this establishment. Pasta and Taglioni sing and dance as charmingly as ever : but the Opera seems to be a little in eclipse since the arrival of the wonderful Paganini. Even on Opera nights there is a constant buzzing of his name throughout the house; really the town is in a state of monomania—*nothing but Paganini* is heard on any hand '. His fourth concert, given on the sixteenth, left the press with hardly anything fresh to say. Like their continental colleagues, the critics had exhausted their resources. But the crowd applauded as usual and another nine hundred pounds went into the fiddler's bank. *The Athenaeum* said ' we thought we had exhausted our vocabulary in our last, in the praise of the Signor, but alas! Language " toils after him in vain." *The New Monthly Magazine* wrote : ' Our pen seems involuntarily to evade the difficult task of giving utterance to sensations which are beyond the reach of language. . . . If we were to declare, as some of our colleagues have maintained, that Paganini has advanced a century beyond the present standard of virtuosity, the assertion would be incorrect—for we firmly believe that all the centuries in the womb of time will not produce a master-spirit, a musical phenomenon, organized like

Paganini '. The first century since that date has produced perhaps greater musicians and possibly equally great technicians; but no one has yet appeared who has combined in himself the attributes of musicianship and technicality with a personality such as was Paganini's. His great secret lay in the identification of himself with the music he was playing, or, as *The Literary Gazette* puts it : ' Paganini's playing partakes of that rare quality of oratory which communicates itself from the speaker to the hearer with greater intensity in proportion as the former is deeply impressed with his own matter. His whole being seems to be in the tones he is producing—the man and the instrument cannot be separated '.

On the day following this concert *The Times* printed a letter from ' an amateur ' who regretted his inability to hear Paganini at the theatre; and he, being sure that there must be many like himself, whose moral principles did not permit them to enter a theatre, asked whether it could not be made possible for Paganini to play at one of the concert-halls. He received a reply in the next issue that showed once more how ready Paganini was, contrary to the general belief, to help the deserving poor :

' Paganini '.

' Sir,—I am happy to inform your correspondent that he will at an early period, have an opportunity of gratifying his wishes, by witnessing a performance of the above distinguished musician at the Hanover-Square Rooms, where he has undertaken, in the kindest manner, to afford his valuable and gratuitous assistance at a concert in aid of the funds of a most useful and benevolent institution—the Adult Orphan Institution. . . .'

At this date Chorley gives us a further note on the violinist's personal appearance : ' In conclusion I must observe that not one of the numerous portraits of Paganini bears any real resemblance to him. His features are delicate and intellectual, whilst their meditative expression, the peculiar tone of his voice, the airy lightness of his small and slender figure, and his dark flowing hair, impart to his whole appearance that air which stamps him as a son of genius '.

On Friday, June 17th, he was engaged to play before the King and Queen at the latter's weekly concert. A story that found its way into a German work of reference runs to the effect that William IV sent to enquire Paganini's fee for performing at Court. The violinist is supposed to have been in a generous mood and asked no more than a hundred pounds. The royal messenger thereupon offered half the amount. Paganini's reply is said to have been, ' His Majesty can hear me at terms more advantageous to himself by attending one of my concerts '. Though the anecdote is neither verified nor denied by any other reference, it seems pretty well established that he charmed a diamond ring out of the not too generous king. Greville in his *Journal* gives us some idea of such a court-concert when he enters a fortnight earlier : ' We dined at the castle. . . . Directly after coffee the band began to play; a good band, not numerous, and principally of violins and (other) stringed instruments. The Queen and the whole party sat there all the evening, so that it was, in fact, a concert of instrumental music '. Such a performance, with the addition of Paganini's solos, would represent the concert of June 17th.

From now onwards the papers seized upon any pretext for printing the most improbable stories. Thus *The Globe* : ' There is a rumour afloat about the Opera-house, that Paganini has already lost his heart, and offered his hand to the lady who stole it. The lady is said to be a pupil of Signor de Begnis, and in her sixteenth year '. Knowing Paganini rather well we may be justified in believing the rumour; but we hear no more about it. A Brighton correspondent, writing to the *Courier,* gives the sensational information that ' Signor Paganini has refused an offer of a thousand guineas from the managers of the Liverpool theatre for six nights '. This is possible, for he did not play in Liverpool until the January of the following year. According to the same Brighton source he ' demanded ten thousand pounds to play fifteen nights at the Vauxhall Gardens, during the last season'. This is much more difficult to believe since there is no record of his having played at those once fashionable pleasure gardens, except for charity. The ancient glories of Vauxhall had departed, and it was very unlikely that the management could afford so expensive a luxury as Paganini, in spite of the assurance of the writer that 'this is strictly true, and that an intimate friend of M. Laporte was, in both instances, the medium of communication with Paganini'. The well-informed correspondent of the *Courier* adds, 'it is understood that Paganini intends to purchase a title when he thinks he is rich enough to afford the price of it'. Does this mean an English title? And did Paganini keep his Westphalian barony a secret from his English public? We do not know more than that none of the English papers of this year mentions his foreign peerage. Had the London press known of the latter, *The Harmonicon* would surely have poked fun at it. As it is, that paper pounced upon the *Courier's* gossip with avidity and suggested that the violinist's future title should be the *Marchese di Cremona*, or 'that he be created the *Duca d'Inghilterra-Stolta*'—the latter a cruel thrust. While dealing with flippant matters it may be amusing to read an anecdote from the *New Monthly Magazine*:

'Paganini is indeed a wonderful man: he has performed a feat which no other man in the world could have accomplished—he has put Brougham down. At a dinner in the Mansion House, the health of the Lord Chancellor having been given, he rose to return thanks:—" Feelings overpower me—proudest moment of my life, and " . . . were on his lips. Paganini, entering the room at the instant, naturally supposed that such applause could not be meant for anyone on earth but himself, and to show instantly how well he deserved it, got upon a chair and commenced his performance. Lord Brougham sat down. It is reported that there were persons so tasteless as to call for the speech in preference to the fiddle. As the scene was a City feast, it is not incredible '.

According to Escudier, Paganini played before a brilliant

gathering of men and women of wit, fashion and learning in the salon of Lord Holland on June 21st. For two hours the famous violinist had kept the enthusiasm of his audience at fever heat when his lordship sprang a dramatic surprise upon his distinguished guests. An eye-witness vouches for the truth of what followed : ' On a signal from Lord Holland, all the candles which illuminated the salon were extinguished simultaneously. In the darkness a woman rose and, in a slow and dramatic manner, improvised one of those sombre legends—weird and terrible—in which the fantastic and the supernatural were the principal ingredients. It was Ann Radcliffe, the most popular of the English writers of romances, the authoress of *The Mysteries of Udolpho,* that tale of spectres and phantoms which made our flesh creep during the long winter nights. . . . To this mournful subject Paganini improvised a running commentary of appropriate music, always fitting the different situations perfectly '. So terrible was the combination of story, accompaniment and darkness—not to mention Paganini's satanic reputation—that the ladies began to faint on all sides. His lordship's little joke had been eminently successful. Unfortunately for this entrancing history of musically-accompanied spooks, Ann Radcliffe died in 1823, and the only suggestion that can make it plausible is that someone else recited a story of that writer.

At Paganini's fifth concert on June 22nd he reached his greatest popularity. The house was packed from wall to wall and his takings exceeded £1,460. *The Athenaeum* said that ' as it was understood to be his last concert, the rush was tremendous—we scarcely remember to have seen so full a house. The consequence is that another concert has been announced for next Monday, when we have no doubt a like assembly will be collected. It is waste of pen and ink to attempt to describe the effects which he produces '. *The Harmonicon* was forced to admit that the audience was ' more enthusiastic than ever ' and that the ' stalls, orchestra and pit were crowded to excess '; while *The Examiner* added that ' It would have required an hydraulic press to squeeze another into the pit '. The last-

named newspaper then drops into poesy, one stanza of which
will serve as a sample of its style:

> ' Of all the beasts which Nature made,
>   With just no other view
> Than to surprise our mortal eyes,
>   And show what she could do;
> Of monsters in the air or deep,
>   Four-footed, furr'd, or finny,
> There's none to be compared at all
>   To Signor Paganini '.

From *The Harmonicon* we learn that the violinist was now ' in
a deplorable state of health, which indeed his looks betray. He
is however under good English medical care '. In spite of his
ill-health he does not seem to have had to cancel any of his
engagements during this visit to England; and though the fifth
concert was supposed to have been the last, he had actually
hardly commenced his work north of the Channel.

On June 23rd *The Times* advertised Lablache's ' benefit
concert ' and announced that Paganini would play. *The
Athenaeum* however adds that ' the lion of the day seems
determined to have the lion's share!—the Signor stipulated for
and received *one third* of the gross receipts at Lablache's
benefit '. This appears to have struck the English press as a
damning proof of Paganini's meanness and avarice. It can
hardly be looked upon in this light, for the object was not
charity, and Lablache was far from being a poor man. In
any case Paganini was a greater draw than Lablache himself.
The objection was not that Lablache was too poor, but rather
that Paganini was too rich. The outcome was that the bass
and Rubini determined not to sing at Paganini's concerts any
more—or Paganini refused to engage them again. At the same
time the violinist seems to have played gratuitously at de Begnis's
' benefit ', *The Athenaeum* saying that ' the chief attraction was
Paganini, who, though he exhibited in one short piece, seemed
equally to delight and astonish the company '. Paganini's sixth
concert took place on the 27th—positively his ' last appearance '

—and on the 30th he appeared for the seventh time—for a ' last ' performance. On this occasion *The Examiner* said : ' His taste is excellent, and his perfection is in his expression . . . Paganini bends in acknowledgement to the band as well as to the audience. We like this : all great artists should claim respect for their arts by honouring their brethren in them '. On July 4th he gave his eighth and ' last ' concert. About a week later he appeared at another benefit concert—Signor Torri's—and was advertised to accompany a recitative and aria of La Pasta's with a violin obbligato.

At the middle of July Paganini conceived the original idea of taking his violin to the east of London, and on the 13th gave a successful concert in the assembly-room of the ' London Tavern '. Three days later he gave another there, and wishing to reduce his expenses, omitted to engage an orchestra. *The Harmonicon,* delighted at an opportunity to practise its sarcasm and stress the violinist's avarice, relieved its patriotic feelings in this strain :

' Paganini was too liberal-minded, too generous to labour only for the delight of the west end of the town ; he took compassion on those east of Temple Bar, nay, east of the Royal Exchange, and gave a concert at the London Tavern. It was fully attended ; but a second attempt at the same place, on the 16th, failed ; and no wonder, for the Signor tried an experiment on the forbearance of the citizens, and actually took only a pianist and one or two second-rate singers with him to make up a half-guinea concert. This was too much even for John Bull—the most indulgent of all creatures to anything foreign—to submit to ; and the miracles on one string will not, we suspect, be exhibited before the wise men of the East, who certainly are not so easily imposed on as those of the opposite quarter '.

Between these two dates he gave his ninth and ' last farewell ' concert at the King's Theatre, still drawing five hundred pounds, though the ' best people ' were already out of town. He thereupon followed some of them to Cheltenham, where he met with an unpleasant reverse.

The success of the two concerts he had arranged to give at this fashionable spa was so great that, as usual, he thought he might squeeze in a third performance on July 21st. The grotesque events that followed are perhaps best related as they were told contemporaneously to the readers of the *Lady's Magazine* :

> ' The house was crammed, when the audience was informed that Paganini had suddenly refused to play unless £200 was paid to him before he left the room where he then was. A ball had been advertised for the same evening; and it appears that Paganini was apprehensive that his concert would be damaged by it, and was desirous of getting rid of the engagement by imposing new terms. The audience rose and to a man demanded their money back; hundreds rushed to the place where Paganini was, and a riot commenced amongst the crowd. A magistrate was soon on the spot, and had great difficulty in restraining them. Paganini at first was declared unwell, but this produced no effect; and finding himself surrounded, he made various proposals to play on profitable terms, which were all rejected. The magistrate employed himself as negotiator, and after protracted discussions, the violinist yielded to the terms exacted by the people as a reparation for the insult and breach of faith of which they considered he had been guilty : they were, that he should perform gratis!—that the prices should be reduced one half; that £25 should be given to the manager of the theatre; and that, after the expenses of the theatre had been paid, the residue should be given to some charitable institution. It was ten o'clock before he came to the theatre, which was crowded by persons whose indignation had not yet subsided and who were determined to exhibit it. But how the superiority of his art was strikingly manifested : he elicited a plaintive air from his instrument, when the rage of the audience was subdued, and nothing was to be heard during the remainder of the night but rapturous applause. The power of Orpheus has been equalled! '

The Harmonicon gave a version of the cause of the trouble differing materially from the one just quoted :

> ' Paganini, in advertising his concerts had stated " that his numerous engagements would render it impossible for him to remain beyond that time"; yet having undertaken to play at the theatre last night, he was accordingly announced. This the residents and visitors of the place considered an act of un-

253

fairness towards the regular subscription balls of the Rotunda, especially as Mr. Jearrad, the proprietor, had relinquished his usual musical entertainment on the previous evening in order that Paganini's talents might have full scope. Immediately the Signor's intention was, therefore, made known, Captain Berkeley and W. L. Lawrance, Esq., took upon themselves to print a handbill calling upon the nobility and gentry to support the established amusements of the town by patronizing the ball last night, considering it merely as an act of justice to the proprietor. The effect of this was to secure a thronged attendance at the Rotunda ball, and so poor an assemblage at the theatre that Paganini refused to perform. . . . '

The Harmonicon concluded later with the joyous remark that ' Paganini actually had to play for nothing as the takings hardly covered the expenses ', and clapped its hands with glee. The reader is at liberty to select whichever version of the affair he pleases—or neither; for this class of journalism was in those days so much a matter of passing a story from hand to hand or from one gossiping correspondent to another, that absolute trust cannot be placed in such reports farther than what concerns the actual results visible to the eye-witness. *The Athenaeum* account of the scandalous exhibition of mob-law in Cheltenham seems to have been prepared from a hash of the two reports given above. *The Cheltenham Journal* which, being on the spot, ought to have had the facts of the case, tells quite a different story : Paganini did not go to the theatre because the manager had not yet brought him the signed contract; the people were incensed because they had been told that Paganini had received £100 on account and had refused to appear until the balance had been paid, which was untrue; the people were foolish and unjust, but when he agreed to play their attitude changed and they became a very friendly audience.

The only piece of information that need interest us at the moment is that Paganini ' left the Plough Hotel at midnight in a chaise and four for London ', as he had to appear in the capital for his tenth and ' last concert '. This spirited dash across England enriched him to the extent of £395. Three days later

—on July 25th—he performed again at the King's Theatre for the eleventh 'and last time', justifying the newspapers' uncharitable remark that 'so long as there was any money to be obtained from the English public, Paganini would go on giving concerts' to wring it out of them. By this time his spoils had dwindled to £343—still a respectable sum for an evening's work, though not to be compared with the princely profits from his first half-dozen performances.

His experiences at Cheltenham and his manner of leaving that town must have come as a shock to his self-esteem; and what he privately thought about the English interpretation of the doctrine of 'courtesy to a foreigner' would probably not have been printed—even in *The Harmonicon*. On his journey back to London through that summer night he must have contrasted his exit with the tumultuous scenes of enthusiasm which often accompanied his return from a concert on the Continent, when he was escorted to his hotel by cheering crowds of admirers. Well; it was all part of an artist's life—especially if the artist occasionally loved money better than he respected his status and his vocation. After eleven concerts in the metropolis he found his audiences and the press tiring of his repeated 'last farewells', and he decided to give them a little rest. During the last week in July and the beginning of August, therefore, we find him in Norwich.

Here again, proposing a third concert after having given two highly successful performances, he provoked a newspaper discussion that shows us once more what a cantankerous set of squabblers our ancestors must have been. No apology will be called for if *The Harmonicon* is again drawn upon for the evidence, because no one could help us to visualise the temper of the times—not to speak of the many little customs that were observed in the profession of public entertainment—so well as the contemporary journalist:

'Signor Paganini has performed at Norwich, where he was engaged during the Assize week by Mr. Pettet. A gentlemanly, but pretty smart attack was made on the latter in the *Norwich Mercury* . . . for having fixed the price of admission so high —15*s.*—and also for giving a *third* performance, two only having been announced, in consequence whereof, the manager of the Norwich theatre sustained a serious loss, " who could not but perceive how injurious these concerts must be to his receipts, and especially as one of them was fixed for the night on which the play had been bespoken for many years past . . . Mr. Smith, the manager, waited on the Mayor, and enquired whether his worship had given permission for more than two performances. . . . The worthy Chief Magistrate gave him his most positive assurance that no third performance had been notified or should take place. The power of the magistrate was however set at defiance, and when the question was discussed at the Court of Mayoralty, the law officers not being prepared to give an opinion as to the power to enforce what has hitherto been considered an undisputed right, the concert went on without interruption." We cannot say that we regret this latter circumstance, as it may put a stop to what we have always considered an unjust exercise of power. . . ."

The verdict of the local press was that Mr. Pettet lost some of his profits as the third concert was Paganini's and not his, and that the fiddler took over eight hundred pounds away with him. Being a local man the agent was much pitied and the editor of the Norwich paper had some scathing things to say about rapacious foreigners in general and Paganini in particular— whereat *The Harmonicon* once more clapped its hands. Fortunately the Rev. John Edmund Cox in his *Musical Recollections* gives us a more pleasant picture of Paganini in Norwich:

' As I had the good fortune then to be able to converse in French, the friends who had engaged Paganini for a round of concerts in Norwich and its vicinity placed me in direct communication with him somewhat in the capacity of a secretary; so that I not only travelled in his company and heard him play at every concert at which he appeared, but I lived in the same hotels and lodgings which had been secured for him. This kind of semi-official position necessitated my seeing much of him during his leisure hours, when he threw off the suspicious restraint which was always apparent in his manner when he was amongst

PAGANINI

Drawn by D. Maclise at the King's Theatre in the Haymarket. The background shows portraits of Lindley, Dragonetti, and others.

strangers, who he imagined were bent on getting as much as possible out of him for their own advantage. Then, indeed, he would evince anything but a hard and ungenerous nature, his manner being not only kind but courteous, whilst any attention that was afforded to his wants or to his comforts was sure to elicit not only looks but words of gratitude '.

Such testimony to his character has a distinct value and should not be dismissed too lightly. It has often been said that he played very rarely off the concert-platform and no one ever heard him practise. Mr. Cox was more fortunate:

' In public he confined himself almost exclusively to the performance of his own music. . . . But in private—*for he had his violin constantly in his hand*—he would sit down and dash off by the hour together snatches from the compositions of the best masters and give readings of such originality to passages that had been heard again and again, as apparently they have never been supposed to possess by any other player. As an instance of this he, one morning whilst I was writing several notes for him, commenced the first motivo of Beethoven's magnificent violin concerto. To write was then impossible, and he, perceiving how entranced I seemed, asked whether I knew what it was. On my replying in the negative, he promised, if it could be managed, that I should hear the whole of that movement before we separated. He then went off at a tangent and I resumed my writing, speedily forgetting all about the promise he had given. On the last night, however, several persons came to take their leave of him; and one gentleman, whom I never saw before or since, and whose name I never could learn, on a signal from the ' master ' sat down at the pianoforte and drawing a piece of crumpled music from the inner pocket of a long black dress-coat . . . began to play. Instantly I was on the alert, for I remembered the notes, and his promise rushed back upon me. Never shall I forget the smile on that sad, wan and haggard face, upon every lineament of which intense pain was written in the deepest lines, when I caught his eye—or the playing into which a spirit and a sympathy were thrown that carried one wholly away '.

The next morning Paganini rose early, long before the time arranged for his departure, entered his post-chaise which stood already packed, and with his valet left Norwich before any of his friends were aware of his intention. Canon Cox firmly believed that this was done to avoid painful leave-takings, and the reverend gentleman was left with a lively sense of pleasure at having known a man who was generous and human, though inordinately ' fond of gold '.

On August 5th Paganini was back in London playing again in the King's Theatre; and so little did he feel the taunts of the press on account of his numerous ' last ' concerts, that he gave another—the thirteenth in London—on August 11th. On the last occasion *The Athenaeum* was still enraptured :

> ' The excitement which Paganini's performances first raised seems in no degree to subside. His concert on Thursday was as well attended as any former one has been. To give any detailed account . . . would be only to repeat that which we have stated over and over again ; we can therefore only say that, as usual, it was perfect and inimitable. With regard to the pieces he played . . . each was so exquisitely, so truly given, as to convince the most sceptical, that distinct ideas may be conveyed to the human mind by the perfection of instrumental performance, and that Paganini possesses this power to a degree which leaves him a solitary man in his art, and places him upon an eminence so difficult of attainment, that we fear it will not again be reached. He will give two more concerts next week, and then positively proceed to Dublin '.

These two appearances—the fourteenth and fifteenth—took place on August 17th and 20th; and though they delighted the music-lovers they disgusted some of the newspapers who probably felt that from a journalistic point of view Paganini had already gone far beyond his nine days of wonder. *The Examiner* was rather sarcastic and asked plaintively, ' Why inflict on us the pain of perpetual leave-takings ? ' Let Paganini play as often as he will—but when he has said farewell, let him depart. And with the same censure the press castigated Taglioni, Potier and others. A few of the papers were cruel enough to suggest what the public had long known—that the word ' farewell ' on the posters was added to increase the takings.

The theory was hardly proved just in Paganini's case, for his last two appearances in London enriched him to the extent of 'only' £409. It is of interest to note that his income from the fifteen London concerts alone, amounted to more than £10,200.

Why Paganini left London just before the Coronation, it is difficult to say; and the only hypothesis that can be advanced is that he signed a contract to appear at the Dublin Festival of August 30—September 3, without thinking of the influx of visitors that the ceremony would attract to the capital. As events proved, he missed very little. The coronation, on account of the modest sum voted for the festivities, was dubbed the 'Half-Crownation' by the wits; and the affair went off with comparatively little brilliance. The £50,000 voted by the House of Commons did not go very far. There was no banquet in Westminster Hall and no King's Champion. A cartoon illustrated the court's economies: the King and Queen proceeding to the Abbey in a hackney coach followed by an omnibus loaded with the King's family by Mrs. Jordan. Neither the Duchess of Kent nor Princess Victoria attended. The atmosphere in London being one of amusement when it was not one of derision, Paganini was better out of it. The Dublin Festival occupied three nights and was voted a complete artistic success. *The Harmonicon*, of course—ignoring the fees paid to Henry Phillips and John Braham—had its usual 'Britain for the British' slogan to air and its customary story of Paganini's rapacity to print: 'The Signor . . . is to have *only* 500 (Guineas), a sum that would rescue at least eighty Irish families from the miseries of hunger during the whole of the ensuing winter. And, let it be borne in mind, not a tenth part of this sum will be spent either in Ireland or England'. It was Paganini's fault that the Irish were hungry, so why should Sir George Smart or the orchestra or the singers forego their fees in order to feed them? Let the unique art of a distinguished foreigner pay the penalty of misgovernment, mismanagement and social unrest. And *The Harmonicon* was a journal devoted to the service of art: a commodity that was supposed to know no frontiers. La

Pasta bought a villa on the Lake of Como with English money, but that escaped the notice of *The Harmonicon*. It is interesting to see William Vincent Wallace among the violinists active at the festival, and to note that Paganini wrote his variations on *St. Patrick's Day* for his Irish tour—one of the trumpet parts bearing the date ' Dublin, September 17, 1831 ' in the handwriting of the performer of the part.

Paganini's opening piece was preceded by a little incident that might have led to unpleasantness had Smart not smoothed things out. It was characteristic of Nicolo to pause for a few moments before commencing to play—settling his instrument comfortably and poising his bow above the strings to collect himself before beginning. These preliminaries tried the patience of the Irish spirits in the gallery, and in the dead silence of expectation the crowded house heard a resonant voice calling down, ' Well, we're all ready '. The audience laughed and Paganini frowned; then, turning to Sir George he asked angrily, ' Que 'est—ce que c'est? ' Not understanding the conductor's explanation he wheeled about and left the platform. It was some little time before he was pacified; but when he did play the customary Orphean result followed. They could applaud in Dublin as enthusiastically as in Vienna, and Paganini once more sunned himself in glory. Before leaving the capital for a tour of twenty-three concerts in Ireland, he received—according to Regli—a piece of jewellery from the Viceroy. He is difficult to follow in Ireland, but we know that he played in Cork on October 1st, and in Limerick a few days later.

Paganini's departure from Dublin was reported in the *Dublin Morning Post,* and the account being characteristic of the odious journalism then fashionable, provides instructive reading:

> ' At one o'clock September 19, the splendid equipage of the modern Orpheus drew up before his lodgings . . . to convey the Signor from the metropolis on his tour through the south of Ireland. Notwithstanding the tremendous torrent of rain which fell at that period, not less, perhaps, than 700 wretched paupers

were found hardy enough to brave the deluge in their anxiety to attend the exit of the star of the Musical Festival, for the benefit of " Charity ". All was silence, patience and good order till his *Excellency* had taken his solitary seat, *closely* muffled up in the vehicle, and the postillion smacked his whip, when a number of the poor unfortunates of the order *mendicant* drew up in battalion before the heads of the leaders and, presenting a bold front, effectually served for a time to check their progress southward. A *bow* hand from inside the carriage waved gracefully to those on " preventive service " as if in acknowledgment of a compliment. But we were sorry to see that the right hand of Paganini seemed to the poor Dublin folk to have lost all its virtue . . . and while the equipage thus remained *in statu quo,* one of them, acting as spokesman, addressed his Italianship, observing. " Ah, then, be my sowl, Mr. Palaga-nini, sure it is not yourself that would be after going away wid your fiddle, wid the curse of the town upon you, widout leaving de poor e'er a halfpenny at all at all, after the fine harvest you reaped among us ". This hint, and a few others still more broad, unloosed the magic strings, not of the Signor's violin, but of his purse ; and having " grinned a ghastly smile " and flinging a couple of sovereigns into the midst of the eager expectants on his charity, he made his escape amid the confusion of the scramble occasioned by his munificent donation to the poor of Dublin '.

The exact date of his return to England is not known, and though his activities in Ireland were followed by a series of fifty concerts in this country and Scotland, only a few of his appearances seem to have been recorded. But ' happy is the land that has no history ' ; when the papers said nothing it was because they had nothing sensational to say. All the world knew that Paganini could play as no one else. During October he was ' received with vast applause ' in the large Assembly Room in Edinburgh, and ' the critics of the modern Athens vied with each other in the warmth of their praise '. Not until he reached Brighton for his concert of December 7th was there any undue excitement; but once arrived in that Hanoverian suburb of London, a situation arose after *The Harmonicon's* own heart.

In the days of William IV it did not take more than six hours for news to travel from London to Brighton, and an artist who could draw so many large audiences to the King's Theatre would be awaited impatiently by the fashionable court-followers of the Sussex resort. A well-known local manager—one Mr. Gutteridge—wisely engaged Paganini for one concert, foolishly agreeing to the violinist's terms of £200—wisely because six hours after his first London appearance Paganini was sure of a triumph at Brighton, foolishly because he knew that the Theatre Royal there could only hold from £100 to £110 when every seat was occupied at the 'usual dramatic prices'. The number of applications for tickets, as soon as the 'nobility and gentry' were informed of Paganini's coming, convinced Mr. Gutteridge that the Old Ship Assembly Rooms would be far too small, and there was nothing left for him to do but hire the theatre at a cost of £40. As the *Brighton Gazette* said, 'Here was at once an expense of £240, to say nothing of Her Majesty's band, the singers, *etc.* . . . It is clear therefore that Mr. Gutteridge had no means of covering his own outlay but by raising the prices. This he accordingly did, making the pit and boxes 10*s*. 6*d*., and the gallery 4*s*'. This occasioned a storm of protest which culminated two days before the date of the concert in an 'insolent placard . . . on the railings of the Steine, of which the following is a copy:

'Public Caution and Notice.

If the gross imposition with which the public are to be gulled next Wednesday keep not people from the Theatre, it is to be hoped their personal safety will.

The theatre in a manner belongs to the public, is a place for their rational entertainment, at a reasonable expense, and not an arena for the avarice of Signor P. or Mr. G.

To the former concerts at the theatre, to that of the Russian Horns (a far greater musical phenomenon) *etc.*, the admission was at playhouse prices.

Let Mr. G. and Signor P. give their concert elsewhere and charge what they will—ay, and let them " Charge home " on the

262

purses of all fools, of which description of persons the musical world in general consists.

The Public are therefore cautioned that this conduct having excited universal indignation, a report has gone abroad that on Wednesday night the Theatre will be Fired, an O.P. row, and general disturbance ensue, and the whole will be a signal for making Brighton a Cheltenham, a Lyons, or Bristol.

Notice . . . . All those who have the sense and spirit to resist this imposition will meet under the Colonnade, Wednesday '.

The *Brighton Gazette* explains in detail all the points of this precious document: ' As to the " avarice " of Signor Paganini or Mr. Gutteridge the former does only what every other man has a right to do—make the most that he can of his talents; while Mr. Gutteridge actually took upon himself a great burden, responsibility and risk in order to oblige that very public which the author of this infamous libel endeavoured to inflame against him '. Messrs. Vining and Bew, the managers of the theatre, were naturally a little concerned for the safety of the building in those days of incendiarism, and the proper steps were consequently taken ' to preserve the public tranquility . . . At six o'clock yesterday evening the people began to collect; and we were glad to see that a considerable number of the police were in attendance to preserve the peace. All went off however quietly, without any attempt at disturbance '. The *Gazette* goes on to give an excellent account of the programme and Paganini's manner of performing it; but we have read such enthusiastic reports before, and there will be no need to reprint this one. A few of the *Gazette's* remarks are nevertheless worth repeating, for they help to strengthen our impressions of his person and the emotional appeal he made : ' He advanced and made his obeisance in his own peculiar and antique style . . . . much has been said of the size of his hand; but it struck us that, however extensive the span may be, that it is rather small than large, though the fingers are long and taper . . . . Then we had the opportunity of judging more fully whether he possessed those great qualities which are essential to form a real musician, or whether he was " the mere quack " which some

263

publications have most unjustly represented him to be. Without fear of contradiction we . . . assert that more real feeling—more pure pathos—was never expressed; and we do not envy those who were unable to sympathize with him in those sadly deep and melancholy passages '. The gathering must have been one of great brilliance, for we are told that ' the King's box was occupied by Lady Broughton and party, and the opposite box by Sir George and Lady Shiffner and party. Among the general company were Lady Gore, Lady Scott and a large party, General Blunden, Lady Blunt, Sir A. Dalrymple, *etc* '. For the first time in Brighton history ' seats were erected on the stage as well as in the orchestra, but still many were turned from the doors '. Indeed, so insistent was the clamour of the disappointed ones that two days later Paganini was compelled to give another recital, this time at the Old Ship Hotel. He charged 10s. for admission and ' no distinction was made for the gallery seats, a thing never before attempted here, even in the halcyon days of Catalani. There were about 260 persons in the room . . . The company was most fashionable . . . If we were pleased or astonished by the performance of Paganini on the Wednesday, we were much more so this evening '. There never were two opinions on the manner in which he could play a slow movement, and the *Gazette's* description resembled all the others : ' Paganini drew forth an exquisite melody, blending sweetness with melancholy. It was like the wailings of a bursting heart, which died away upon the ear in softness and sorrow . . . '

George Augustus Sala tells a pretty story of Paganini's enigmatical nature when he recounts his mother's experiences with the great violinist. Madame Sala was a well-known vocalist then resident in Brighton, and she sang at both of Paganini's concerts there. Left a widow, she could always be certain of exceptional talent at her ' benefit ' concerts, and on one occasion her programme was adorned with the names of Malibran and Paganini. It might have interested *The Harmonicon* to know that although Paganini insisted upon a nominal fee of twenty-five guineas, Malibran was avaricious enough to ask for thirty. In spite of these expenses the concert was a great success, and in the morning following the function Madame Sala, accompanied by little George, went to pay the two artists. In his *Life and Adventures,* Sala says that they called on Malibran first:

> 'The renowned singer smiled, patted me on the head, chucked me under the chin, told me to be a good boy and very calmly took the thirty-one pounds ten shillings which with trembling hands my mother placed on the table. She had a good cry, poor woman, in the fly which conveyed us to the Old Ship, where Paganini was stopping. I can see him now—a lean, wan, gaunt man in black, with bushy hair—something like Henri Rochefort, and a great deal more like Henry Irving. He looked at me very earnestly, and somehow . . . I did not feel afraid of him'.

In a tale he wrote for one of the *Bow Bells Annuals,* Sala says he *was* afraid of the demon fiddler; but the sidelight which the paragraph sheds upon the character of Paganini makes it well worth reading:

> 'Paganini frightened me as usual . . . but much more terrified by him when my mother repaired to his lodgings to pay him five and twenty guineas, his hire . . . Most of the great artists of the day—Pasta, Blasis, Curioni and Braham—commiserating her lone condition, had been only too glad to give her the benefit of their services for nothing; but Paganini was known to be the most avaricious of mankind, and he had gloomily refused, when going into the orchestra to play, to abate one penny of the sum which he had covenanted to receive. "Take your little boy with you, Madame Sala, when you pay Paganini; perhaps *that* will soften him a little", was the shrewd counsel of Sir Charles D——. I was the smallest and the chubbiest of my tribe, and they pilloried me in the largest and most symmetrically frilled collar that an Italian iron could turn out. Then, duly washed, combed and made spruce, my parent took me in her hand and led me to the Old Ship . . . We were ushered . . . into the presence of the mighty musician, who was at breakfast and was gnawing a large and terribly underdone mutton chop . . . Then

my mother, alluding so far as she in delicacy could, to her large family and her small means, proceeded to count out, sovereign by sovereign and shilling by shilling, Paganini's fee . . . I can see, with the eye of memory, the whole man before me now; his gaunt, angular form; his black elf-locks falling in weird confusion over his neck and shoulders; his cadaverous face and shaggy brows; his long, hairy hands with the veins standing out like cordage. I can see the glare—so it seemed to me— which, when he raised his pent-house brows, darted upon the pile of money, and the spasmodic avidity with which he extended his bony digits and swept the pile towards him. It was only five and twenty guineas . . . and I remember that, when he had pocketed the money, he concluded the consumption of his chop, drained a large cupful of black coffee at a draught, and wiped his lips on the table-cloth. " 'E a very nice little boy", he was good enough to say, alluding to myself; " but time is bad and there is no monish in de vorld; no, never no monish at all ". My mother rose with a heavy heart to depart. " Stop, little boy", cried the great violinist while he beckoned to me with a skinny finger which any one of the witches in *Macbeth* would have been proud to own. " Stop, take dis, it vill buy you a cake ". He thrust a crumpled piece of paper into my hand; rose from his chair; and without more ado bolted—that is the only word suited to the action—into his bedroom. He had given me a bank-note for fifty pounds. Superstitious people used to whisper that Paganini had sold himself to the enemy of mankind, spiteful people used to decry him as a greedy and flinty-hearted miser, libellous people used to hint that he had poniarded a man once in Genoa and had narrowly escaped the gibbet. I only know how he acted towards my mother; and the remembrance of that circumstance has always tended to confirm me in the wholesome opinion that there is nothing more unsafe than to trust to appearances '.

Had the distinguished novelist and journalist been able to see into the mind of the violinist, he might have beheld the portrait of another widow—a very old widow in Genoa who could not write.

On December 15th the *Brighton Gazette* said that ' Signor Paganini left on Sunday for Bath, having engaged to perform on the Monday at Bristol, after which he proceeds to fill numerous engagements, including one at Manchester and

Liverpool '—and for once a newspaper prediction concerning Paganini was right. The *Bristol Gazette* for December 8th carries the Theatre Royal advertisement which says: ' The Manager has the honour to announce that he has concluded an engagement with Signor Paganini to perform in two Grand Concerts on Monday, December 12, and Wednesday, December 14'. But here also an attempt was made to interfere with the attendance by some unfortunate out-of-work violinist or a crank with the then fairly common anti-foreign bee in his bonnet; and here again it took the form of a poster:

' *Paganini.*

To the Citizens of Bristol.

' Fellow Citizens,—It is with feelings of unqualified disgust that I witness the announcement of Signor Paganini's Perform- ance to take place in this City. Why at this period of Distress? With the recollection of so many scenes of misery still fresh in our minds and while Subscriptions are required to the extent of our means in order to feed and clothe the poor: Why is this foreign Fiddler now to appear? For the purpose of drawing those resources which would be infinitely better applied in the exercise of the best feeling of man—Charity. Do not suffer yourselves to be imposed upon by the Payment of Charges which are well worthy the name of extortion; rather suffer under the imputations of a want of Taste than support any of the tribe of Foreign Music-Monsters, who collect the Cash of this country and waft it to their own shores, laughing at the infatuation of John Bull.

PHILADELPHUS '.

As events proved, the Bristol music-lovers spent their spare cash on their own pleasures, and as many of them as the theatre would hold went to Paganini's concerts. He produced the usual ' astonishment, wonder and delight ', especially after his G-string work, which was ' loudly encored '. The conscience of the audience seems to have been clear enough; perhaps its mem- bers had already sent their donations to the relief-funds—a contingency which seems never to have occurred to ' Philadelphus'. This plan to ruin Paganini's chances of success having failed, an attempt was made to pin on to the violinist the onus of having again imposed usurious terms. This was countered by the following letter in the *Bristol Gazette* of December 14th:

'Sir,—An erroneous impression has gone abroad as to Signor Paganini's engagement with the manager of the Bath and Bristol Theatres. The fact is, the Agent of the Manager wrote to the Signor and *offered three-fourths* of the nightly receipts if he would come to Bath and Bristol. Signor Paganini *accepted the offer*. The augmented prices were also proposed by the Manager's Agent . . . .

FAIR PLAY'.

What he did during the second half of December we have no idea, and we lose sight of him until his appearance in Liverpool is recorded early in January, 1832. Our source of information is an anonymous biography published at Liverpool later in the same year: 'The spirited managers of our Theatre Royal having . . . engaged Paganini, that celebrated artist made his appearance for the first time before a Liverpool audience on Monday, January 9th, and his performance having exceeded the utmost expectation even of his friends, the lessees were induced to re-engage him for three additional nights, commencing on Monday, 23rd'. All four concerts created the same furore as we witnessed in Munich or Stuttgart, and although the price of admission was higher than that of any other city except London, they were 'attended by all the beauty and fashion, not only of the town but of the neighbourhood. Williamson Square was nightly crowded with equipages; and all who went to hear him returned enraptured'.

After his first concert in Liverpool he went to fill engagements in Manchester, writing on January 15th an interesting letter from this city to Germi, giving his friend an account of his doings during the past few months—useful information where his memory did not play him false. In addition it gives us an excellent idea of how he travelled:

> ' The devilish enthusiasm which my instrument has produced in the concerts I have given, has determined me to give six more next week. I shall then make a tour through some other towns, and return to London by February 20 next, on my way to Paris, to embrace my dear Achillino, who is doing well, and is in excellent hands. When once I get hold of him again I shall not part with him, for he is my greatest joy.
>
> On leaving London for Ireland, what a lot of concerts I gave!—commencing with the festival at Dublin and then in other cities in Ireland, Scotland and here in England. Sixty-five concerts commencing on August 30, 1831, and ending on January 14, 1832! Remember, I was ill for six weeks, and gave no concerts—so that the sixty-five concerts I gave in the space of three months, passing through thirty cities, accompanied by four people on horseback and the singer Signora Pietralia. I have with me a certain Cianchettini who plays the cymbals, a secretary, a very prepossessing young Englishman, who travels before me to arrange for my concerts; also a stupid fellow who acts as porter, and a good domestic. I hired a splendid carriage in London . . . If I had come to London twelve years ago, I could easily have made a fortune; but now one does not, owing to the poverty which everyone experiences . . . . To-morrow I go to Leeds, and shall give a concert on Tuesday evening; on Friday and Saturday I shall give further concerts at Manchester; Monday, and the 23rd, 24th, 25th, at Birmingham; 30th, a concert at Chester, and then in three or four more cities where there are musical students '.

It was at about this period that he learned of his mother's passing. Who can say what effect this news had upon a man of Paganini's temperament, a man who had loved her with a devotion and a constancy that he exhibited to no one else in the world. ' I have poured forth bitter tears for the beloved mother lost to us ', he writes to his sisters—' and I am still weeping '. He consoles them with the pious hope that her ' prayers to the Saviour ' will bring about their reunion in the hereafter. It will be well to remember these sentiments when, eight years later, the orthodoxy of his Christianity was called into question.

Generously he instructs his sisters to continue drawing the pension he had allowed his mother, and promises to further the interests of his nephew.

But Paganini had booked many engagements and he was not permitted to break them for the purpose of mourning his dead. As his letter indicated, he was soon in Leeds, where he was so successful that a large sum was given to charity from the takings. The auditorium was filled seven hours before the commencement of the concert, and Paganini's profits on that occasion were probably greater than at any other single recital. He then returned to Liverpool, gave his remaining three concerts there, and probably proceeded thence to Birmingham. Here his advent drew such crowds into the city from the surrounding districts, that all the hotels and inns could not house the amateurs who arrived, nor was there stabling sufficient for their horses. This was early in February. By the fifth of March he was playing in Winchester, after having performed at several other places on his journey south, and on the sixth he was in Southampton. Two days later he left England for Paris, having been in these islands for very little under ten months and having given—as far as they can be traced with certainty—about one hundred and forty public concerts.

CHAPTER XXII

(March 9th, 1832—Feb., 1834)

THE restless spirit of Nicolo Paganini allowed no response to the body that housed it. His stay in the British Isles had been as well filled with lucrative engagements as any artist could wish. Yet on the very evening of his arrival at Le Havre he gave a concert there. 'At last I shall hear a little music', he is reported to have said on landing; but whether this was intended as a compliment to French art or a reference to his own recital of the same day, is not clear. That he had no special reasons for praising the English orchestras of that day as he had done the French, already emerges from the criticism to which our bands were subjected by the native press. One passage from *The Athenaeum* will suffice to show their shortcomings :

'The trio is still a vulgar exhibition of mistaken feeling and acting . . . Is there no " gran-maestro " to correct these violations of taste and feeling? . . . We were amused with a triple authority of beating time. The prompter with a small crayon, with evidently an entire control over the choristers, the gran-maestro, Signor Costa, with arm uplifted urging the singers to sing faster than necessary, and lastly the leader with his long bow moving in the air like the telegraph at the Admiralty. We notice all this particularly to bear us out in the truth of the observations of our notice on the opening of the theatre. Here are three persons assuming the same authority : in the midst of all this distraction Dragonetti comes in for a fourth and, with one of his powerful sforzandos cements the whole tottering fabric. Let Mons. Habeneck or Valentino from the Académie de Musique, or Mr. Guhr from Frankfort be engaged for one little month to give us an idea of a " conductor's " duties, and the band would be fifty years advanced in discipline'.

271

Such an accompanying instrument would possibly have been the reason for Paganini's remark.

He reached Paris at a terrible time. The cholera was raging; strong men fled to the country in horror; the less robust were dying on every side. This puzzling man who, with his intestinal complaints and other troubles, should have been especially careful to avoid infection, stayed in the capital and calmly made arrangements for a series of ten concerts. Commencing on March 25th with a recital at the *Italiens* he secured the usual applause and homage; and though the receipts—through the difficulties of the period—were not nearly so generous as on his first appearance in Paris, they were still considerable. On April 8th he wrote a letter addressed to one of the Ministers: ' Harrowed by sorrow at the misfortunes which overwhelm humanity, I am desirous of giving a concert—the proceeds of which are to be consecrated to the victims of the cruel plague which is desolating the capital '. According to *Le Moniteur* of the 13th, ' M. le Ministre du Commerce et des Travaux Publics ' accepted Paganini's offer and placed one of the larger halls at his disposal. Writing to Germi the courageous benefactor said, ' I shall give a concert next Friday for the benefit of the sick. Rossini has fled through fear; but I, on the contrary, fear nothing through a wish to be useful to humanity '. What can we say to a sentiment of this kind? We cannot suppose that he was being heroic only to impress so old a friend as Germi who knew him so well. Can it be that for over a century the whole of the cultured world has misunderstood Paganini?— accusing him of posing when excruciating pain almost prevented him from standing; expressing disgust with him for his meanness and avarice at the very moment when he was giving his services to charity; making cruel fun of him because continued suffering had scored his face with lines and disillusionment had left traces of bitterness and sorrow on his features. The concert for the relief of the cholera-victims took place at the Opéra and brought a net gain of 9154 francs to the fund—a large sum for such times. He aroused tremendous enthusiasm, as much in recognition of his courage and generosity as for the perfection of his performance; and the official account of the function says that he ' responded to the acclamations of the crowd with as much modesty as feeling '.

When *The Harmonicon* heard that Paganini had played for charity its rage knew no bounds :

' Paganini *gave* a concert at Paris . . . for the benefit of the poor. When he was in that city last year, he gained about £6000 sterling by his performances. While in the British Isles he netted at least £20,000. But he gave no concert for charitable purposes here ! No, No !—the English, the Scotch, and the Irish are only fit to be fleeced and abused; praise and gratuitous performances are reserved for our neighbours '. This contains as many lies as so short a paragraph well could; and what makes *The Harmonicon's* action in thus baiting Paganini more odious is the circumstance that its contributor knew the statements to be false. If we, a century later, can read in the newspapers of the time the records of Paganini's charity in all the three countries named, surely the editor of *The Harmonicon* was able to do the same. Nor was that paper the only English institution that had not learned its manners : At the anniversary dinner of the Royal Society of Musicians, when a donation of ten guineas to its funds from Paganini was announced, it was ' thought so excessively mean an acknowledgment of the generosity of the English nation . . . that it was received with groans and hisses '. Unperturbed by this venom Paganini was not to be prevented from visiting England again. In the meantime he gave seven more concerts in Paris between April 27th and June 1st.

On his journey to England he gave a concert at Boulogne on June 18th attended again by some unpleasantness. He had agreed to employ the local amateur Philharmonic Society to supply the orchestra for his accompaniments; but when that body insisted upon a large number of free tickets, he refused to oblige. His excuse was that the hall was not large enough to allow him to grant free admission to so many and leave any

273

profit for himself. As the amateurs refused to make any concessions Paganini decided to employ a professional band. The amateurs, furious at being deprived of the opportunity for accompanying so distinguished a performer, endeavoured to coerce the professionals to cancel their engagement by threats of boycott. This praiseworthy intention being frustrated, the amateurs found the money to buy tickets and attended the concert for the sole purpose of hissing the violinist. Fortunately there were enough admirers present to drown the noise of the malcontents with their applause. The concert was a success after all, and the amateurs, as the local paper said, won for themselves the questionable distinction of having hissed Paganini. But the affair was too unusual for *The Harmonicon* to miss, though the admiration that the paper expressed for the player's musical qualities may surprise us:

> ' The musical amateurs of Boulogne have contrived to distinguish themselves in a way that will certainly signalize them from their brethren in every other part of Europe. They have *hissed*, actually and loudly *hissed*, Paganini. The illustrious artist, despising, as he well might, such petty spite, entrusted his revenge entirely to his bow and his fingers, whose magic effects soon reduced to a pitiable silence those who had come to offer him so gross an insult, and called down the rapturous plaudits of all the rest of his delighted audience '.

When Paganini reached England for the second time at the end of June, 1832, he found the Cholera in possession. The epidemic rolled across the capital claiming ten thousand victims of whom half died. This scourge, the lateness of the season, the absence of novelty, and the comparatively few new works offered, were probably the reasons for the great reduction in the sums earned by the violinist. His total profits from twelve concerts given at Covent Garden between July 6th and August 17th amounted to about two thousand five hundred pounds; a sum which cannot compare with that produced by his first visit, though by no means a bad reward for less than six weeks of work. The opinion of the press remained unchanged, *The*

Examiner reporting : ' Paganini's concert drew a full house. His performances increase in attraction, and the more they are heard the more they are admired '. The objection that Paganini was a foreigner was still raised, though it was left to a short-lived so-called comic paper, *The Original,* to show the courage necessary for admitting that reason :

> ' Paganini is arrived and, while our present number is passing through the press, will no doubt be exhibiting his wonderful talents and gathering " golden opinions " from crowds of admirers. We do not grumble at the patronage of Paganini, who is a man of genius and deserves it ; but we do grumble that all the patronage and profit is now picked up by foreigners ; and we do grumble that when Sheridan Knowles had his benefit, not one of those titled patrons of foreign excellence could find it in their hearts to patronize their gifted countryman . . . '

which, in its moderation and justice, might well have served many of *The Original's* higher-class contemporaries as a model.

In the third week of July, *Galignani's Messenger,* a popular English paper published in Paris, reported that ' Paganini has met with an accident which will prevent his performing for some time. On Monday he cut the thumb of his left hand, and it is supposed in playing on Tuesday some rosin entered the wound and caused suppuration ; it is hoped he will be able to perform next week '. The injury proved trifling and not more than a week elapsed before Paganini was again at Covent Garden. The mishap, however, inspired the humorist on the staff of *The Original* with a real flash of genius :

' *A Note of Enquiry, Addressed to Paganini.*

' Grant me reply, great Fiddler, to a word
Of question, by my sympathy preferr'd ;
　　　Ah ! do not fail—
This wound that dooms thy fiddle to be dumb,
Which part of thy extraordinary thumb
　　　Doth it assail?
Doth it at side, or joint, its mischief make?
Or is it, like the money thou dost take,
　　　Down on the Nail? '

On August 10th Mr. Laporte had 'the satisfaction to announce that he has prevailed on Signor Paganini to relinquish some of his Provincial Engagements and that he will give three more concerts at this theatre' (Covent Garden). The satisfaction of *The Harmonicon* was not so apparent and the futility of its ravings become almost amusing:

> 'Signor Paganini, the *lion,* and a most ravenous one, of the day, having performed his four "positively last" nights, has been prevailed on to "defer his country engagements" and play three times more, which performances were peremptorily to be his *final last.* The Signor, with Signora Pietralia and Mr. Bennett for his coadjutors, is filling Covent Garden Theatre with dupes, and his pockets with money, and reasonable people with wonder at English gullibility, while our summer theatres are losing two hundred pounds a week each'.

This extracted from *Galignani* the apposite remark: '*The Harmonicon* is always peculiarly amusing in its endeavour to bring Paganini into bad odour. It reminds us of the futile attempts of Polyphemus in the cave to rival the thunder of Jove'. Referring to Paganini's 'farewell' concert of the 17th the writer of the last says:

> 'This miraculous artist has also, we regret to say, brought his concerts to a close. He has played new things and outdone former doings; we hope he will still hold the public by the button and give *more* "last" concerts. His new piece of two movements, commencing with an *Andante Cantabile amoroso* and concluding with a *rondo brillante,* displays, beyond anything yet heard, his incredible perfection as a solid player. Here was no one-stringed exploit, no guitar effects, no harmonics; he played the fiddle in the accustomed way, as any Mori or de Beriot would have played it, the only difference being that where they would have been *knocked up,* fairly exhausted, and out of breath, he was fresh and vigorous, and as able to go on as ever. . . . He displays the strength and command of any six performers'.

A short tour of southern England followed, commencing on August 23rd at Canterbury. Monday the 27th he arrived at the

Old Ship Hotel in Brighton for the second time and played in the Assembly Room to ' about three hundred fashionables '. The *Brighton Herald* tells us that he was assisted by ' a very clever young lady, only seven years of age, Miss E. Jonas, a pupil of Mr. Field from St. Petersburgh '. Our old friend the *Brighton Gazette,* having said all it could the previous year, contented itself, after a few stereotyped remarks, by adding: ' The performances of Signor Paganini are now too well known to require a lengthened notice '. Under its heading ' Fashionable Chronicle ' it tells us, quite rightly, that the violinist returned to town the following day, having to appear at Southampton on the evening of the 30th and the morning of the 31st. We can follow him through Winchester (September 4), Southampton again (7th), Portsmouth (10th and 11th) and Chichester (12th). He then seems to have returned to London, probably to pick up his Achillino. On September 17th he writes in good spirits to Germi: ' This year I reached London late, when the season was over. Nevertheless, I gave eleven concerts at Covent Garden at a time when it usually is closed. It only required the advertisement of my violin to have the theatre full; for my playing they say has become more miraculous than ever—as the caps and handkerchiefs in the air, and the infernal cheering, prove to me '.

England was now accustomed to Paganini—one half to admire him, and the other half to jeer:

> ' Who are those who pay five guineas
> To hear this tune of Paganini's?
> Echo answers—" Pack o'ninnies " '.

The violinist arrived back in Paris on September 27th and allowed himself a fortnight's rest. During the first three weeks of October he gave three concerts at Rouen, two at Le Havre, and one or two others, harvesting roughly twenty thousand francs. He returned to Paris on October 23rd. We will now hear very little of him until the spring of the following year when he once more appeared before a Parisian audience at a series of concerts. He most probably spent the winter of 1832-33 quietly—resting and writing—and devoting a little more time than usual to Achillino who, now in his eighth year, must have grown into an interesting and intelligent companion. A few days before Christmas the Paganinis removed from their lodgings at No. 237, rue St. Honoré to the *Hôtel di Malta*.

In the spring of 1833, while Paganini was giving his Parisian concerts, a situation arose that was the beginning of a long and bitter persecution. Henrietta Smithson, the Irish actress who had been presenting Shakespearean plays with an English company at the Odéon, failed, and a concert was arranged for her benefit. All the best-known artists in Paris—Hiller, Chopin, Liszt, and more—immediately came to her assistance. Paganini, for what reason no one can say, refused to be associated with the benevolent action of the others. He may have been unwell or he may have been prevented by engagements that could not be broken—the fact remains that he did not perform on behalf of Miss Smithson, and those who were only too ready to rend him at once seized the opportunity. It was to this refusal that most of his posthumous reputation for selfishness can be traced. *L'Europe Littéraire* wrote that ' Paganini knew how to take seven or eight hundred thousand francs from England . . . The magic of his bow is more powerful than the sceptre of many a monarch . . . Miss Smithson begs for a little help from her couch of pain and . . . Mons. Paganini refuses '. The violinist's antagonists made all the capital they could out of the affair. The curious aspect of the case, however, is that Berlioz, who married Miss Smithson the same year, bore Paganini no sort of ill-feeling. Why the man who played for the Cholera-victims in Paris, for the flood-victims in Prussia, for the distressed Poles and the adult orphans in London, should have refused to help the bride of Berlioz, must remain a mystery. But *The Harmonicon* took notice of it. and promised Paganini empty theatres when next he came to England. Already in February that paper had printed :

' We are certain to be honoured by another visit from Signor Paganini after Easter . . . It was to me a matter of certainty, demonstrable upon moral principles, that while anything is to be got in this country, the hero of one string will be drawn to our shores by metallic attraction . . . . It is really " too bad " to be lavishing thousands upon a foreigner '.

Paganini was not the only one who harped on one string. As soon as he arrived in London early in May he was taken to task by a correspondent who complained to *The Times* that he had refused to play at the Gambatti benefit concert in Paris. Paganini, writing from an address in Newman Street on May 9th, denied the allegations and explained the circumstances in a manner that would convince anyone but him who refused to be convinced, adding :

' But in self-defence I may be allowed to state, that I have played for charitable institutions in different parts of England, Scotland and Ireland, that when called upon to assist decayed musicians, their widows and orphans, on my first arrival in London, I did it without a moment's hesitation, and this year I felt happy on having arrived just in time to do the same, though even before my début '.

To show to what lengths of misrepresentation the party-spirit provoked some of the writers for the press, it will be necessary to say only that while *The Harmonicon* reported the pit at one of Paganini's concerts to be ' not half full, the gallery not a third, and the boxes almost empty ', *The Observer* said that he played before ' an overflowing house '.

A provincial tour followed his London appearances, but none calls for special mention, except perhaps the concert he gave in the ballroom of the ' Lion ' at Shrewsbury on Thursday, August 15th (not on his way to Ireland in 1831, as Sitwell states in his life of Liszt). On this occasion he was assisted by ' those highly celebrated vocalists Miss Wells and Miss Watson, likewise Mr. Watson, composer to the Theatre Royal, *etc.*' Mr. Watson was an American resident in London, and in that ménage Paganini lodged when in town on this visit and the next. His innocent

279

association with the wickedly immoral Miss Wells and Mr. Watson was later to cause him a good deal of trouble.

In the autumn Paganini returned to Paris in the greatest need of rest after his strenuous work and the anxieties caused by a constant defensive against the frequent attacks upon his character. In his absence a Mr. Freeman sued him in the Middlesex Sheriff's Court for thirty guineas, being his fee as interpreter at the rate of two guineas a day. The defence was that the charge was exorbitant. The jury found for the plaintiff. But one or two interesting pieces of information were elicited at the hearing reported in *The Times* for November 28th. In cross-examination: ' The Signor played at Vauxhall at a concert given for the relief of the distressed Poles. He played in the Rotunda in the Gardens . . . He refused to play in the open air . . . The Signor played gratuitously . . . The Signor played gratuitously at the Royal Gardens last season also, in aid of the funds of the Ear Dispensary . . . '

Early in December Paganini was seriously ill, but had recovered sufficiently to attend a concert of Berlioz' on the 22nd of the month. This was the first time that these two men met; and Berlioz, looking upon Paganini as a mature artist, entered in his *Mémoires* :

' . . . and finally, to complete my happiness, a man—after the audience had left—a man with long hair and piercing eye, a strange and ravaged visage, one possessed of genius, a colossus among the giants, one whom I had never seen before, and one whose appearance troubled me at first glance—such a man awaited me alone in the hall, and stopped me to press my hand and to load me with glowing eulogies that fired my heart and brain : it was *Paganini* '.

This acquaintance ripened into friendship. Paganini was enraptured by the *Symphonie Fantastique;* he was also very fond of the viola as a solo instrument. Dwelling upon these two themes he conceived the brilliant idea of commissioning Berlioz to write a symphony for him with a solo part for his favourite Stradivari viola. Berlioz apparently did his best, for the result was ' Harold in Italy '; but it did not please Paganini. It did not give him the opportunities he sought. In his *Mémoires* Berlioz wrote : ' Scarcely was the first section written before Paganini wanted to see it. Noticing the rests in the viola part he said, " That won't do; I am silent too long in that; I must play all the time ". I said, " What you really want is a concerto for the viola, and in that case, you can best write it yourself ". He did not reply though he seemed disappointed, and he left without speaking of my symphonic sketch any more '. Paganini may have lost a viola solo, but the world profited by the possession of ' Harold '.

For the major part of that winter Paganini withdrew himself from the public gaze, treated his suffering body and rested his harassed mind, still spurred on by his relentless ambition and his unconquered spirit.

CHAPTER XXIII

TAKING Paganini's life as a whole we can never rank him among the really happy men. He had had his supremely happy moments: when he believed he had found the life-companion of his dreams; when he enjoyed the company of his child; when he regarded his bank-balance; when he heard the enthusiastic plaudits of huge audiences. Now—at the age of fifty-one—what could he show for a life of striving? A suffering body, a large fortune in cash and securities, and a collection of brilliant concert-notices. His heart was as empty as ever; his soul still yearned for a haven of peace where he could rest in the society of dear ones who understood his nature. His castles in the air had long collapsed; there was nothing left to him now but work—the unchanging round of engagements that would help him forget his unattainable ideal. By the end of January, 1834, he felt fit to launch out on a new tour of conquest, and he made arrangements to visit Belgium.

Leaving Paris on February 20th he worked his way towards Brussels. He found the whole territory hostile. All the stories of his meanness, his avarice and his alleged crimes were collected, elaborated and worked up by the press into a veritable campaign against the invader. The Catholic papers dwelt upon the sinister aspects of his life and warned their readers to ignore him. The risk of coming under the influence of Satanic spells was even considered. Paganini played to halls that were almost empty. The musicians were proud of the Belgian school of violin playing and would have nothing to do with him; the rest were indifferent. At Brussels the sparse audience in the

282

Theatre de la Monnaie laughed uproariously when he appeared; indulged in cat-calls; hurled opprobrious remarks, and jeered at him for a 'black skeleton'. That cultured people should descend to such depths of cruelty and brutality must remain an unsolved mystery to all right-minded enquirers; that they should pay for the privilege of crucifying him must always be inexplicable to the most experienced students of human psychology. We can scarcely register Paganini's fiasco in Belgium as a defeat, for he was hardly heard; the only conclusion we can arrive at is that that country, after three years of national independence, must still have been capable of the most glaring violations of the elementary rules of decent behaviour, taste, and hospitality. The only pleasurable moments that fell to Paganini were those he spent in the company of François Joseph Fétis, just then appointed to the directorship of the Brussels Conservatoire. This eminent musical historian remained a lifelong friend of the violinist; and when he wrote his biography of Paganini he drew a merciful veil over the period of the Belgian tour.

Disgusted with the treatment he had received, he fled to England for consolation. There at least the people were just, even if some few of them enjoyed their cruel jokes and cheap gibes. All at least sat silent while he played; he was given what every human being in a civilized country has the right to expect: a fair hearing. But his success was not that of his earlier visits; his health was bad; the novelty of his mystery had worn off; only the violinists were attracted to his concerts. He appeared at the Adelphi Theatre on April 7th and at the Hanover-Square Rooms on the 8th. His third concert was postponed through his illness. The suggestion of Berlioz seems to have taken effect, for there is evidence of his having written a composition for the viola which he played at his last concert in London—*The Athenaeum* saying: 'His precision and brilliancy (upon the viola) as displayed in double-stop passages, harmonics, and arpeggi of extraordinary difficulty, were most amazing'. The solo part of the manuscript is dated, 'Londra, Aprile, 1834'. It was during this last visit to London that

283

Troupenas called on Paganini to negotiate for the publication of his works, but the price asked was so enormous that the publisher, though accustomed to deal in huge contracts, was obliged to refuse. Paganini once told Fétis that he intended publishing his compositions himself; but nothing came of the plan, and only his first five opus-numbers appeared during his lifetime. Little more is known of this tour. He was approached by the committee responsible for the music performed during the Oxford 'Commemoration Week', but no arrangements were made, probably again owing to his extravagantly high terms. From Liverpool he wrote a sad letter to Achille, left in London; he considered the journey a disastrous one; he longed to see his son again.

He left London on June 26th and had scarcely reached Boulogne before another blow fell on his devoted head. The rabble that composed the Watson household, where he had lodged in London, involved him in a scandal that his reputation could ill afford to have attached to itself. Foolishly but innocently he took an interest in Miss Watson's voice and suggested that she go to Paris where he would train it. Mr. Watson objected. But the glamour of Paris was an attraction that the calculating Miss Watson could not resist; and when Paganini arrived at Boulogne he found a crestfallen young vocalist and her irate father, who had been informed of her plan and who reached the French port early enough to intercept his daughter. The rest of the story was told with all its sordid details in the *Annotateur Boulonais*: Miss Watson's age was given as sixteen, Paganini was accused of having encouraged her to leave her home secretly and meet him in France, and much more not at all to the credit of the violinist. Nicolo, now furious at the barbs directed against him by fate, turned at bay and laid about him vigorously. He gave the *Annotateur* his version of the affair without mincing words:

> ' Sir,—Being accused of abducting a young lady of sixteen, my injured honour requires me to . . . bring the truth to light . . . Mr. Watson, as well as Miss Wells—who is not his wife—and

his daughter, had contracted with me for several concerts. This agreement did nothing to impoverish Mr. Watson, for it was kept by me, not only with great fidelity, but even in a manner against my own interests. On my last journey to London I was forced to pay the costs of the hotel which ought to have been met jointly. Later on I lent Mr. Watson £50. For the fourth time in five years he was imprisoned by his creditors, and I, out of my own purse, supplied £45 to secure his freedom. My contract allowed me to give a farewell concert for my own benefit; but, at his request, I waived my right and gave the recital for his daughter's benefit so that his creditors should not seize the profits. I reserved for myself only £50. His daughter handed to him £120 from the proceeds of this concert. This, Sir, was the way in which I treated Mr. Watson. I only learned too late how well his past history illustrated his character. He is a man who for fifteen years allowed his lawful wife to suffer in abject misery at Bath; who drove from home a son whose mother preferred death to witnessing the infamy of his father; who treated his daughter in the most inhuman fashion, and in whose presence he lived a life of the most disgraceful licentiousness. Can you give this man the benefit of credence? . . . Recognizing in Miss Watson a great aptitude for music . . . I suggested taking her as a pupil, assuring her father that after three years of study she would gain independence and be in a position to help her family, and above all, her miserable mother. My plan, one moment rejected and the next accepted, at last remained in the air. I then left England . . . Miss Watson, not sixteen, but eighteen years of age, was already active at the theatre . . . Disregarding her future, her father preferred to have her at home, where she received the most humiliating treatment in reward for her share of the concert-work, and where she occupied a position lower than that of the meanest servant, forced to obey the commands of Miss Wells, the mistress of her father . . . In order to escape from such a scandalous life she remembered my suggestion and voluntarily came to me for protection . . . Thus I did not kidnap Miss Watson . . . If I had wished to be guilty of this, I could have taken her away quite easily when her father was in prison . . . and she was free and alone, for Miss Wells left the house every evening to join her imprisoned lover . . . I assert emphatically that my behaviour has been quite undeserving of censure, that my intentions were honest and free from self-interest, and that they conformed with the rules which order help to the oppressed on the grounds of morality and religion '. (Freely translated and abridged.)

Quite a long discussion ensued and the ultimate outcome is unknown. Several papers in England and France took the matter up and the consensus of opinion inclined to the view that Paganini acted imprudently in associating with such people and foolishly in attempting to help such a daughter as Mr. Watson's, and that the young lady was not abducted but rather 'literally ran after him'. Unfortunately a dog with a bad name is as good as hanged, and it would have required more than one exculpating letter to the *Annotateur* to wash Paganini quite clean in the eyes of very many. Miss Watson eventually returned to America where she toured as a singer and 'ex-fiancée of Paganini', using occasional stories of alleged matrimonial offers from the great violinist as advertising material.

Paganini reached Paris early in September to find a distinctly antagonistic atmosphere. L'affaire Watson, following on l'affaire Smithson, was all that was needful to set a whole pack of curs snarling at a lion no longer in his prime. The poor inhabitants of Saint-Etienne had suffered severely by floods, and Paganini had not given a concert to swell the fund instituted for their assistance. Jules Janin led the attack in the *Journal des Débats* in the bitterest manner. In the issue of September 15th he wrote an article, venomous and heartless, from which the following is an extract:

' With what enthusiasm we received him when he first came to us! . . . With what violent transports did we welcome him! . . . For him we forgot for a moment our greatest artists— even Baillot. For him, when the fear of the Cholera kept us in our houses, we went out contrary to our doctors' orders . . . to hear him play the prayer from *Moïse*. We have done for Paganini all that could be done for a grand artist. It was a passion that went to the lengths of folly. But all at once this passion subsided, this folly ceased, without leaving a vestige. All at once we ceased to desire to hear the prayer from *Moïse*, and the black man who played it to us so willingly and for so high a price, placed his soul in his violin and his violin into its case; he made his most profound bow and departed. He understands that for us he is dead . . . '

Then Janin says that this monster, though he may be a great violinist on the platform, is but a vulgar speculator off the stage; that when he returned from London loaded with gold he refused to aid the poor English actress. ' Then was Paganini judged in accordance with his true worth; he lost all credit with us '. He enlarges upon the sufferings of the women of Saint-Etienne and paints a terrible picture of the ogre who refused to play for them, and another of the divine Paganini had he but done so. Comment and defence are alike unnecessary. In the eyes of Janin, Paganini was the only man whose duty it was to help the distressed. Paganini addressed a reply to the paper which was referred to but not printed. The *Journal* said that his excuse was that he had been ill and had, moreover, already given two concerts for charity. ' His reply would have been different had he been offered ten louis for every bow-stroke '. But why insist further; this ' grotesque something ' refused to come to the aid of suffering humanity; ' to argue further with an Italian would be a dishonour to France '. Paganini, insist-ing that he had the right to see his letter in print, gained his point. The *Journal* inserted his short defence. In effect it amounted to this : he had been unwell and for three months had not played at all; his health required that he return to his native country, but no one had the right to assume that he was unwilling to play in aid of the poor. Long afterwards Janin learned that he had been misled by idle gossip as completely as so many others had been, and to his credit it must be placed that he apologized handsomely for the cruel injustice he had done Paganini: ' To my shame I confess. . . . I was wrong though public sentiment supported me. . . . The great artist was perfectly justified in wishing to show his generosity when he could and would '. The amends came too late.

Worn out by work and wounded in spirit, Paganini for the

first time in his life experienced fear. He realized that his powers were waning; he felt that if he was to continue his activity he would have to recover his strength and renew his courage. Medical advice no doubt caused him to look forward to a winter in Paris with dread; and as soon as his reply to the *Journal des Débats* was printed, he left the city he had entered so triumphantly three and a half years earlier. With all possible speed he travelled to Genoa; and exactly six and a half years after leaving his native land, he recrossed the Italian frontier.

Like a Roman general returning triumphantly from a long campaign, Paganini was greeted by his countrymen, wherever he showed himself, with the greatest joy and pride. He was in no mood to be lionised; he did not even wish to play publicly. These circumstances in themselves should be enough to prove how desperately he was in need of repose. He hunted northern Italy for a haven where he could rest from travel, devote himself to the preparation of his works for publication, and give his son a chance of regular education and a little private home-life. After viewing many properties that had appealed to him during earlier tours, he finally decided upon the ' Villa Gaione ' with the surrounding estate, about four miles from Parma, and bought it. During October he took possession and, except for an occasional excursion to a neighbouring town to give a concert for charity, he remained in his villa, nursing himself and trying to combat the cough that was now troubling him more and more. A trip to Genoa added a gold medal to his collection from the city council of his birthplace as a sign of recognition for the glory he had brought his country. On November 14th he gave a concert in aid of the poor of Piacenza—his first public appearance in Italy since he left Milan in 1828. On December 12th he was invited to play at the birthday festivities of Marie Louise, Duchess of Parma, and once more turned courtly heads with excitement. The gracious Austrian princess no doubt chatted with him of Napoleon, of Elisa, of Vienna; she commissioned him to establish the orchestra of the Ducal Theatre on a practical and efficient foundation, and gave him full authority to effect any reforms he deemed necessary. In return for these services she bestowed upon him a magnificent diamond ring.

The glitter and flattery of a court called forth a flicker of his old spirit; he once again saw himself attracting uncountable thousands of foreign admirers by the magic of his unique art. He wrote to Germi: ' I have always wanted to spend a winter in Russia, and go to America—as that other world has so often requested—and unite the joys of seeing new places with that of earning another million *scudi*. With a sympathetic girl at my side it would certainly be an admirable plan '. Poor Paganini! —his three original obsessions still hold him in thrall and delude him with visions of conquests that he is not destined to make.

During 1835 his old love for Milan reasserted itself and he spent the year between that city, his birthplace, and his villa. He was in Genoa in February when he composed sixty variations on *Barucaba*, dedicated to Germi. On July 28th his old friend and patron, the Marchese Giancarlo di Negro, inaugurated a splendid festival at his villa near Genoa, and in the presence of a distinguished gathering, had a marble bust of the violinist unveiled with great pomp, while the Marchese A. Brignole-Sale delivered an impressive oration. An elaborate banquet followed, and Nicolo and Achille were fêted by a brilliant company. The prophet was honoured in his own land, and in his satisfaction Paganini forgot for a moment the Belgian nightmare and the bitterness of Janin. This year the Cholera devastated northern Italy, and once more the irresistible charm of the famous Guarneri drew thousands from the pockets of Italian audiences for the relief of the sufferers. Reports of this activity became muddled in the foreign press, the rumour went the rounds that Paganini had himself fallen a victim of the dread disease, and a flood of premature obituary notices appeared.

On November 27th Paganini's brother Luigi is mentioned for the last time, *The Times* of that date giving the contents of his Will:

'The brother of the celebrated violinist, whose death was recently announced, has left property, it is stated, to the value of 400,000 francs. His passion for music was almost as great as his brother's, although it does not appear that he played any instrument. By his will he has bequeathed a handsome annuity to a young woman who resided with him; but the bulk of his property is divided between two musicians—one *chef d'orchestre* at Florence, and the other filling a similar situation at Verona. The deceased alludes to his brother, but considering that he is sufficiently provided for, he is not named among the legatees, who are confined to the beforementioned three persons'.

Luigi Paganini became a well-known connoisseur of old violins, and so learned in the lore of *lutherie* that he was generally referred to as ' Dr.' Paganini.

In the first week of January, 1836, the great artist was honoured by another knighthood, this time that of the Order of St. George, at the hands of the Duchess of Parma. He evidently stayed some time in the domains of Marie Louise, for on May 3rd we find him writing to Germi. At this moment one subject only occupied his mind—the legitimation of Achille by an order of the Italian courts. Germi had suggested the placing of Achille with the Jesuits for education, but Nicolo rejected the proposition with determination. His note reads: ' (on account of my) rheumatic pains, I am obliged to carry out the Le Roy treatment; but as soon as I am recovered I shall set out for Turin, and having obtained what I require for my peace of mind (the legal recognition of Achille), I shall make my Will. . . . If you had ever read the smallest amount of Botta's History of Italy, you would never have advised me to place my boy with the Jesuits '.

On March 15th the Roman musical society of St. Cecilia elected him to honorary membership; but he was in no condition to enjoy such honours. His health now began to fail with a more alarming rapidity, and he was advised to seek a more southern clime. Towards the end of the year he is found in Nice—actually giving another concert there on December 17th. On the 23rd he wrote to Germi again : ' My violin is decaying with me; but after the six or eight concerts that I intend giving in Marseilles, I shall recover. I am endowed with more courage than strength; but I am content to have taken up my instrument once more, and to have shown myself in public again '. The proposed concerts in Marseilles were never given; but while we admit the indomitable courage of the man, we must wonder what it could have been that persisted in hounding him from the sick-chamber to the concert-platform.

On April 27th, 1837, he made his Will, but he had not the slightest intention of dying. He must have made a partial recovery, for he appeared a few times in Piedmont in the early part of the summer. On July 9th he gave a concert at Turin with the assistance of the famous guitar player Luigi Legnani, the proceeds being destined for charity. This was the last time that the incomparable Nicolo Paganini appeared in public as a violinist. At the age of fifty-five his career as a virtuoso was ended; his real sufferings had hardly begun.

CHAPTER XXIV

THE SETTING STAR
(July, 1837—Feb., 1839)

EARLY in 1837 Paganini had been approached by a pair of speculators who planned to float a company for the exploitation of a place of public entertainment. They felt that Paganini's reputation was still great enough to make his name an asset. They were sufficiently plausible to convince him that by lending his name and, of course, a certain sum of money, the project would provide a rich source of income when his playing days came to an end. The venture was a gamble and he knew it; but conducted as it should have been, and with Paganini's regular performances as an added attraction, the 'Casino Paganini' should have been a great success. The prospectus provided for amusements and recreations of every kind: Music, dancing, the fine arts, conversation, lectures, reading; but the main object, though kept in the background at the outset, was to provide a locale for gambling. Whether Paganini knew the risk he was running when he gave his name to the Casino and contracted for a specified number of personal appearances, is not certain; but, keen and cautious business-man as we know him to have been, it is hardly likely that he was entirely ignorant of its nature. A magnificent site on the Chaussée d'Antin—occupied by a palace belonging to the Duke of Padua—was bought, and construction commenced. By November it was ready for a grand opening ceremony. Paganini had been installed in a splendid suite of rooms on the premises and lived like a lord—for a very short time. The government refused to grant a gaming licence, and the organisers were compelled to depend upon concerts for their income. It goes without saying that so grandiose a scheme could not be carried out with such limited means. The ornate salons were deserted; the aristocracy and the intellectuals were not interested in the paintings or the reading-rooms; Paganini was too ill to play. The desperate speculators, finding it impossible to meet their obligations, called upon Paganini to save the venture with his magic. He had agreed to play twice a week; but the unfortunate man, with his laryngeal trouble now developing rapidly, could not appear at all. Berlioz, writing in the *Chronique de Paris* before the opening of the Casino, said: ' As to the personal share of the celebrated violinist in the musical activity of the establishment, it is confined to this: Paganini, on certain days, walks round the gardens three times—if the weather is fine '. On November 25th the Casino was opened to the public—a public that wished to gamble for high stakes or hear Paganini play. Their desires were satisfied in neither particular, and the undertaking failed ignominiously.

Paganini, useless as an artist and a pitiable object to behold, took modest lodgings for himself and Achille, deeply involved in a labyrinth of law-suits, cross-examinations, and domiciliary visits by the police. He was the innocent victim of speculators who took what they must have known were unwarrantable risks. It was a cruel disillusionment. His golden dreams of a happy old age, secured by a steady income, vanished like a puff of smoke. He grew weaker, and the affection of his throat reduced his voice to a barely-audible whisper. He was not even able to play his violin. For the first time in his proud life he saw himself beaten. Desperately he gazed about him—this man who in the arrogance of his prime once said: ' How many Paganinis do they think there are in the world? '—and he lowered his arms and hauled down his flag. The papers, it is true, still printed a good deal about him; but it was to announce financial losses, his illness, his misfortunes. He was sued for damages; the court returned a verdict against him; he was to pay a fine of six thousand francs for every time he should have performed and did not. The total sum involved in this finding amounted to 20,000 francs. He appealed. The higher court heard his counsel sympathetically and altered the fine to 50,000 francs, which with the costs came to 60,000. Every day new plaintiffs and prosecutors rose up against him, and only by paying his fines and costs did he escape ending his career as he was supposed to have begun it—in prison.

Writing to Germi in the spring of the following year he said, ' The society of the Casino is composed of robbers and assassins, and has gone bankrupt; the sixty thousand francs are lost. He entered a nursing-home—' Les Néo-thermes '—and made a valiant attempt to recover his health and strength. The process was slow and discouraging. There were days when he was so terribly ill that, unable to move and almost voiceless, he refused to see anyone. At other times—and he still had occasional ' good ' days—he would promenade the covered walks or play billiards, once a favourite recreation of his. Sometimes he did a little composing assisted by the guitar; the violins rested in their cases.

It was now the spring of 1838. As the weather improved he got about a little more, and even paid visits to friends in Paris, sat in the music-shops where people would gaze at him, haggard and emaciated, dreaming of a future filled with new successes for his art. In June this strange man, ashamed of his surrender of the previous year, once more hoisted his colours. He wrote to Germi: ' I am feeling stronger and shall probably cross over to London; in that case I shall tell them that it is the last time I am to appear before the world and that I wish to devote my last musical energies to them '. Why he chose London for this honour we cannot say; perhaps he thought that the ' gullible ' English, as *The Harmonicon* was pleased to call them, would be sentimental enough to pay handsomely for these absolutely ' final last ' farewell concerts. But our flippancy rings false; it has a sombre undercurrent of sad minor chords in a flat key; Paganini never went to London again; his physical condition was hopeless.

It was probably during this year that Paganini took his famous Guarneri to the equally celebrated J. B. Vuillaume for repair.

When he last used the instrument—in Turin—he noticed a tonal defect that he wished to have remedied, no doubt in view of his proposed journey to London. One fine day when he was feeling tolerably well, he walked into Vuillaume's workshop in the rue Croix-des-Petits-Champs with his violin-case in his hand. The instrument was examined by the expert and an operation deemed necessary. The violin would have to be opened and Paganini stood aghast. After long hesitation he agreed to allow Vuillaume to repair the instrument on condition that he worked under its owner's eye. The luthier consequently came to the ' Néo-thermes ' with his tools. Paganini sat at the end of the room; seized the knee of one crossed leg in his hands and rested his chin on them; watched the operation with deep anxiety. The chisel was introduced between the table and the rib; a slight cracking noise; Paganini bounded from his chair. Every movement of the tool brought fresh beads of perspiration to the brow of the tortured man, who loved this fiddle more than he cared for any other inanimate thing in the world. He said, ' it was as if the chisel were entering my own flesh '. The operation was completely successful and Paganini was quite satisfied with the result. At the same time Vuillaume made a replica of the instrument, which Paganini bought for five hundred francs. A little later, when Vuillaume called upon the grateful artist, the latter said : ' The cure is complete '; and going to his desk he produced a very fine snuff-box set with precious stones which he offered to the violin-maker with the words, ' I have had two boxes made like this : one for the physician of my body, and the other for the surgeon of my violin; my gratitude is equal in both cases, and the souvenir given should be the same '. Friends made Vuillaume suspicious as to the value of the present, saying that Paganini was far too mean to give anyone a real gold box set with real diamonds. The luthier took it to a jeweller for valuation and found, to his astonishment, that the gift was worth about 1,800 francs. It was possibly one of the many presentation-boxes that Paganini had received from Royal hands.

In 1838, too, Sir Charles Hallé, then a youth of nineteen, made the acquaintance of Paganini, and in his autobiography has left us an interesting account of the violinist as he appeared to the casual observer of that time :

'To return to 1838, a year so rich to me in reminiscences. I must say a few words about a man, in his way the most remarkable of his time—Paganini. He was one of the wonders of the world to me, so much had I read and heard about him, and I deeply deplored that he had given up public playing, and —so I was told—even chose his lodgings so that the sound of his violin could not be heard outside. The striking, awe-inspiring, ghost-like figure of Paganini was to be seen nearly every afternoon in the music shop of Bernard Latte, Passage de l'Opéra, where he sat for an hour, enveloped in a long cloak, taking notice of nobody, and hardly ever raising his piercing black eyes. He was one of the sights of Paris, and I had often gone to stare at him with wonder until a friend introduced me to him, and he invited me to visit him, an invitation I accepted most eagerly. I went often, but it would be difficult to relate a single conversation we had together. He sat there, taciturn, rigid, hardly ever moving a muscle of his face, and I sat spell-bound, a shudder running through me whenever his uncanny eyes fell upon me. He made me play to him often, mostly by pointing with his bony hand to the piano without speaking, and I could only guess from his repeating the ceremony that he did not dislike it, for never a word of encouragement fell from his lips. How I longed to hear him play, it is impossible to describe, perhaps even to imagine. . . . On one never-to-be-forgotten occasion, after I had played and we had enjoyed a long silence, Paganini rose and approached his violin-case. What then passed in me can hardly be imagined; I was all in a tremble, and my heart thumped as if it would burst my chest; in fact, no young swain going to his first rendez-vous with his beloved could possibly feel more violent emotions. Paganini opened the case, took the violin out, and began to tune it care-fully with his fingers without using the bow; my agitation became almost intolerable. When he was satisfied, and I said to myself, with a lump in my throat, " Now, now, he'll take the bow," he carefully put the violin back and shut the case '.

The taciturnity mentioned by Hallé has often been called moroseness with no justification. Had Paganini been morose he would not have asked the young man to come and see him so often; Paganini was silent because he was almost aphonous— because the effort of speaking caused him intolerable pain. How tragically had the lively anecdotist of the Italian dinner-party at Prague been changed in nine short years!

In December, 1838, Paganini came once more in contact with Berlioz in circumstances that bordered on the romantic. On the sixteenth of the month Berlioz, himself an invalid and desperately poor, gave a concert at which his 'Harold in Italy' was produced. The *Journal de Paris* tells us that at the end of the performance ' Paganini, who had come to hear the symphony for the first time, advanced and threw himself at the feet of Berlioz, crying as well as he could, for he was voiceless, " It is prodigious." ' Berlioz, in his *Memoires* gives a more detailed version :

' When the concert ended I was worn out, covered with sweat, and trembling, when, at the entrance to the orchestra Paganini, followed by his son Achille, approached me with lively gesticulation. On account of his illness he had then already lost his voice entirely, and only his son could hear, or rather guess, his words. . . . He made a sign to the boy who, mounting on to a chair, placed his ear close to his father's mouth and listened attentively. Achille then stepped down, and turning to me said : " My father commands me to assure you, Sir, that during the whole of his life he has never been so deeply impressed at a concert; that your music has bewildered him; and that, if he had not controlled himself, he would have placed himself at your feet to thank you." At these strange words I made a gesture of incredulity and confusion, but Paganini seized me by the arm and said with the remnant of his voice, " Yes, yes." He dragged me back to the platform, where there were still a number of my musicians, and kneeling down, he kissed my hand. I need not say how astonished I was; I state the facts, *voilà tout* '.

Two days later Paganini addressed two letters : one to Berlioz, enclosing a cheque for 20,000 francs, and the other to Baron de Rothschild to this effect :

' Monsieur le baron,—I beg you to give to the bearer of this,

M. Hector Berlioz, the 20,000 francs which I deposited with you yesterday. You will infinitely oblige,

Faithfully yours,
NICOLÒ PAGANINI '.

Berlioz, imprisoned by illness, wrote a most grateful and flattering letter of thanks. He now had the means at his disposal that would permit him to recover his health and produce some epoch-making works with a tranquil mind. The first result was the symphonic poem ' Roméo et Juliette ' which he dedicated to Paganini. As soon as he was able to go out, he called on his benefactor at the ' Néo-thermes ' and a very touching scene was enacted. Many stories explaining this munificent gift were circulated—twisted of course to place Paganini in as disadvantageous a light as possible. The sum of the allegations was that some unknown person had supplied the money, while Paganini had meanly taken the credit for it. Fundamentally this story was true, though Paganini, without betraying his trust, could hardly help having the credit forced upon him *malgré lui*. The most recent research has not improved upon Hallé's version of the truth:

> ' Armand Bertin, the wealthy and distinguished proprietor of the *Journal des Débats*, had a high regard for Berlioz and knew of all his struggles, which he, Bertin, was anxious to lighten. He resolved therefore to make him a present of 20,000 francs, and in order to enhance the moral effect of this gift he persuaded Paganini to appear as the donor of the money. How well Bertin had judged was proved immediately; what would have been simple graciousness from a rich and powerful editor towards one of his staff, became a significant tribute from one genius to another, and had a colossal *retentissement*. The secret was well kept and never divulged to Berlioz. It was known, I believe, to but two of Bertin's friends besides myself, one of whom was Mottez, the celebrated painter; I learned it about seven years later when I had become an intimate friend of the house, and Madame Armand Bertin had been for years one of my best pupils '.

This was the last that Paris saw of the man who a little more than seven years ago had ' driven all her musicians mad '. The winter climate of the Seine neighbourhood was more than he could stand. As fast as his condition would allow he travelled south to Marseilles. On February 17th, 1839, he wrote to Germi:

> ' I delayed my departure from Paris because of the calumnies of a rogue who made complaint to the King's procurator that I sought to assassinate him in my house by means of four armed murderers in disguise. The examination of the various witnesses occupied almost two months, so that I could not leave. At last, however, the case was dismissed, as it ought to have been, and the fraud of the rogue was discovered '.

At Marseilles, once more looking over the blue Mediterranean, Paganini entered upon the last chapter of his eventful life; when the torch that had blazed so triumphantly was to be dimmed by the shadow of dark wings.

CHAPTER XXV

THE FLICKERING LIGHT
(Feb., 1839—May, 1840)

WHEN Paganini reached Marseilles he was a man condemned to death by all the medical opinion he sought; but he fought on, refusing to believe that a man could die so long as he willed to live. Tuberculosis of the larynx was a disease in the face of which the doctors of 1839 were helpless. His other complaints, painful and inconvenient though they were, might have allowed him to live a few years longer. He lodged with a friend who did all that was humanly possible to make him comfortable. Occasionally he played the guitar, jotted down fugitive musical ideas that occurred to him, conversed with Achille or his servant by writing notes, and, it is said, even took part now and then in classical string-quartets. But his ' good ' days were now few and separated by longer intervals of terrible weakness. Fétis tells us—on the evidence of eye-witnesses—that one day he ' seemed to revive and performed a quartet of Beethoven, his particular favourite, with the greatest energy '; but such exertions were usually followed by periods of prostration. Strange it may appear to us that the man who ignored all the canons of the traditionalists when exhibiting his personal talents to a wondering public, should turn to Beethoven for solace in his last hours. And it was probably his love for compositions cast in a more heroic mould as much as his devotional feeling that took him, despite his increasing weakness, to hear a Requiem of Cherubini. A few friends living in Marseilles cheered him with their welcome company—the notary Brun with whom he was staying, and Giuseppe Galofre with whom he formed one of the most cordial friendships of his life. On April 16th *The Times* informed its readers that 'Paganini is dying: the physicians despair of being able to prolong the days of that eminent artist, who appears to have lived for some time past by positive enchantment'. But as the weather became warmer he rallied again; the *Semaphore* of Marseilles writing on May 16th that 'the health of this celebrated violinist is improving daily'. By June 21st he felt strong enough to visit a church and assist at a celebration of the Beethoven Mass. New hope of a recovery induced his doctors to try further treatment, and in July he undertook a spa ' cure ' followed by a visit to the sulphur springs of Vernet-les-Bains. *Le Moniteur* announced his arrival on August 22nd accompanied by his Guarneri and Dr. Lallemand, who reported that Paganini was scarcely more than an emaciated shadow of his former self. The patient was ordered baths from the Elisa spring at a temperature of 72 degrees. We may learn a little of his life at Vernet if we take the trouble to look up the *Perpignan Journal* for August:

> ' Having lost all his teeth, the celebrated maestro eats with the greatest difficulty. At table his meat is minced for him, either by one of his neighbours or his servant. His days are passed entirely in playing billiards or walking with a friend. He is much amused when reading the *Charivari*, but his gaiety soon passes off; and he then sinks into a state of depression, the result no doubt of his illness, and seeks for solitude. With his cap on his head and his cane in his hand he retires to the environs of the baths and remains plunged in deep meditation, interrupted sometimes by sudden movements as if he wished to shake off reflection. He then strikes the ground repeatedly with his feet, like a man who, on rising from his seat, is afraid that his legs will give way under the weight of his body '.

Towards the end of September he returned to Marseilles very little benefitted by his stay at Vernet, except, perhaps, in so far as change of scene and routine helped him to escape from his thoughts for fleeting moments. He seemed consumed with impatience; the restless urge of a man who feels subconsciously that his mission has not yet been fulfilled; the spurring of a restless and ambitious spirit to one more astounding act; to make one more sensational return to the limelight so that he might say farewell as befitted an artist of his theatrical temperament and unconquerable will—in a blaze of triumph. To play as he had never played before and make his final bow to the accompaniment of thunderous applause and the last snapping of his silver G-string. But this crowning joy was denied him.

At the beginning of October he decided to visit his birthplace once more, probably submitting to the ordeal of travel in the hope that the sea-voyage would strengthen him. He reached the old harbour he remembered so well, in a state of nervous collapse. We are able to learn nothing of his doings in Genoa beyond the fact that he wrote to Galofre : ' Being in much worse health than I was at Marseilles, I have resolved upon passing the winter at Nice '.

The well-known Riviera resort, then still an Italian possession, was destined to be the last asylum for his body, weakened as it was by disease and wearied by his unremitting labour. His mind, however, still struggled to rise above these frailties and to permit itself the luxury of hope. Count di Césole, faithful to his friend to the last and helpful to Achille when the boy most needed a guiding hand, came to see him every day and even obtained some instruction on the violin. There were days when the waiting enemy in ambush made his proximity felt; on such a day he wrote to Genoa that he hoped to go to Tuscany to breathe, before he died, the air that sustained Dante. At other times his spirits rose again; and at such a moment he would write as he wrote to Berlioz; ' If Heaven permits it, I will see you once more in the spring, and I hope that my condition will improve here—this is the only hope left to me '. The Nice correspondent of the *Gazette Musicale* wrote on January 11th, 1840; ' I see M. Paganini almost every day . . . he still shows considerable vigour and I sometimes hear him playing his muted instrument, when he is alone. He still speaks of a new method for the violin which he wishes to publish, and which will materially shorten the time needed for study'. It must have been at this period that Sivori came to see him, and once again the master heard the pupil play. Sivori was presented with the copy of the Guarneri that Vuillaume had made; and when Paganini's Will was read it was found that he had bequeathed one of his Stradivaris to the pupil whom he considered to be the only exponent of his own style.

These slight improvements in his health were but of a passing nature, and each was succeeded by still greater weakness and the development of more alarming symptoms. His features became more sunken than ever, and his voice was reduced to an almost soundless breathing which only Achille could interpret into words. Escudier is responsible for the story that Paganini was one day seated at his bedroom window watching the setting sun; the clouds were coloured with reflections that shone in purple and gold; a warm breeze carried up to him the scent of flowers. The slanting rays of the westering sun fell upon a fine portrait of Byron hanging on a wall of the room. The sensitive eye of Paganini was drawn to the picture of a man for whom he had the deepest and sincerest respect. On one of his visits to Florence he had met Byron—though not in the year to which Escudier assigns the meeting—and there was something in the wayward and unhappy writer that found a responsive chord in Paganini's sympathetic nature. On this evening his gaze rested long and speculatively upon the portrait. Rising from his chair, his head held proudly erect, he seized his violin and expended his last energies in improvising a poem in sound that was his homage to the heroic poet who slept at Missolonghi. Paganini was conquered by his weakness as the last chord rang out on the still air, and his bow remained motionless in his stiffening fingers. Those who heard him on that occasion—Césole among them —say that this was the most exalted music Paganini ever made. Immediately afterwards he took to his bed and never left it again. On April 4th, and again a fortnight later, he wrote to Germi; but the spirit of Hope revived no more in him. He could do no more than write of his feebleness, of his loss of appetite, of his painful symptoms. On May 24th the curé came to offer him the last consolation of the Church. At once the proud spirit of the doomed man flamed up; he was not yet ready to die. Father Pietro Caffarelli retreated before Paganini's impatient gesture, and he came no more.

On May 27th Paganini suffered from repeated paroxysms of coughing which left him exhausted. He fell into a fitful slumber that gradually became more calm. When he awoke he seemed a little refreshed. He made signs to those about him to withdraw the bed-curtains and open the windows wide. The moon, rising in the velvet sky of the Mediterranean, sent silver paths across the rippling water and soft beams on to the coverlet of his bed to touch those magic fingers with ghostly radiance. A thousand memories seemed to crowd upon him at once; he saw an ocean of faces, innumerable eyes fixed upon him in rapt attention; he heard the thunder of applause; he felt the chaplet of bays placed upon his head by fair hands; beads of perspiration broke from his brow; he gazed about him wildly. At last his eye fell upon that which he sought—the violin which always hung near his bed. Slowly his hand was stretched forth to hold once more the instrument he had loved best throughout his painful and glorious pilgrimage—his friend in joy and triumph, his consolation in disillusionment and suffering. Lightly his fingers brushed over the vibrant strings and the hand that had charmed thousands into breathless silence fell beside his lifeless body. And as the vibrations from those four eloquent strings died away tremulously in the stillness, it was as if the whole of his world had said ' Goodnight ' . . . . Paganini, at the age of fifty-eight, had gone to learn the truth.

On June 1st the Will of Paganini was opened and read. It disposed of a fortune of roughly two million lire (about £80,000), a large amount of property and securities in France, England, Italy, and the Kingdom of the Two Sicilies, and a valuable collection of jewellery and instruments. After providing munificently for his two sisters he directed that the life-annuity of twelve hundred francs to Antonia Bianchi be continued, and that his favourite Guarneri be preserved in the

Municipal Museum of Genoa. Everything else was to go to Achille absolutely. Paganini's son inherited the German barony and was enjoined to keep the Villa Gaione and its contents in good order as an heirloom to be bequeathed with the barony to the eldest male descendant. Giambattista Giordani, Lazzaro Rabizzo, and Pietro Torrigiani of Genoa were appointed executors. Paganini's lifelong friend Luigi Guglielmo Germi, at his own request, was not among the beneficiaries under the Will. We may suppose that Germi assisted Paganini in drawing up the document which was written in 1837 after Achille's status had been legitimised by court-order. We may also imagine that it was only after a long argument that Paganini agreed to leave Germi out when disposing of his property. But he hoped that Achille would always follow the advice of this genuine and disinterested friend. The Marchese Lorenzo Parento was named as the boy's guardian. Before closing his testament Paganini wished that no musicians perform a requiem and that his funeral be conducted without pomp. Baron Achille Paganini, who had been his father's constant companion and, latterly, his help, fought hard to retain his favourite instrument. He saw how it had been cared for and had witnessed the love that had been bestowed upon it. This violin was the last thing touched by the man who had struggled so long against pain that his son might inherit a fortune. The city fathers of Genoa refused to waive the right given them by Paganini's Will. The new baron offered the city the fine marble bust that Varni had made, in place of the violin; the mayor again refused. In 1851 the son at last parted with his father's precious companion, and to this day it stands in a glass case surrounded by other relics of the great man, with the Stradivari which he bequeathed to Sivori lying before it.

.   .   .   .

When great men die their torches, before being extinguished, light an altar-fire from which their successors borrow the illumination that guides their footsteps to still greater flights. Paganini's light was not of this order. His meteoric fire, dazzling all who beheld it, could help his followers but little. Except for a few not indispensable technical effects, and an indication as to what lengths instrumental virtuosity might be developed, the world of music has not profited by his presence on its stage. His greatness, his uniquity, lay not in the grandeur of his creations so much as in his manner of reproducing his ideas. This manner, like the peculiar imagination that directed it, was a faithful reflection of his own feelings, his own varied experiences, his own personality—his Ego. That surely was mercifully unique. For who would wish to acquire the means of repeating his performance at the price he was called upon to pay?

He commenced paying in his earliest youth when an all-absorbing passion for his instrument diverted his mind from all other interests. Gradually he identified himself with his art, and an egotism developed of which he was not conscious. And later—his physical wild oats sown and his mind refined by association with brilliant men and cultured women—he formulated his ideal of womanhood that was an almost non-existent combination of beauty, grace, learning, taste, and angelic patience. This ideal he sought all his life.

Endowed with mechanical perfection in his art, he was enabled to say through his instrument all that was denied utterance through the usual channels of expression. At each failure in his quest after the ideal, he complained to the world in tender Adagios, in tempestuous Allegros, and in cynical Scherzi. He and his violin were so far one that he hardly knew whether he was pouring out his soul before a world that would not pity him, or whether he was doing it for his own relief, his own satisfaction, and overwhelming himself with his own pity. This it was that developed the egotism which was impersonal—the egotism whose existence he did not suspect.

At times he could detach himself from his musical monomania and indulge in witty or philosophical conversation that called only his intellect into play. Intimate friendship he could form only with the few whom he felt he could trust with the secret of his sorrows. He needed most of all a companion whose tenderness would compensate him for the roughness of the way and the weariness of his body; but his complete absorption in his vocation prevented him from rewarding such tenderness in a manner that would ensure its endurance. His success with his audiences was due to the circumstance that, by allowing his own feelings to dominate his style of performance, he made his listeners feel. And as his reactions to suffering and joy were peculiar to himself, so was his technique of interpreting them into terms of sound unique. There will be no necessity to refer again to his physical pain; this only gave him the emaciated body that induced ridicule from a public that should have expressed pity and made allowances. Paganini was a 'strange individual' and his was an 'enigmatical personality' only when the unsatisfied longings of his mind and soul were not understood. To those who really knew him he was lovable and human, generous and just. Above all, he was a staunch and grateful friend. At the same time there was a decided streak of suspicion in his composition—whether purely individual or national, we cannot say—and there were very few among his friends whom he really trusted.

Generous and tolerant where his fellow-artists were concerned, he was extremely critical of his own performance; he never suffered under any of the delusions common to the artists whose egotism was of a more personal order; and when his playing was not up to his usual standard he was the first to admit it. His dejection on such occasions was as deep as his elation was unbounded when he scored his most brilliant successes. In this at least he was quite human. Trustworthy witnesses like A. B. Marx, who met Paganini at the Mendelssohns' hospitable board in Berlin, always found him perfectly normal and companionable in spite of the disquieting effect of his peculiar personal appearance. As to his generosity very much might be written; scores of writers give their personal experiences when in his society, and all differ in their judgment. According to one, he would seek a restaurant where his dinner cost no more than two francs and whence he would purloin a pear or piece of bread to eat at home; according to another he often took two rooms at an inn when one would have sufficed, had his meals at the best restaurants, always took good wine, and gave adequate tips. We can only come to the conclusion that, like most other human beings, Paganini was generous when the mood was upon him, and very careful with his money at other times. Possibly all the witnesses told the truth, their varying evidence applying to different periods of his life.

While freely acknowledging the learning and virtues of his more intellectual acquaintances, he treated the unlettered lower classes with undisguised contempt—probably owing to the fact that he had himself risen by his own efforts and had no patience with those who were content to remain in their original ignorance. Of personal vanity he showed no trace. In private life he was simple and unaffected; and writers of many nations describe his bearing in public as having been modest and unassuming. How conscientiously he fulfilled his obligations to his audiences, we know—even at the cost of his comfort and health. His wardrobe was scant, old-fashioned, and plain; but he always insisted upon clean linen of good quality. He travelled with very little luggage and was content, in his earlier years at least, with the most humble lodgings so long as his rooms were out of range of street-noises. When travelling he sat warmly clothed in the corner of his vehicle, either in animated conversation with his travelling companion or silently planning a new work. It was probably his fear of draughts and dust that compelled him to keep the windows of his carriage closed, for arrived at his quarters he would have all the doors and windows opened wide.

Obstinate and proud, he never brooked dictation from anyone. Where his affection alighted he could be as self-sacrificing as any man; and in spite of the meanness so often attributed to him, there is abundant evidence, only recently discovered, of very great charity of which the world knew nothing. A large number of distinguished men and cultured women, highly placed in society and honoured in the world of learning, found it worth their while to cultivate his friendship; and if the public at large preferred to satisfy their baser instincts by elaborating every libellous legend that was told of him, instead of seeking to know him better—so much the worse for that public. It is not possible for us to form any very different opinion of Paganini; he commanded the respect, and enjoyed the friendship of too many critical and discerning men for us to think any less highly of him.

Such was the man who died on May 27th, 1840. Yet when his eyes were closed and his courageous spirit left the body that was too weak a vessel to hold it, there was no priest to be found who would say, ' Peace be to his ashes '. The impiety of his world had still one more indignity with which to reward his memory for the many benefactions he wrought and the pleasure he had given to innumerable thousands.

CHAPTER XXVI

'DANSE MACABRE'
(May, 1840—1926)

WE have to reconcile ourselves to the natural law that all men, even the greatest and best, have to die; but when they depart we place their deserted bodies out of sight with decent haste so that the sufferings and the sins of the flesh may be forgotten and the mind of the mourner allowed to remember only the good they did and the pleasure they gave. Yet in the whole history of mankind—certainly in that of the nineteenth century —it is to be doubted whether so disgusting an exhibition of cruelty and callousness, not to say of impiety, has ever been permitted as was shown at the burial of Nicolo Paganini. For a longer period than he lived on earth, the insulted corpse of the great virtuoso was made the desecrated shuttlecock of those canons made by man which went under the name of religion's guardians. For years a gabbling, hypocritical, and fickle world —including the thousands who but a short time earlier had called the living man 'illustrious', 'incomparable', 'divine'— stood by mutely while his bones were literally thrown into one inadequate ditch only to be hauled out again and flung into another, still more degraded and unsuitable.

The untutored savages of the darkest ages burnt or buried the bodies of their dead and made sacrifices to their helpless idols that the sins of the departed might be forgiven and their souls admitted to life eternal. Not so those who had profited by the enlightenment and culture of the nineteenth century, whose spirits had been illumined by the flaming torch of the Christian faith and made merciful and tolerant by the example of Golgotha. Because three days before Paganini died he curtly dismissed the priest whose few stereotyped words, uttered in Latin, would have given his soul its passport to heaven. Why he refused the curé's offices we shall never know. Possibly his unconventional mind could not welcome an invitation to settle his earthly accounts with a man to whom its innermost workings must always have remained inexplicable; perhaps he preferred —as he said in his will—to recommend his spirit ' to the immense pity of its Creator '; most probably, like most victims of a tubercular disease, he did not suspect the nearness of death. Whatever the reason, the fact remains that he died without having satisfied the requirements of the Roman Church.

From the moment Paganini's eyes were closed, objections against his burial in consecrated ground were raised. The bishop of Nice, Monseigneur Antonio Galvano, alleged that there was no documentary evidence of the deceased musician's religious beliefs, although his will ordered the Capuchin fathers to celebrate a hundred Masses for him. On the shoulders of the Conte di Césole fell the responsibility for disposing of his friend's body. All kinds of evidence was produced to show that Paganini had been a good Catholic; it was countered by a priest's allegation that on the walls of the dead man's room hung profane pictures; the faithful di Césole asserted that holy pictures were also displayed; the argument produced no result. After permission for burial in a Catholic cemetery had been withheld, the body, which had been lying in state in the count's villa, was removed to the hospital at Nice. Here this distinguished example of the race created in God's image, but from which the divine spark had fled, attracted a continuous succession of visitors—some drawn to the bier by a desire to show a last sign of respect to the honoured artist, some by idle curiosity. The clergy of Nice, treating the man who had died without absolution as one excommunicated, objected again, and the bishop ordered the removal of the coffin under military escort to the lazaretto of Villafranca.

In this beautiful spot all the old legends of demoniac possession were resuscitated by the ignorant peasantry and fisherfolk; supernatural sounds were perceived, the restless spirit of the great violinist was heard playing ghostly music, and terror spread over the neighbourhood. Whoever had to pass the leper-house after dark hastily crossed himself and hurried away. The executors for the dead man approached the local ecclesiastical tribunal which upheld the decision of the bishop of Nice. On April 1st, 1842, the *Augsburg Gazette* wrote that the question was still before the courts and that the authorities had ordered the facts of the case to be laid before them for revision. The bishop of Nice was not to be moved; as *The Times* for February 16th, 1843, said, that prelate, 'holding to the gross bigotry which denounced the artist when dead, of whom, when living, the Romish Church made such liberal use', still refused to give his permission 'for the entrance of Paganini's remains into consecrated ground'. The episcopal court of Genoa was now appealed to, and the judgment of the lower tribunal was reversed. Nice, however, was not satisfied, and appealed against this verdict to the court of Turin, which upheld Genoa. Three appeals only were allowed by law, and the bishop of Nice, not to be thwarted in his determination to observe the letter of the law, appealed to Rome. All these negotiations dragged on for years, and in the meantime the body of Paganini awaited the pleasure of the obstinate prelates.

The many complaints that now came from Villafranca compelled di Césole to seek another resting place for the coffin, and it was perfunctorily interred near the wall of an olive-oil factory. It was not yet permitted to lie in peace even here. Waste products trickling from the refinery fouled the grave of Italy's hero and his body had once more to be exhumed. The heart sickens at the thought of the undignified wanderings of this ill-fated corpse. They are even difficult to follow. Possibly some of the stories—especially that which gave the coffin a temporary grave on one of the Iles des Lérins, in a hole still called after the violinist's name—may not even be true. Count di Césole and baron Achille did not rest from their labours. At last the commissioners appointed by the Holy See decided against the appellants from Nice, and in 1843—three years and three months after Paganini's death—the permission of the church was given for his Christian burial. Marie Louise—his last patroness —now remembered the Knight of St. George whom she had herself created, and ordered the body to be admitted into the territory of Parma. Gratefully baron Achille, now eighteen years of age, conveyed his father's bones to a villa on his own estate in the Polcevera valley near Genoa. In May, 1845, the body was taken into the Duchy of Parma and re-interred in the churchyard adjoining the Villa Gaione.

This was not yet the end. At different times the remains were dug up, re-embalmed, buried again. Long after the death of his father baron Achille—after expending large sums—succeeded in holding a memorial service, conducted by the violinist's nephew, baron Attila, in the church of the Madonna della Steccata, belonging to, or largely used by, the knights of St. George. At last a requiem was said for the repose of the famous Piedmontese; and eventually, in 1876, his dust was buried in the graveyard of Parma. In 1896 the bones of the artist were yet again brought to the light of day, encased in a new coffin, buried in the new cemetery at Parma, and surmounted by an elaborate monument of marble columns and a portrait-bust, dedicated to a father's memory by a devoted son.

It might be thought that the clay which had been Paganini now deserved undisturbed tranquillity. The Italian authorities were evidently not of that mind. If we consult a recent 'Baedeker' for Northern Italy we will read that in the *Camposanto* of Genoa, near the tomb of Mazzini, can be seen 'the grave of Paganini, whose remains were brought here in 1926'.

CHAPTER XXVII

THE position occupied by Nicolo Paganini as a violinist and composer for his instrument should be defined clearly enough by the contemporary opinions reprinted in the foregoing pages— and no amount of fresh research can increase our knowledge in this respect. All that can be done to-day is to decide which particular aspects of violin-technics existed before his time to be developed by him in a normal manner, and which of them may be said were 'invented' by him. The lessons to be learned from almost every page of musical history should warn us not to use the words 'invented' and 'discovered' too easily. Harmony was supposed to have been 'invented' by Dunstable until careful research discovered that he was but a link—even though he were a glorious link—in a long evolutionary chain. Certain chords were supposed to have been 'discovered' by Monteverdi until we found that much earlier composers already used them. Great men in the musical art—men who dominated their respective eras—were great not so much because of their discoveries as on account of the use they made of the features they found provided by their predecessors. Double-stopping passages had been written long before Paganini's time; but no one ever attained to his technical facility in their performance. This ease of manipulation permitted him to write successions of still greater extent and difficulty. Where he did add new effects to the violinist's materia technica was in the domain of bowing, left-hand pizzicato, and single and double harmonics. Whether the second and third of these three departments of technical display are to be considered beautiful or not, must remain a matter of personal taste. No one has the right to say that this or that technical effect is artistic or inartistic; but

314

those who think as Spohr thought will look upon them as
'tricks', just as some of Paganini's contemporaries did. It was
in extending the range of his instrument, in demonstrating what
surprising results could be obtained by a combination of natural
talent and hard work—in short, in showing new paths for the
development of instrumental virtuosity, that Paganini's greatest
merit lay. The majority of his contemporaries are agreed that
Paganini used such effects as means and not as an end; and he
certainly is not to be blamed if so many of those who sought to
emulate him lost sight of the musical object and concentrated
upon the display of mere technical finish.

In the enormous variety of new bow-strokes exploited by
Paganini lies a much more legitimate reason for honouring his
memory. The technic of the bow lagged far behind that of the
left hand when Paganini appeared. By the time he died prac-
tically all of the strokes he used with such electrifying effect,
were adopted—in some cases with modification and in others
without—by all the important schools of violin-playing, though
their successful employment was always restricted to the few
who possessed the requisite flexibility and control. The passages
which he wrote in pizzicato for the left hand, and those in
single and double harmonics, have been played by many virtuosi
since his time; but—even taking into account the enthusiasm
aroused by such technicians as Kubelik and Kocian on their
first appearance—no one has ever produced the emotional
effects attributed to Paganini by writers whose word we are
compelled to accept. We have seen throughout the whole of
Paganini's public career that his greatest successes were achieved
as much by his dramatic and emotional power and versatility
as by his amazing exhibition of mechanical fluency. It is on
this account that no second Paganini has appeared. On
this account, too, he can never be taken as a model; he will
be imitated only when a personality like his appears, endowed
with his physical, mental, and spiritual attributes. And the
combination will be found to be rare enough.

It is very much to be doubted if his extraordinary facility

315

was, to as great an extent as is generally supposed, the result only of frantic practising. We know that he experimented with certain passages with a patience that is scarcely believable; but the potentiality for the eventual conquest of the most difficult of his problems on the fingerboard lay already in the peculiar adaptability of his body, the suitability of his organs, and the ease with which his mental processes and his physical reactions collaborated. There can be not the slightest doubt but that there existed in him an unusually high degree of musical intelligence from his earliest years: in his fifth year his rhythmic sense was already sufficiently developed to enable him to detect the faults in his father's performance. Dr. Francesco Bennati, the eminent physiologist who examined Paganini so thoroughly, was of opinion that 'without the peculiar conformation of his body, of his shoulders, arms and hands, he could never have become the incomparable virtuoso we admire to-day'—and there is more in this than is generally admitted. 'His left shoulder is higher than the other, a circumstance that makes his right side appear much longer than it is, when he stands erect with his arms hanging by his sides. The elasticity of the shoulder tendons, the relaxation of the muscles which connect the wrists with the forearms, the base of the hands with the phalanges, and all the joints with each other, can easily be observed. His hand is no larger than the normal, but thanks to the elasticity peculiar to all its parts, his span is doubled. By these means, for example, he can—without altering the position of the hand—bend the upper joints of the fingers of the left hand in a lateral direction, and with the greatest ease and rapidity. Paganini's art lies in his having developed by tireless study the gifts with which nature had endowed him'.

Whatever has been said of Paganini's 'tireless practising' must apply to his early years—certainly not later than about 1805. After that time no one ever heard him practise in the usually accepted sense of that word. He often said that he 'had practised enough and could now do with a little rest'; and it seems that all the exercise he needed in later years was provided by his concerts themselves. Stories of amateurs who resorted to all kinds of subterfuge in order to hear him at his studies are legion. The London musicians were just as anxious to solve the mystery of Paganini's mastery as were his colleagues of Berlin, Frankfort, and Vienna. But he allowed no one to catch a glimpse of his solo parts, and always jealously guarded the music both before and after rehearsal. There is the entertaining story of the determined Englishman who followed the artist from town to town in the hope of hearing him practise, and thus arrive at his 'secret'. After many fruitless attempts he at length obtained a room next to that in which Paganini lodged. Peeping through the key-hole he saw the violinist seated on a couch; the violin was taken from its case and placed under the chin; but the bow, to the great disgust of the eavesdropper, was left in the case. After the left hand had been exercised a little and certain distances had been measured, the violin was returned to its case, and the practice was over.

He was equally disappointing at rehearsal. The members of the orchestra were always agog with excitement, thinking that their privileged positions would enable them to learn something of the virtuoso's technical methods; but the lesson was never forthcoming. Paganini would indicate the required tempo for the introduction, play a few very tame passages to keep the accompaniment to the speed he desired—passages generally quite different from those introduced at the concert—and when the brilliant cadenza was reached he would play the first few notes, turn abruptly, and with a meaning smile say airily, 'Et cetera, Messieurs'. He lost his temper easily if the band did not grasp his intentions as quickly as he thought they should; but when they were fortunate enough to divine his purpose, he would overload them with praise—his favourite expression on such occasions being, 'Bravissimo, you are all virtuosi'. At the end of the rehearsal he took the orchestral parts away with him to prevent them being copied; and the only way in which the then common pirates could work was to write down the themes as well as they could at the performance, adapt an accompaniment more or less like the original, and publish the result. *The Athenaeum* for December 24th, 1831, printed a significant paragraph in illustration of this practice: 'It appears that while so many were listening in rapture to this celebrated player, others, and of some fame too, were noting down his solos as performed. When the musical annuals made their appearance, this was so palpable that Paganini was advised to proceed against the parties, and one of them, a music-seller in Bond-street, is understood to have paid a sum of money by way of compromise'.

Very few of Paganini's works were published during his life-time—only those contained under the first five opus numbers: *Twenty-four Caprices,* op. 1, for solo violin; *Twelve Sonatas,* opp. 2 and 3, for violin and guitar; and *Six Quartets,* opp. 4 and 5, for violin, viola, guitar and violoncello. The *Capricci* were long considered impossible of performance, and not until Paganini arrived in Paris was it seen how feasible they were. Apart from their mere technical difficulty, they possess a distinctly musical worth. The next series of works to be published (Opp. 6—14) did not appear until 1851; but even then the greater part of Paganini's writing remained unpublished. The works printed posthumously were: *Concerto in E-flat,* op 6; *Concerto in B-Minor,* op. 7, ending with the *Campanella* rondo; *Le Streghe,* op 8; *God Save the King,* op 9; *Carneval di Venezia,* op. 10; *Moto Perpetuo,* op. 11, *Allegro di Sonata*; *Non più Mesta,* op. 12; *I Palpiti,* op. 13; and sixty variations on the air *Barucaba* (op. 14; written at Genoa in February, 1835, in three books). Without opus number, three airs with variations on the G-string, the fantasia on the prayer from *Moise,* and a few less important works, appeared. For unaccompanied violin his *Nel Cor più non mi sento* was also printed.

By far the greatest part of Paganini's unpublished music is now preserved in the Heyer Museum at Cologne. In 1910 baron Achille II (Nicolo's grandson) disposed of his illustrious grandfather's musical possessions by public auction in Florence. The manuscripts were offered by him to the museum at Genoa and declined on account of the price asked. The Heyer collection acquired them from the antiquarian who secured them in Florence. Besides these manuscripts there still remain three more concerti unpublished. In the Heyer catalogue (compiled in admirable manner by Georg Kinsky) are a number of interesting entries relating to manuscripts of the historical importance of the *Napoléon* sonata for the G-string, the *Scena Amorosa* on two strings (written for the countess at Lucca), a *Sonata Varsavia* (based on a theme used in the fifth concerto), the *Storm,* and the *Maria Luisa* sonata for the G-string.

Whether Paganini really developed a course of study for the violin differing from that used by the other schools, we have no means of deciding. In his conversations with Schottky he always insisted that he had worked out such a plan. He claimed that he used it in part when he instructed Sivori. Schottky tells us that Paganini repeatedly assured him that with his method a young man could be fully trained in three years to a degree of proficiency usually attained after ten years of study. ' I often asked him if he were joking . . . and each time he answered : " I swear to you that I am speaking the truth, and authorize you to say as much in the biography. Only one solitary person, who will now be about twenty-four years old, Signor Gaetano Ciandelli at Naples, knows my secret. He had played the cello for a long time in a very mediocre manner, so that his performance was considered of the everyday order, and passed without special notice. But as the young man interested me, and I wanted to favour him, I made him acquainted with my discovery, which had so good an effect upon him that in the course of three days he was quite a different person, and the change in his playing was considered miraculous ". One will readily believe that I shook my head dubiously at this ; but Paganini persistently assured me of his earnestness when making the declaration '. To the day of his death Paganini flirted with the idea of giving his ' discovery ' to the world ; but, if such a thing really existed as a practicable plan, it perished with him.

In the course of his career Paganini—having ample funds at

his disposal—brought together a collection of instruments that would to-day be worth a fortune. When he was in Prague in 1828 he told Schottky that he possessed ' a veritable treasure-hoard of valuable instruments, of which I take only the smallest part with me on my travels. The Stradivari which I have left in Italy, and which I consider to be the father of all violins, has a tone almost as big as that of a contrabass, so distinguished is it by its power. I would not part with it at any price—not even for the 3800 francs that was paid for Viotti's violin in 1824. Side by side with this I place my excellent cello (also by Stradivari). At Milan I have also left a beautiful Amati and a Guarneri, the latter a little on the small side, but still possessing a charming tone '. The full tale of his instruments was told in 1910 when all those not bequeathed by will were sold in Florence: Seven Stradivaris (1692, 1678, 1695, 1724 (2), 1725, and 1726); one by Giuseppe Guarneri (1734), one by Andrea Guarneri (1670), one by Guarneri del Gesù (1742), two by Nicolas Amati, one by Tononi, and one by Ruggeri. In addition there were two Stradivari celli (1712 and 1728), one by Ruggeri (1734), and a Stradivari viola dating from 1731. A noble collection of instruments now dispersed to inspire their present owners with the patience and persistence of the man who once cherished them as things that needed no more than the touch of his hands to make their speech almost human.

.   .   .   .

Paganini said, ' Bisogna forte sentire per far sentire ', and in that is summed up the secret of his almost supernatural power over all who heard him. The instrument, the composition, and even his stupendous technical achievements—all fade into the background, leaving behind them just a man; to impart his human message by means of his own intense feeling.

INDEX

321

NICOLO PAGANINI

A Bibliography
Compiled By Frederick Freedman

NICOLO PAGANINI

A Bibliography
Compiled By Frederick Freedman

Aarvig, C. A. *Paganini-Legenden*. Copenhagen: W. Hansen, 1935. 104 pp.

Abbado, Michelangelo. In: *Enciclopedia Treccani* [analysis of compositions].

————. "Ho visto Nicolò Paganini," *La Lettura* [Milan] (August 1941).

————. "Nicolò Paganini," in: Claudio Sartori, ed. *Enciclopedia della Musica*, 4 vols. (Milan: Ricordi, 1963–64), III, 353–5.

————. See: "Omaggio."

————. "La 'Scordatura' negli strumenti ad arco o Niccolò Paganini," *La Rassegna musicale* XIII/5 (May 1940), 213–26.

Abbiati, Franco. "Miracolo a Parigi. Il 'Quatro Concerto' per violino e orchestra di Paganini ricuperato nella sua stesura integrale ed eseguito alla sala Pleyel," *La Scala* 61 (December 1954), 33–8; 131–3.

Abell, A. "Famous Violinists of the Past," *Musical Courier* LVIII/8 (August 1908), 9–11.

Alver, Alfred W. "New Light on Paganini," *Guitar Review* 2 (1947), 1–2f.

————. "New Light on Paganini," *The Strad* XL (1929–30), 408–9, 473–4, 535–7, 599–600, 663–5.

Amsler, Marc. "La lettre de Paganini à Berlioz ou les perplexités d'un collectionneur," *Scripta manent* I/2 (1956/57), 9–14.

Anders, Gottfried Engelbert. *Niccolò Paganini: sa vie, sa personne, et quelques mots sur son sécret*. Paris: Delaunay, 1831.

Armando, Walter G. *Paganini: eine Biographie*. Hamburg: Rütten & Loening, 1960. 382 pp.

B., F. "Ein Meisterwerk Paganinis entdeckt," *Die Woche* [Berlin] XXXIX/15 (1937), 26.

Bachmann, Alberto. *Les grands violonistes du passé*. Paris: Fischbacher, 1913.

———. "Nicolò Paganini, sa vie, ses oeuvres et son influence," *Mercure musical* (December 1907; January 1908).

Balestreri, Giuliano. *Di tanti palpiti*. Genoa: 1940.

———. "Paganini direttore d'orchestra," *La Rassegna musicale* XII/12 (December 1939), 491–503.

Bandini, A. R. "The Greatest Fiddler of Them All: Nicolò Paganini, 1782–1840," *The Catholic World* CLI [=902] (1940), 138–48.

Barát, Endre. *Boszorkánytánc: Paganini életregénye*. Budapest: Zenemükiadó Vállalat, 1962. [Fiction.]

Bargellini, Sante. *La chitarre di Paganini*. Rome.

———. "Paganini and the Princess," *The Musical Quarterly* XX/4 (October 1934), 408–18.

———. "Paganini à Lucques (d'après des documents inédits)," *La Revue musicale* X/4 (February 1929), 162–5.

Belgrano, T. *Imbreviature di Giovanni Scriba*. Genoa: Istituto Sordomuti, 1882.

Bennati, Francesco. "Notice physiologique sur Nicolò Paganini," *Revue de Paris* (May 1831).

Berri, Pietro. "La malattia di Paganini," *L'Almanacco del Medico* (1938).

———. *Il calvario di Paganini*. Savona: Liguria, 1955.

———. *Paganini: documenti e testimonianze*. Genoa: Sigla Effe, 1962. 189 pp.

———. "Paganiniana," *Bollettino Ligustico* III (1958), 129–38.

———. "Ricette di Paganini," *Rivista municipale Genova* XXXVI/7 (1959), 32–7. [Also in: *La Lettura del Medico* XVII/12 (1959), 308–16.]

———. "Testimonianze su Paganini e contributi elvetici," *Svizzera Italiana* XIX [=138] (1959), 1–13. [Also in: *La Scala* 123 (February 1960), 13–20.]

————, and Zdeněk Výborný. "Paganiniana: Tema e variazioni," *Rivista municipale Genova* XXXV/5 (1958) , 24–9.

Bianchi, Renzo. "Il trillo del diavolo; vita dei Niccolò Paganini," *Radiocorriere* 31–7, 40, 43–4 (1957) .

Biographie von Nicolo Paganini. Zurich: 1846.

Blondel, Augusta. "The Terrors of Superstition; the Last Days of Paganini," *Menorah* XI/9 (September 1891) , 126–41.

Boero, G. B. *Genealogia di Paganini.* Genoa: [National Committee], 1940.

Bonaventura, Arnaldo. "Gli autografi musicali di Niccolò Paganini," *La Bibliofilia* XII (April 1910) , 1–31.

————. *Niccolò Paganini.* Genoa: A. F. Formiggini, 1915. [Other editions: Modena: 1911; Rome: 1923; Modena: 1939.]

————. "Nuovi ricordi di Niccolò Paganini," *La Bibliofilia* XI (June–July 1909) , 127–32.

Bonavia, Ferruccio. "A New Life of Paganini," *Monthly Musical Record* LXVI (1936) , 83–4.

————. "Nicolo Paganini," *The Strad* LI [=601] (May 1940) , 11–3. [Also appeared as: "Paganini: Died May 27, 1840," *The Musical Times* LXXXI [=1168] (June 1940) , 252–4.]

Bone, Philip J. "Paganini and the Guitar," *Hinrichsen's Musical Year Book* VII (1952) , 475–85. [Also appeared as: "Nicolo Paganini and the Guitar," *The Strad* LXV (August 1954) , 104–8; (September 1954) , 136; (November 1954) , 224.]

Boschetti, Ottavio. *Al celebratissimo Barone Cavaliere Nicolò Paganini.* Parma: 1835.

Boschot, Adolphe. *Une vie romantique; Hector Berlioz.* Paris: Plon-Nourrit, 1919.

Botti, Don Ferruccio. *Paganini e Parma. Note storicocritiche.* Parma: Scuola Tipografica Benedettina, 1962.

————. *Spigolature d'archivio; spunti di cronaca e storia dagli archivi parrocchiali parmensi.* Parma: Scuola Tipografica Benedettina, 1952–58. 2 vols.

Bouffier. *Die Violine und ihre Virtuosen.* Berlin: 1890.

Brémont, Anna Elizabeth, comtesse de. *The World of Music; the Great Virtuosi.* New York: Brentano's, 1892.

Brennecke, Wilfried. "Paganini in Kassel," *Musica* IX/4 (April 1955), 131–2.

Bromfield, Louis. "Paganini's Secret Exercise Falls to Young Violinist," *Musical America* XXXVI/5 (May 1922), 5.

Bruecker, Hermann. "Paganini in Kassel," *Die Musik* XIX (1927), 864–6.

Bruni, O. *Niccolò Paganini, celebre violinista Genovese: Racconto storico.* Florence: Galleti & Cocci, 1873. [Also 1904 ed.]

Calmeyer, J. H. "The Mysterious Wizard of the Violin," *Etude* LXXII/5 (May 1954), 25; LXXII/7 (July 1954), 25.

Campo, H. *Niccolò Zaganini. Eine Parodie.* Breslau: 1829.

Catalogo No. 84. Collezione del celebre violinista N. Paganini. Florence: 1910.

Chalupt, René. "*Paganini, le magicien,* par Renée de Saussine," *La Revue musicale* XIX [=183] (April–May 1938), 323.

Chiesa, Mary Tibaldi-. See: Tibaldi-Chiesa, Mary.

Codignola, Arturo. *Paganini intimo.* Genoa: Municipio de Genova, 1935. 691 pp. [Important study of Paganini's 287 letters.]

Codignola, Mario. *Arte e magia di Nicolò Paganini.* Milan: Ricordi, 1960. 106 pp.

Cohn, Arthur. "On Epic, a First of Rich Importance—Paganini: 'The 24 Caprices' Played on the Viola by Emanuel Vardi," *The American Record Guide* XXXI/9 (June 1965), 966–7.

Colombo, Gianluigi. "Paganini pianista," *La Scala* 127 (June 1960), 12–3.

[Concerto No. 1, in D major, Op. 6, for Violin and Orchestra. Program Notes appear in the following:
Chicago Symphony Orchestra Program Notes (April 21, 1949), 9.
Cincinnati Symphony Orchestra Program Notes (April 2, 1954), 551–5.
New York Philharmonic—Symphony Society Notes (October 22, 1950); (November 29, 1951).
Philadelphia Orchestra Program Notes (January 13, 1950), 367; (March 27, 1953), 622–5.

San Antonio Symphony Program Notes (December 1, 1962), 15.

San Francisco Symphony Notes (April 4, 1962), 17.]

Conestabile della Staffa, Giovanni Carlo, conte. *Vita di Niccolò Paganini da Genova, scritta ed illustrata da Giancarlo Conestabile.* Perugia: Tip. di V. Bartelli, 1851. 317 pp.

————. *Vita di Niccolò Paganini; nuova edizione con aggiunte e note di Federico Mompellio.* Milan: Società editrice Dante Aligheri, 1936. [=Studi e ritratti, 14.] 646 pp. [Major revision of previous work; important work.]

Cooke, James Francis. "Musical Showmanship," *Etude* LXXIII/4 (April 1955), 16.

Copertini, Spartaco. "Il segreto di Paganini," *Il Piccolo di Parma* (April 14, 1920).

Corte, Andrea della. "Caratteri dell'uomo Paganini," *La Rassegna musicale* (July–August 1940), 301–12.

Courcy, Geraldine I. C. de. "Beiträge zur Biographie Paganinis," *Die Musikforschung* XIX/3 (July–September 1966), 305–8.

————. *Chronology of Nicolo Paganini's Life; Chronologie von Nicolo Paganinis Leben.* (English and German text; German trans. by Hans Dünnebeil.) Wiesbaden: Erdmann, 1961.

————. "Mystifikation um Paganinis Viertes Violinkonzert," *Musica* IX/3 (March 1955), 132–4.

————. "A New Look at Paganini," *American String Teacher* XI/3 (1961), 14.

————. "Niccolò Paganini," in: Friedrich Blume, ed., *Musik in Geschichte und Gegenwart* (Kassel: Bärenreiter, 1949–69), X, 630–3.

————. *Paganini, the Genoese.* Norman: University of Oklahoma Press, 1957. 2 vols. [Most recent, though not entirely adequate, English-language work on Paganini.]

————. "Paganini's Posthumous Calvary," *American String Teacher* XIV/3 (1964), 16–7.

————. "Ein unbekanntes Werk von Paganini," *Musica* IX/10 (October 1955), 512–3.

Dancla, Charles. *Notes et Souvenirs.* Paris: Delamotte, 1893.

Dawson, Frederick. "Paganini in Leeds (January, 1832)," *Publication of the Thoresby Society* [*Leeds, England*] XXXIII/3 (1936), 447–58.

Day, Lillian. *Niccolo Paganini of Genoa.* New York: Macaulay, 1929. 318 pp. [Another ed.: London: Gollancz, 1967. 298 pp.]

della Corte, Andrea. See: Corte, Andrea della.

Dent, A. "Paganini" [condensed from Preludes & Studies], *The Musical Digest* VIII (1950). 178–81.

Desverges et Varin. *Paganini en Allemagne apropos anecdotiques en l'acte.* Paris: 1831.

Dewelster, J. "La legende de Paganini le diabolique," *Musica* [*Chaix*] 73 (April 1960), 7–11.

———. "Nicolo Paganini, le sorcier du violon," *Musica* [*Chaix*] 71 (February 1960), 18–21.

Dolejsï, Robert. "Finger Calisthenics and the Paganini Legend," *American String Teacher* XIII/4 (1963), 17–21.

Donoghue, O. *Paganini à Boulogne sur mer.* Paris: [n.d.]

Dorian, Frederick. "Paganiniana: Divertimento by Alfredo Casella," *The Musical Quarterly* XXXIV/2 (April 1948), 254–6.

Doring, Ernest N. "A Faked and an Authentic Portrait of Nicolo Paganini," *Violins & Violinists* XV (May–June 1954), 134–7; (November–December 1954). [German version as: "Wie sah Paganini aus? Über echte und gefählschte Bilder des Meisters," *Musica* IX/3 (March 1955), 103–7.]

Dubourg, George. *The Violin.* London: Cocks & Co., 1836. [Partly serialized as: "The Italian School," *Violins & Violinists* XIV (March–April 1953), 77–85; (May–June 1953), 105–7; (July–August 1953), 173–80; (September–October 1953), 224–9; (November–December 1953), 262–4; XV (January–February 1954), 32–5; (March–April 1954), 84–8; (May–June 1954), 132–4; (September–October 1954), 227–30.

Eberhardt, Goby. *Mein System des Übens für Violine und Klavier auf psychophysiologisher Grundlage.* Dresden: G. Kühtmann, 1907.

———. "Nicolo Paganini," *Bühne und Welt* (1906).

Eberhardt, Siegfried. *Paganinis Geigenhaltung; die Entdeckung des Gesetzes virtuoser Sicherheit; Buchschmuck und illustrationen von Ernst Huxdorf.* Berlin: A. Fürstnen, 1921.

Ehrlich, Alfred Heinrich. *Berühmte Geiger der Vergangenheit und Gegenwart.* Leipzig: A. H. Payne, 1893.

————. *Die Geige in Wahrheit und Fabel.* Leipzig: [n.d.]

Escudier, Léon. *Mes souvenirs: les virtuoses.* Paris: E. Dentu, 1868.

Escudier, Märie Pierre Yves, and Léon Escudier. *Vie et aventures des cantatrices célèbres; précédées des musiciens de l'empire et suivies de la vie anecdotique de Paganini.* Paris: E. Dentu, 1856.

Evanoff, G. "Paganini—1782-1840," *Canon: Australian Music Journal* XIII (October 1959) , 72-3.

Farga, Franz. *Paganini, der Roman seines Lebens.* Zürich-Rüschlikon: A. Müller, 1950. 191 pp. [Fiction.]

Fastofsky, Stuart. "Duetto fiorentino," *Musical America* LXXIV/4 (April 1954) , 23.

Fayolle, François. *Paganini et de Bériot, ou avis aux artistes qui se destinent à l'eseignement du violon.* Paris: Legouest, 1831.

Felice Da Mareto, P. "Ancora del processo ecclesiastico a carico di Nicolo Paganini," *Parma per l'arte* IX/1 (1959) , 15-23.

Ferrarini, Mario. "L'orchestra di Paganini e i direttori del suo tempo," *Musica d'oggi* XXII/6 (June 1940) , 155-60.

Ferris, George Titus. *Great Violinists and Pianists.* Rev. ed. New York: D. Appleton, 1895. [Chapter on Paganini.]

Fétis, François Joseph. *Notice biographique sur Niccolò Paganini, suivie de l'analyse de ses ouvrages et précédée d'une esquisse de l'histoire du violon.* Paris: Schönenberger, 1851. 95 pp. [English translation as: *Biographical Notice of Nicolo Paganini, Followed by an Analysis of His Compositions, and Preceded by a Sketch of the History of the Violin.* Trans. by Wellington Guernsey. London: Schott, 1852. 68 pp. 2nd ed.: London: Schott, 1876. 90 pp.]

"Fiddler's Will," *Time* LXII (October 19, 1953) , 88.

Fiechtner, Helmut A., and Joachim Herrmann. "Das wiederentdeckte Paganini-Konzert," *Musica* IX/2 (February 1955) , 65-6. [About D minor violin concerto.]

Finck, Henry Theophilus. *Masters of the Violin*. New York: Mentor Assoc., 1916.

Fiorentino, [Raffaello Buonajuti?]. "Paganini und seine Werke," *Wiener Abendpost* (March 19, 1852).

Fitz-James, M. de Miramon. See: Miramon Fitz-James.

Flesch, Carl. "Apropos of Paganini's Secret," *The Strad* L [=593] (1939), 205–7.

Flodin, Robert W. *The Meaning of Paganini*. San Francisco: Morgan Print Co., 1953.

G., G. *Paganini*. Rome: 1840.

Gasperini, [Guido?]. "Brevi notizie su un periodo poco noto della vita di Nicolò Paganini," *La Rinascita musicale* (July–August 1919).

Gerber, Ernst Ludwig. *Neues historisch-biographisches Lexikon der Tonkünstler* . . . (Leipzig: A. Kühnel, 1812–14), IV, 47. [One of the earliest biographical notices.]

Germi, [Luigi Guglielmo]. "Unbekannte Briefe Paganinis an Germi," *N. Bad. Landeszeitung* (March 27, 1909).

Gervasoni, Carlo. *Nuova teoria de musica ricavata dall'odierna pratica*. Parma: Stamperia Blanchon, 1812.

Gerzfeld, J. *Paganinis Geige*. Riga: 1898.

Giazotto, Remo. See: "Omaggio."

Gottschalg, Alexander Wilhelm. "Nicolo Paganini," *Chorgesang* (October 1907).

Grew, Eva Mary. "Niccolò Paganini," *Musical Opinion* (May 1940), 343–4.

Grove, E. S. "The Perils of Paganini," *Music Journal* XXIII/5 (May 1965), 38–9.

Guadagnino, Luigi Maria. "Immagini di Paganini," *La Scala* 23 (October 1951), 42–4.

Günther, A. *Paganini in Lucca*. Munich: 1929.

Guhr, Carl Wilhelm Ferdinand. *Ueber Paganini's Kunst, die Violine zu spielen; ein Anhang zu jeder bis jetzt erschienenen Violinschule nebst einer Abhandlung über das Flageoletspiel in einfachen und Doppeltönen*. Mainz: B. Schott's Söhnen, 1829. [French version as: *L'art de jouer du violin de Paganini*.

338

Appendice à toutes les méthodes qui ont paru jusqu'à présent. Avec un traité des sons harmoniques simples et doubles. Mayence: Les Fils de B. Schott, 1829. 69 pp. English version as: *Paganini's Art of Playing the Violin, with a Treatise on Single and Double Harmonic Notes,* trans. from the German by Sabilla Novello, and revised by C. Egerton Lowe. London: Novello, [1915]. Earlier English version: London: Novello, 1831.]

————. "Paganini à Francfort en 1829," in: C. F. Schmidt, *Mittheilungen* (Heilbronn: 1901).

————, and Gottfried Weber. "Paganinis Kunst, die Violine zu spielen," *Caecilia* XI (1820), 76–86. [French trans. by Fétis, *La Revue musicale* (December 1829).]

Guichard, Arthur de. "Some Interesting Data and Personal Notes About Paganini," *Musical Observer* XIX/8 (1920), 18, 25.

Halski, Czeslaw Raymond. "Paganini and Lipiński," *Music and Letters* XL/3 (July 1959), 274–8.

Hamerton, R. J. "Paganini," *Musical Gem* (1832).

Harrison, Richard. "A Renowned Fiddler," *Musical Opinion* (July, August & September 1888).

Harrys, Georg. *Paganini in seinen Reisewagen und Zimmer, in seinen redseligen Stunden, in Gesellschaftlichen Zirkeln und seinen Konzerten.* Brunswick: Vieweg, 1830.

Haweis, Hugh Reginald. "Paganini," in his: *My Musical Life* (London: W. H. Allen, 1884), 339–88.

————. *Good Words* [three articles about Paganini].

Heald, W. F. "No Rest for Paganini (the Strange Wanderings of His Body After Death)," *Musical Courier* XL/8 (September 1954), 33.

Hedouins, O. *Mosaïque. Peintres. Musiciens.* Valenciennes: 1856.

[Heine, Heinrich]. "Paganini," *Bollettino bibliografico musicale* I–II (April 1927), 10–16.

"Heinrich Heine über Paganini und Liszt," *Neue Zeitschrift für Musik* CXVII/4 (April 1956), 222.

Héritier, Louis François L'. See: L'Héritier.

Heron-Allen, Edward. *Fidiculana. I. The Violin. II. Nicolo Paga-*

nini and His Guarnerius. III. Early Violin Schools. IV. Old Violin Frauds. London: Printed for the author by Mitchell & Hughes, 1890. 64 pp. [=His *De Fidiculis Opuscula, Opusculum* IV.]

Hertens, G. "Argentina," *Violins & Violinists* XII (December 1951), 347.

Herzog, Friedrich W. "Paganini—Mythos und Wirklichkeit," *Musik* XXXII (May 1940), 264–5.

Hiller, Ferdinand. *Künstlerleben.* Köln: 1873.

"History of a Violin," *Music and Musicians* IX (August 1961), 19.

Holde, Artur. "An Unknown Paganini Letter," *Music and Letters* XXVIII/4 (October 1947), 338–40.

Holmes, [William G.?]. *Notes Upon Notes.* London: [n.d.]

Hubbard, Elbert. *Little Journeys to the Homes of Great Musicians.* New York: G. P. Putnam's Sons, 1903. [Chapter on Paganini.]

Hüttel, Walter. "Niccolò Paganini. Zum 175. Geburstag des Meisters," *Musik und Gesellschaft* VII (1957), 601–3.

Huschke, Konrad. "Paganini und Spohr; Ein Kapitel Geigergeschichte," [*Neue*] *Zeitschrift für Musik* CXV/11 (November 1954), 636–7.

Iampoliski, I. M. See: Yampol'sky.

Imbert de Laphalèque, G. See: L'Héritier, Louis François

Istel, Edgar. "The Secret of Paganini's Technique," *The Musical Quarterly* XVI/1 (January 1930), 101–16.

———. *Nicolo Paganini; mit einem bildnis nach der kreidezeichung von Lyser.* Leipzig: Breitkopf & Härtel, 1919. 60 pp.

"Italy: Paganini's Violin Played Upon by Zino Francescatti," *Violins & Violinists* XIV/6 (November-December 1953), 252.

Jacobsen, Maxim. *The Mastery of Violin Playing.* English text prepared by Gemma Farmer. 2 vols. New York: Boosey & Hawkes, 1957. [See: II, 4–7.]

Jacomb, C. E. "The Resources of a Violin," *The Strad* LX (June 1949), 41–2; (July 1949), 73–4.

Jampolskij, Izrail' Markovič. See: Yampol'sky.

Jarosy, Albert. *A New Theory of Fingering (Paganini and His Secret),* English version by Seymour Whinyates. London:

Allen & Unwin, 1933. 70 pp. [French original as: *Nouvelle théorie du doigté (Paganini et son secret)*, Paris: 1924. German version as: *Paganinis Lehre*, Berlin: 1921.]

Kapp, Julius. *Nicolò Paganini.* 15., erg. Aufl. Tutzing: Hans Schneider, 1969. 183 pp. [Earlier eds.: Berlin & Leipzig: Schuster & Loeffler, 1913; 13. ed. Stuttgart: Deutsche Verlags-Anstalt, 1928. 234 pp.]

Kestner, A. *Römische Studien (Paganini in Italien).* Berlin: 1850.

Kinsky, Georg. "Paganinis musikalischer Nachlass," in his: *Musikhistorisches Museum von Wilhelm Heyer in Köln,* 4 vols. (Leipzig: Breitkopf & Härtel, 1910–16), IV [Musik-Autographen], 402–47.

Kirkendale, Warren. "Segreto Communicato da Paganini," *Journal of the American Musicological Society* XVIII/3 (Fall 1965), 394–407. [Important discussion of Paganini's use of artificial harmonics in double stops.]

Klein, Josef B. A. *Paganinis Übungsgeheimnis; Lehrgang des geistigen Übens für Anfänger sowie für Fortgeschrittene als Weg zur wahren Virtuosität. Das Naturgesetz im Bewegungsgeschehen für alle Streichinstrumente.* Leipzig: Steingräber Verlag, 1934.

Kmoch, V. "Scordatura 'Secret' of Paganini," *The Strad* LXXVIII (June 1967), 67.

Kobbé, Gustav. "The Devil and Paganini," *Musician* XI (1906), 219–21.

Kohut, Adolpf. *Aus dem Zauberlande Polyhymnias, Neues über Paganini.* Berlin: 1892.

Komroff, Manuel. *The Magic Bow; a Romance of Paganini.* New York/London: Harper, 1940. 362 pp. [Fiction.]

Krick, George C. "Niccolò Paganini, Guitarist,"*Etude* LVIII/8 (August 1940), 567–71.

Kross, Emil. *Studium der 24 Capricen.* Mainz: Schott, 1900. [English version as: *The Study of Paganini's Twenty-Four Caprices; a New Descriptive Treatise Based Upon Paganini's Secret Methods, Explaining How These Famous Studies Can Be*

Mastered by All Violin Players. Trans. by Gustav Saenger. London & New York: C. Fischer, 1908. 53 pp.]

Kuechler, Ferdinand. "Goether über Paganini," *Geigenspiel-Rundschau* 18 (1936), 29–30.

Küster, Johann Heinrich. "Einiges über die Ausübung der Flageolettöne auf der Violine," *Allgemeine Musikalische Zeitung* XXI/42 (October 20, 1819), 701-7.

Kuhnert, Adolfo Artur. *Paganini: romäns, tulkojusi Lücija Kalnini.* Riga: "Grämatu draugs," 1934. [5th ed. Leipzig: Reclam, 1938. 247 pp.]

Kuznetsoff, Konstantin, and Izrail Yampolsky. "[Paganini as a Man and Artist]," *Sovetskaia Muzyka* VIII (August 1940), 60–73.

Lahee, Henry Charles. *Famous Violinists of To-Day and Yesterday.* Boston: The Page Co., 1916. 384 pp.

Lancellotti, Arturo. "Paganini," *Revista de musica* III (1929), 85–96.

Langle, F. de. *Elisa, Soeur de Napoléon I.* Paris: Denoel, 1947.

Laphalèque, G. Imbert de. See: L'Héritier, Louis François.

Lazzareschi, E. *Il soggiorno di Niccolò Paganini a Lucca.* Lucca: Artigianelli, 1940.

Lewin, R. "Left or Right?" *The Strad* LX (December 1949), 233-4.

———. "The Secret," *The Strad* LX (September 1949), 137-8; (October 1949), 169–70.

L'Héritier, Louis François. *Notice sur le célèbre violiniste Nicolò Paganini,* par G. Imbert de Laphalèque [pseud.]. Paris: E. Guyot, 1830. 66 pp. [English version as: *Some Account of the Celebrated Violinist N. Paganini,* trans. . . . with additional notes. London: Chappell, Clementi, Collard & Collard, 1830. 66 pp.]

"Library of Congress Gets Paganini Letters," *The Music Magazine and Musical Courier* CLXIII/12 (December 1961), 2.

[Lipiński, Karol.] "[Lipiński and Paganini in Padua]," *Tygodnik Wielkopolski Naukowy, Literacki i Artystyczny* [Poznan] (1873).

Listemann, Bernhard. "The Art of Paganini," *Violinist* X/2 (1910), 24–30.

Lobe, Johann Christian. "Der Wundermann auf der Geige," *Gartenlaube* (1872).

Loveland, J. D. E. "The Strange Obsequies of Paganini," *Monthly Review* XXV/3 (December 1906), 81–9.

Luin, Elisabet Jeannette. "Divagazioni su Paganini all'estero (Nel centenario dell morte)," *Musica d'oggi* XXII/5 (May 1940), 126–9.

Lyser, Johann Peter. *Phantasie aus B-moll.* Hamburg: 1830.

———. "Paganini," *Lesefrüchte* (1830).

Macmillan, F. "Paganini's Lost Secret Revealed at Last," *Musical Courier* LIV/12 (December 1907), 16–7.

Manassero, Aristide. "La vita e l'arte Nicolo Paganini su nuovi documenti," *Nuova antologia* V/139 (February 16, 1909), 591–605.

Mandelli, Alfredo. *Carlo Bignami e Niccolò Paganini.* Milan: Ricordi, 1893.

[Manén, Joan]. "Paganinis erste Grabstätte," *Geigenspiel-Rundschau* 27 (1938), 32.

Mantovani, Roberto. *Le Secret de Paganini.* Paris: 1922.

Marbach, G. "Der Zaubergeiger," *Neue Zeitschrift für Musik* CXVIII/1 (January 1957), 10.

Marcelli, J. *Aux violonistes. Petit traité de violon pour le développement paride de la technique et de la sonorité par l'application du secret de Paganini et l'art de travailler.* Croix: L'auteur, 1937.

Marchisio, Cesare. "Il tributo d'omaggio dell' Italia e del mondo a Niccolò Paganini nel primo centenario della morte (1840–1940)," *Genova: rivista municipale* XX/8 (July 1940), 27–48. [Offprint issued separately as: "La celebrazione del primo centenario della morte di Niccolò Paganini, 1840–1940."]

Martens, Frederick Herman. *Paganini.* New York: Breitkopf & Härtel, 1922. 27 pp.

Marx, Adolf Bernhard. *Erinnerungen. Aus meinem Leben.* Berlin: O. Janke, 1865.

Meckel, C. "Paganini und Spohr, ein Vergleich," *Neue Zeitschrift für Musik* (1901).

Meisel. "Der falsche Virtuose oder das Konzert auf der G-Saite," *Passe in 2 Aufzügen. Musik von Glaser.* Vienna: 1828.

Mell, Albert. "Paganiniana in the Muller Collection of the New York Public Library," *The Musical Quarterly* XXXIX/1 (January 1953), 1–25.

———. "[Review of] Cantabile and 6 Sonatas (Centone de Sonata) for violin and guitar (recording)," *The Musical Quarterly* XLVI/4 (October 1960), 557–9.

———. "[Review of] *Paganini the Genoese,* by G. I. C. de Courcy," *The Musical Quarterly* XLIV/4 (October 1958), 524–31. [Important review.]

Mengozzi, G. C. *Niccolò Paganini a Rimini.* Rimini: Zangheri, 1952.

Meynell, Esther Hallam. *Time's Door.* New York: Macmillan, 1935. [Fiction.]

Miramon Fitz-James, M. de. *Paganini à Marseille.* Marseille: Fuéri, 1841.

Mompellio, Federico. "Il quinto concerto di Paganini," *Musicisti Piemontesi e Liguri Academia Musicale Chigiana* XVII (1959), 99–105.

———. See also: "Omaggio"; Conestabile.

Montanelli, Archimede. *Paganini a Forlì.* Forlì: 1930.

Morazzoni, Giuseppe. "Iconographia Paganiniana," in: *Catalogo della Mostra di cimeli Paganiniani* (Genoa: 1940).

Morelli-Gallet, Wina. "Das Originaltestament Nicolo Paganinis," *Österreichische Musikzeitschrift* XV/1 (January 1960), 25–7. [Also as: "Das Wiener Originaltestament Nicolo Paganinis," *Musik und Gesellschaft* XI (December 1961), 734–6.]

Moscheles, Ignaz. *Aus Moscheles' Leben.* Leipzig: Duncker & Humblot, 1872–1873.

N., G. "Altes und Neues über Paganini," *Das Orchester* (June/August 1885).

Narayn, D. "The Search for Guarnerius del Gesu," *Violins & Violinists* XXII/1 (Spring 1961), 2–3.

"Neizvestnoe pis'mo N. Paganini [An Unknown Letter from Paganini to A. F. S. Pacini]," *Sovetskaja Muzyka* XII (1957), 65–7.

Némethy, Ferenc. *Paganini, a "Sátán hegedüse," halálának százéves fordulójára irta.* Budapest: Rózsavölgyi és társa, 1940. 181 pp.

"Neznamý konzert N. Paganiniko," *Hudebni rozhledy* VIII (1955), 33.

Nicolai, Gustav. *Arabesken für Musikfreunde* (Leipzig: Wigand, 1835), II, 187–326.

Nicoll, K. G. "Correspondence," *The Strad* LXVI (February 1956), 396.

"Nicolo Paganini," *Slöjd och Ton: tidskrift för Stränginstrumentmakare* XXXIII/2 (1963), 23–4.

"Nieznany list Paganiniego," *Ruch Muzyczny* XI/10 (November 1967), 9.

Niggli, Arnold. "Nicolo Paganini," in: Waldersee, P., *Sammlung musikalische Vorträge* IV (1882). [Re-issued (?) also: Leipzig: 1892.]

"Omaggio a Nicolò Paganini," *Il Secolo XIX* [Genoa] (May 28, 1940). [Contains articles by Ildebrando Pizzetti, Remo Giazotto, Federico Mompellio, and Michelangelo Abbado.]

Ondřiček, František. "Am Sarge Paganinis," *Musica* XI/2 (February 1957), 72–4.

Onoranze a Niccolò Paganini, nel 1° Centenario della morte, sotto l'alto patronato del Duce. Programma delle manifestazioni. Genoa: 1940.

Orestad, Ivar. "Paganinis Violin," *Slöjd och Ton: tidskrift för Stränginstrumentmakare* XXIX/1 (1959), 14–15.

Ormay, Imre. *Wenn Paganini ein Tagebuch geführt hatte....* Budapest: Corvina Deutscher Verlag für Musik, 1967. 181 pp.

Ortlepp, Ernst. *Grosses Instrumental- und Vokal-Concert. Eine musikalische Anthologie.* Stuttgart: F. H. Köhler, 1841.

"Paganini, direttore d'orchestra," *Musica d'oggi* XX (1938), 126–7.

"Paganini fund," *Neue Zeitschrift für Musik* CXVI/10 (October 1955), 39. [Discusses sonata in D major for violin and guitar.]

"A Paganini Gift to Vecsey," *Musical Courier* LXXXIII/15 (1921), 25.

"Paganini, the Guitarist," *Music* XXVII (November–December 1949), 58.

"Paganini: History of a Wooden Shoe," *Music Journal* XXVII/5 (May 1969), 66–7. [originally appeared in *Once a Week* (October 13, 1866); also in Boston weekly, *Every Saturday*.]

"The Paganini Museum," *Musical Courier* XLVI/15 (1903), 9.

Paganini: Variations poétiques. Lyon: 1831.

[Paganini, Niccolò]. "[Autobiographie]," *Allgemeine Musikalisches Zeitung* XXXII/17 (April 28, 1830), 269–71.

"Paganini's Fingering and Catalogue of His Works," *Hinrichsen's Musical Year Book* VII (1952), 77–82.

"Paganini's Fourth Violin Concerto," *Violins & Violinists* XVI/2 (March–April 1955), 56.

"Paganini's Leben . . . von J. M. Schottky," *Allgemeine Musikalische Zeitung* XXXII/25 (June 23, 1830), 397–402.

Paganini's Method of Producing the Harmonic Double Stops. London: 1840.

"Paganini's Prison Life," *Musician* VII (1902), 63.

"Paganini's Secret," *The Strad* LX (November 1949), 202.

"Paganini-Ausstellung in Genoa," [*Neue*] *Zeitschrift für Musik* CXV/1 (January 1954), 46.

"Paganiniana [Futile Efforts to Discover Cast of Paganini's Hands]," *Violins & Violinists* XVI/4 (July–August 1955), 150.

Paganiniana. A cura del Civico Istituto Colombiano [Mostra giorno di Genova, 12 ottobre]. Milan: L. Alfieri, 1953. 89 pp.

Pelicelli, N. "Musicisti in Parma dal 1800 al 1860," *Note d'archivio per la storia musicale* XII/6 (November–December 1935), 317ff.

Pfeiffer, Emmi. "Documenti inediti intorno a Paganini," *Note d'archivio per la storia musicale* X/3 (July–September 1933), 201–4.

Phillips, Henry. *Musical and Personal Recollections During Half a Century.* London: C. J. Skeet, 1864. 2 vols.

Phipson, Thomas Lamb. *Biographical Sketches and Anecdotes of Celebrated Violinists.* London: R. Bentley, 1877.

Piastro, Michel. "The Paganini Mystery," *Symphony* II (April 1949), 4.

Pintacuda, Salvatore. *Genova. Biblioteca dell'Istituto Musicale "Nicolò Paganini"; Catalogo del Fondo Antico.* Milan: Istituto Editoriale Italiano, 1966. [=Bibliotheca Musicae, 4.] [Cites more than 200 Paganini letters and documents.]

Pirani, Eugenio di. "Nicolo Paganini; Biographische Skizze," *Neue Zeitschrift für Musik* LXVI (November 28, 1900).

Pizzetti, Ildebrando. *Niccolò Paganini.* Turin: Edizioni Arione, [n.d.]. 36 pp.

————. See: "Omaggio."

Podenźani, Nino. *Il Romanzo di Niccolò Paganini.* Milan: Casa editrice Ceschina, 1940. 420 pp.

Polko, Elise Vogel. *Niccolò Paganini und die Geigenbauer. Mit dem portrait Paganini's.* Leipzig: B. Schlicke, 1876. 228 pp.

Polo, Enrico. "A proposito di cimeli paganiniani dispersi," *Musica d'oggi* XVIII (1936), 392–3.

"A Portrait of Paganini," *Violins & Violinists* XV/6 (November–December 1954), 271–2.

Powroźniak, Józef. *Paganini.* Krakow & Warsaw: Polskie wydawnictwo muzyczne, 1958. [=Maie monografie muzyczne, 9]. 220 pp.

Prod'homme, Jacques Gabriel. *Paganini.* Paris: H. Laurens, 1907. 126 pp. [Another ed., Paris: 1927. English version trans. by Alice Mattullath as: *Nicolo Paganini; a Biography.* New York & Boston: C. Fischer, 1911. 67 pp. Latter originally appeared serially in *Musical Observer* II/9–10; III/1–12; IV/1–8 (1908–10).]

Pulver, Jeffrey. *Paganini, the Romantic Virtuoso.* London: H. Joseph, 1936. 328 pp.

[Raaben, L.] [*The Lives of Famous Violinists.*] Leningrad: Muzyka, 1967. 312 pp. [Contains biographical account of Paganini.]

Regli, Francesco. *Storia del violino in Piemonte*. Turin: E. Dalmazzo, 1863.

Reis, Kurt. *Paganini*. Milan: Vallardi, 1956. 311 pp.

Rellstab, Ludwig. *Aus meinem Leben*. Berlin: 1861.

Reuchsel, Maurice. *Un violoniste en voyage: Notes d'Italie. 3. ed., ornée de 8 gravures hors texte*. Paris: Fischbacher, 1907. 63 pp.

Richter, Hermann. *Dämonischer Reigen; ein Paganini-Roman*. Leipzig: Janke, 1938. 285 pp. [Fiction.]

Richards, C. C. "Paganini's Guarneri," *The Strad* LXV (July 1954), 72.

Rinaldi, Mario. "Una scoperta che non scopre nulla," *Rassegna Dorica* X (1939), 357–8. [The tomb of Paganini.]

Rizo-Rangabe, A. "Correspondence: Paganini," *The Strad* LXVIII (May 1957), 28.

———. "Correspondence: Paganini's Technique," *The Strad* LXVII (July 1956), 96.

———. "Nicolo Paganini [Moses' Prayer]," *The Strad* LXVIII (February 1958), 380.

Rosenthal, Albi. "[Reviews of] *Paganini: documenti e testimonianze* by Pietro Berri; and *Nicolo Paganini: Chronology of His Life* by G. I. C. de Courcy," *Music and Letters* XLV/1 (January 1964), 53–56.

S., E. *Biographical Sketch of Nicolo Paganini*. (By the Paris correspondent of the late *Foreign Literary Gazette* as originally inserted in the *Lady's Magazine* for April 1831). London: 1831.

St. Andree, O. G. de. "Neues Paganini-Konzert," *Musica* XIV/1 (January 1960), 38.

Salzedo, S. L. "The Centenary of Paganini," *The Strad* L [=597] (January 1940), 347–9. [Appraisal of Paganini's technique drawn from contemporary commentary.]

———. "Paganini and Ciandelli," *The Strad* L (1939), 109–11.

———. "Paganini's Birthplace." *The Strad* L [=599] (March 1940), 411–3.

———. *Paganini's Secret at Last*. London: Nicholson and Watson, 1946. 39 pp. [Partially issued serially as: "Paganini's Secret at Last," *The Strad* (September 1948), 106–8; (January 1949), 202–4; (February 1949), 233–6.

Salvaneschi, Dino. *Un violino, 23 donne, ed. il diavolo: la vita ardente di Niccolò Paganini.* Milan: Corbaccio, 1938. 286 pp.

Sand, George [pseud. of Mme. A. L. A. D. Dudevant]. "Paris' Reaction to Paganini Described," *American String Teacher* XI/3 (1961), 14–5.

Saussine, Renée de. *Paganini le magicien.* Paris: Gallimard, 1938. 252 pp.

———. *Paganini.* Geneva: Milieu du monde, 1950. 262 pp. [English trans. by Marjorie Laurie, with preface by Jacques Thibaud as: *Paganini.* London: Hutchinson, 1953. 264 pp. American edition of same: New York: McGraw-Hill, 1954. 271 pp. Swedish trans. by Kajsa Rootzén as: *Djävulens violinist. En bok om Paganini.* Stockholm: Wahlström & Widstrand, 1955. 227 pp. Italian trans. as: *Paganini.* Milan: Nuova Accademia, 1958. 295 pp.]

Schonberg, Harold C. "Violin Concertos by Paganini," *The New York Times* [Sunday edition] CV/section 2 (December 4, 1955), 17. [Review of recordings.]

[Schottky, Julius Max.] *Paganinis Leben und Charakter nach Schottky; Dargestellt von Ludolf Vineta.* Hamburg: bei Hoffmann und Campe, 1830. 52 pp.

Schottky, Julius Max. *Paganini's Leben und Treiben als Künstler und als Mensch.* Prague: J. G. Calve, 1830. 410 pp. [Reprinted: Prague: Taussig & Taussig, 1909. Another reprint: announced.] [Earliest major study of Paganini.]

Schuetz, Friedrich Carl Julius. *Leben, Charakter und Kunst des Ritters Nicolò Paganini. Eine Skizze.* Ilmenau: B. F. Voigt, 1830. 98 pp.

Schweizer, [Gottfried?]. "Auf den Spuren Paganinis," *Das Musikleben* VII/12 (December 1954), 444–5.

Sear, H. G. "The Influence of Paganini," *The Music Review* IV/2 (May 1943), 98–111.

Šefl, Vladimír. "[Caprices for solo violin] 24x Paganini," *Hudebni Rozhledy* XIV/21 (1961), 920.

Shedlock, John S. "The 'Nel cor' Variations of Paganini," *Monthly Musical Record* XXV (1895) , 79.

Siber, Julius. *Paganini*. Berlin: 1920.

————. "Paganinis Glockenkonzert und Juan Manén," *Geigenspiel-Rundschau* 25 (1938) , 29–32.

————. "Paganinis Hexentanz; eine Studie über das Teuflische und Groteske in der Kunst," *Geigenspiel-Rundschau* 17 (1936) , 1–8.

————. "Die Teufelsmesse Paganinis; eine Skizze," *Geigenspiel-Rundschau* 18 (1936) , 24–9.

Slonimsky, Nicolas. "Scène Amoureuse," *Etude* LXIX/1 (January 1951) , 5.

Spivacke, Harold. "Paganiniana," *The Library of Congress Quarterly Journal of Current Acquisitions* II/2 (February 1945) , 49–67. [Also issued separately as: *Paganiniana*. Washington: Government Printing Office, 1945. 19 pp.] [Survey of the Maia Bang Hohn Collection of Paganini documents at the Library of Congress.]

Spohr, Louis. *Selbstbiographie*. Cassel: 1860. 2 vols. [English trans. as: *Louis Spohr's Autobiography*. London: Longman, Green, Longman, Roberts, & Green, 1865 (Reprinted: New York: Da Capo Press, 1969) .]

Stedman, Jane W. "A Fiddling Devil," *Opera News* XXIX/16 (February 27, 1965) , 14–6.

"Die Stimme des Lesers: Zur 'Daguerrotypie' von Paganini," *Musica* IX/6 (June 1955) , 296–7.

Stratton, Stephen Samuel. *Niccolò Paganini; His Life and Work*. London: "The Strad," 1907. [=The Strad Library, 17.] 205 pp. [Originally issued serially in *The Strad,* 1904–6.]

————. "Paganiniana," *Musical World* (December 1907) .

————. "Die Paganini-Ausstellung in Turin," *Das Orchester* (June 5, 1898) .

————, and Julius Kapp. *Nicolo Paganini*. London: 1913.

Tibaldi-Chiesa, Mary. *Paganini, la vita e l'opera; con 14 illustrezoni e 18 facsimili di autografi musicali inediti*. 3. ed. Milan: Garzanti, 1944, 484 pp. [1st ed., 1940.]

Tibaldi-Chiesa, Mary. "Paganini e gli operisti contemporanei,' *L'Opera* II/5 (October–December 1966) , 33–6.

Tiby, Ottavio. *Paganini a Palermo.* Palermo: Cappugi e Mori 1949.

Tintori, Giampiero. "Nicolò Paganini," in: Claudio Sartori, ed. *Enciclopedie della musica,* 4 vols. (Milan: Ricordi, 1963–64) III, 355–6.

Trifiletti, Igino. "Niccolò Paganini ed Ufo Foscolo," *Uomini* VIII/5 (1957) , 12–3.

Urbschat, Emil. *6 gelöste Rätsel der Paganini-Technik.* Bielefeld: E. Urbschat, 1951. 8 pp.

Valensi, Théodore. *Niccolò Paganini, 1784–1840.* Nice: E. L. F. Jacques Dervyl, 1950. 248 pp.

Vardi, Emanuel. "Recording Paganini's 'Caprices' on Viola Presented Unique Problems," *American String Teacher* XV/1 (1965) , 23–4.

Vernarelli, Gerardo. *Nicolò Paganini nei disegni di un impressionista contemporaneo. Sotto gli auspici del Comitato nazionale nel I centenario dalla morte di Nicolò Paganini.* Rome: F. Gerra, 1940. 15 pp.

Vineta, Ludolf. See: [Schottky]

Vinogradov, Anatolii Korneliyevich. *The Condemnation of Paganini,* trans. from Russian by Stephen Garry. London & New York: Hutchinson, 1946. [Fiction.]

Výborný, Zdeněk. "Der 'Fall Paganini,' " *Die Musikforschung* XVII/2 (April–June 1964) , 156–62.

———. "Lettere di Paganini inedite o poco note," *Revista municipale Genova* XXXII/11–12 (1955) , 18–20.

———. "Nicolò Paganini e Giovanni Ricordi," *Musica d'oggi* VI/3 (1963) , 98–108.

———. "Ondříček e Paganini," *La Scala* 80 (July 1956) , 21–4, 77–8.

———. "Paganini a Carlsbad," *La Scala* 100 (March 1958) , 51–7.

———. "Paganini as Music Critic," *The Musical Quarterly* XLIV/4 (October 1960) , 468–81.

———. "Paganini—heute gesehen," *Musica* XIII/11 (November

1959), 702–4. [Italian version in *Rassegna musicale Curci* XIII (1959), 10–12.]

——. "Paganini sconosciuto: L'agenda rossa," *La Scala* 117–18 (August–September 1959), 43–50, 85–6.

——. "Paganini sconosciuto: Il compositore," *La Scala* 108 (November 1958), 26–30.

——. "Paganini sconosciuto: epistolario intimo," *La Scala* 135 (February 1961), 16–24.

——. "Paganini sconosciuto: L'uomo," *La Scala* 120 (November 1959), 28–36, 93–4.

——. "Paganini sconosciuto: Il virtuoso," *La Scala* 113 (April 1959), 19–25, 93–4.

——. "Paganini und Beethoven," *Die Musikforschung* XIII/3 (July–September 1960), 325–8. [Italian version in *La Scala* 123 (February 1960).]

——. "Paganini und die Romantik; Zur Psychologie der Beziehungen des Kunstlers und seiner Zeit," *Musica* IX/10 (October 1955), 476–8.

——. "Paganini und 'il poeta declamatore,' eine Episode aus dem Leben des 'Teufelsgeigers,'" *Neue Zeitschrift für Musik* CXXIV/3 (March 1963), 95–8.

——. *Paganini v Karlovych Varech.* Pilzen: Vydalo Krajske nakladatelstvi, 1961. 79 pp.

——. "Paganini visto da un famoso violinista polacco," *Bollettino storico Piacentino* LIV/4 (1959), 132–8.

——. "Paganini vom Arzt gesehen," *Musica* X/11 (November 1956), 804–5.

——. "The Real Paganini," *Music and Letters* XLII/4 (October 1961), 348–63.

——. "Das sechste Notizbuch Paganinis," *Die Musikforschung* XVIII/2 (April–June 1965), 187–95.

Waldemar, Charles. *Liebe, Ruhm und Leidenschaft; der Lebensroman des Niccolo Paganini.* Munich: Bong, 1959. [Fiction.]

Wasielewski, Wilhelm Joseph von. *Die Violine und ihre meister.* 5. Aufl. Leipzig: Breitkopf & Härtel, 1910.

Weber, Karl Maria von. *Briefe an den Grafen Karl von Brühl;* hrsg. von George Kaiser. Leipzig: Breitkopf & Härtel, 1911.

Weinstock, Herbert. "Larger than Life," *Opera News* XXVI/1 (October 28, 1961) , 9.

Weissmann, Adolf. *Der Virtuose.* Berlin: P. Cassirer, 1918.

Wendt, M. "The Rise and Decline of Virtuosity in the Nineteenth Century As Traced Through the Art of Violin Playing," *American String Teacher* XVI/4 (1966) , 30; XVII/1 (1967) , 14.

Wheeler, Opal. *Paganini, Master of Strings.* New York: E. P. Dutton, 1951.

Wilkowska-Chomińska, Krystyna. "Chopin i Paganini," *Muzyka* IV/4 (1959) , 101–10.

Wimbush, Roger. "Et Cetera," *The Gramophone* XLV [=538] (March 1968) , 479. [About the D minor violin concerto.]

———. "Paganini," *The Gramophone* XLV [=536] (January 1968) , 371.

Witting, Carl. *Geschichte des Violinspiels.* Cologne: H. vom Ende's Verlag, 1900.

[Wyss, Georg von]. *Biographie von Nicolo Paganini.* Zürich: Gedruckt bei C. Kull, 1846. [*=Neujahrsstück der Allgemeine musikgesellschaft in Zürich,* XXXIV (1846) , 1–20.]

Yampol'sky, Izrail Markovič. "Neizvestnoe pismo N. Paganini [An Unknown Letter of N. Paganini]," *Sovetskaja muzyka* XII (1957) , 65–7.

———. *Niccolo Paganini — zivot i rad.* Moscow: Izdavacko drzavno muzicko preduzece, 1961.

———. "Paganini—gitarist," *Sovetskaya Muzyka* XXIV (September 1960) , 133–8.

Zacharewitsch, Michael. *The Ladder to Paganini's Profound Mastery: Technique.* London: Novello, 1952. 95 pp.

———. "A Paganini Manuscript," *Music and Letters* XXI/2 (April 1940) , 179–80. [Also appeared in *The Strad* LI [=601] (May 1940) , 22–4.] [Discovery of an unknown Paganini *Fantasia* for unaccompanied violin.]

Zur Erinnerungen an Louis Eller. Dresden: R. Kuntze, 1864.